THE FIRST
20 HOURS

'Great opportunities are worthless without skills. No more excuses!
Kaufman proves that we all have the capacity to become experts'
Scott Belsky, founder, Behance, and author of *Making Ideas Happen*

'If you're like me, you'll get so inspired that you'll stop reading to apply
this approach to your own procrastinated project. After reading the
first five chapters I tried his technique to learn a new programming
language, and I'm blown away with how fast I became fluent'
Derek Sivers, founder, CD Baby, sivers.org

'this inspiring little book, Josh Kaufman argues that you can get good enough
at anything to enjoy yourself in just 20 hours. All that's standing between
you and playing the ukulele is your TV time for the next two weeks'
Laura Vanderkam, author of *168 Hours* and *What the Most
Successful People Do Before Breakfast*

'With the amount of information and change in the world today, the person
who can adapt and learn the most quickly will be the most successful. Kaufman
breaks down the science of learning in useful, entertaining, and fascinating ways.
If you care about keeping your job, your business, or your edge, this book is for you'
Pamela Slim, author of *Escape from Cubicle Nation*

ABOUT THE AUTHOR

Josh Kaufman helps people make more money, get more done, and have more fun. His first book, *The Personal MBA,* is an international bestseller. He lives in Colorado.

www.personalmba.com

THE FIRST

20 HOURS

How to Learn
Anything . . . *Fast*

JOSH KAUFMAN

PORTFOLIO
PENGUIN

PORTFOLIO PENGUIN

Published by the Penguin Group
Penguin Books Ltd, 80 Strand, London WC2R 0RL, England
Penguin Group (USA) Inc., 375 Hudson Street, New York, New York 10014, USA
Penguin Group (Canada), 90 Eglinton Avenue East, Suite 700, Toronto, Ontario, Canada M4P 2Y3
(a division of Pearson Penguin Canada Inc.)
Penguin Ireland, 25 St Stephen's Green, Dublin 2, Ireland (a division of Penguin Books Ltd)
Penguin Group (Australia), 707 Collins Street, Melbourne, Victoria 3008, Australia
(a division of Pearson Australia Group Pty Ltd)
Penguin Books India Pvt Ltd, 11 Community Centre, Panchsheel Park, New Delhi – 110 017, India
Penguin Group (NZ), 67 Apollo Drive, Rosedale, Auckland 0632, New Zealand
(a division of Pearson New Zealand Ltd)
Penguin Books (South Africa) (Pty) Ltd, Block D, Rosebank Office Park,
181 Jan Smuts Avenue, Parktown North, Gauteng 2193, South Africa

Penguin Books Ltd, Registered Offices: 80 Strand, London WC2R 0RL, England

www.penguin.com

First published 2013
001

Photographs by the author

Printed in Great Britain by Clays Ltd, St Ives plc

A CIP catalogue record for this book is available from the British Library

ISBN: 978–0–670–92191–1

www.greenpenguin.co.uk

MIX
Paper from
responsible sources
FSC
www.fsc.org
FSC™ C018179

Penguin Books is committed to a sustainable
future for our business, our readers and our planet.
This book is made from Forest Stewardship
Council™ certified paper.

ALWAYS LEARNING   **PEARSON**

For Lela

Contents

■ ■ ■

A Note to the Reader

The lyf so short, the craft so longe to lerne.
—GEOFFREY CHAUCER, *PARLEMENT OF FOULES*, 1374

■ ■ ■

"There's so much I want to do . . . and so little time." The story of modern life.

Take a moment to consider how many things you want to learn how to do. What's on your list? What's holding you back from getting started?

Two things, most likely: time and skill.

Here's an uncomfortable truth: the most rewarding experiences in life almost always require some level of skill. Skills take time and effort to master—time we don't have, and effort we're reluctant to contribute.

"I'll get around to it someday, when I find the time."

It's easier to sit in front of the television or surf the web, frankly . . . so that's what most of us do, and our desires remain dreams.

Here's another uncomfortable truth: many things aren't fun until you're good at them. Every skill has what I call a *frustration barrier*—a period of time in which you're horribly unskilled, and you're painfully aware of that fact. Why start something when you know you're going to be bad at it?

Wouldn't it be great to be able to master new skills with less angst? To break through the frustration barrier quickly, so you can get to the rewarding part? To spend less time slogging through confusion and doubt, and more time having fun?

Is it possible to acquire new skills less painfully, in a way that requires far less time and effort?

I speak from experience: yes, it's possible.

This book is about my personal quest to test the art and science of *rapid skill acquisition*—how to learn any new skill as quickly as possible. The purpose of this book is to help you acquire new skills in record time.

In my experience, it takes around twenty hours of practice to break through the frustration barrier: to go from knowing absolutely nothing about what you're trying to do to performing noticeably well.

This book is a systematic approach to acquiring new skills as quickly as possible. The method is universal. It doesn't matter whether you want to learn a language, write a novel, paint a portrait, start a business, or fly an airplane. If you invest as little as twenty hours in learning the basics of the skill, you'll be surprised at how good you become.

Whatever skill you wish to acquire, this book will help you acquire it in less time and with less wasted energy. With a bit of focused, strategic effort, you'll find yourself performing well quickly, without the fist-pounding frustration.

In this book, we'll start with the principles of rapid skill acquisition: how to go about acquiring new skills as quickly as possible. These ideas and practices aren't complicated, so they won't take long to learn.

Then, I'll explain how to use these principles in the real world by showing you how I acquired the following six new skills in twenty hours or less each, with no more than ninety minutes of practice per day.

- Developing a personal yoga practice
- Writing a web-based computer program
- Relearning to touch-type
- Exploring the oldest and most complex board game in history
- Playing a musical instrument
- Windsurfing

I hope that this book encourages you to dust off your old "want to do" list, reexamine it, and commit to learning something new.

Josh Kaufman
Fort Collins, Colorado,
USA

For updates about the material in this book, visit http:// first20hours.com/updates.

THE FIRST 20 HOURS

A Portrait of the Author
as a Learning Junkie

I get up every morning determined to both change the world and have one hell
of a good time. Sometimes this makes planning my day difficult.
—E. B. WHITE, ESSAYIST AND AUTHOR OF
CHARLOTTE'S WEB AND *THE ELEMENTS OF STYLE*

■ ■ ■

Hi. My name is Josh Kaufman, and I'm a learning addict.

My home and office shelves are piled high with books, tools, and unused equipment of all sorts, most of which are slowly accumulating dust.

I have a "to learn" list hundreds of items long. My Amazon.com shopping cart currently has 241 items in it—all books I want to read. I can't walk into a bookstore without leaving with three or four new books, to be added to the 852 volumes I already own.

Every day, I come up an idea for another project or experiment, which I add to my ever-growing "someday/maybe" list. Looking at everything I want to learn how to do feels overwhelming, so I don't look at the list very often.

I want to learn how to improve my publishing business. I want to learn how to shoot and edit videos. I want to produce an audio program. I want to learn how to give better seminars and teach better courses.

I have ideas for a new product, but I don't know how to build it. I have ideas for new computer programs, but I don't know how to create them. I have more potential writing project ideas in my head than the time and energy to write them.

I want to learn how to draw. I want to learn how to white-water kayak. I want to learn fly fishing. I want to learn rock climbing. I want to be able to play the guitar, the ukulele, the piano, and the electric violin.

There are games I've been interested in for years, like Go, but I haven't learned how to play them. I have games that I already know how to play, like chess, but I'm not very good at them, so they're not much fun, and I don't play them very often.

I like the idea of playing golf, but every game I've played turned into a stoic exercise in laughing off embarrassment. (I usually say I play marathon golf: by the end of eighteen holes, I've run a marathon.)

It seems as though every day I add some new skill to the list of things I want to be able to do, ad infinitum. So much to learn, so little time.

By nature, I'm a do-it-yourself kind of guy. If something needs to be done, I'd rather give it a go myself than look for help. Even if someone else could do it faster or better, I'm reluctant to rob myself of the learning experience.

To complicate matters, Kelsey, my wife, runs her own business, publishing continuing education courses for yoga teachers. Business is good for both of us, so there's always a lot to be done.

To make life even more interesting, we welcomed our daughter, Lela, into the world. Lela is nine months old as I write this.

Before Lela was born, Kelsey and I decided that if we were going to have kids, we wanted to make raising them ourselves a priority. One of the major reasons I quit my former management-track job at a Fortune 500 corporation was to have the flexibility to work from home, set my own schedule, and spend as much time as possible with my family.

Kelsey and I share parenting responsibilities equally. Since we're a two-business household, Kelsey works in the morning, while I take care of Lela. In the afternoon, Kelsey takes care of Lela, and I work until dinnertime. That gives me around twenty-five hours each week to work, plus whatever time I can snatch while Lela is napping.

After Lela was born, I felt like I barely had enough time to get my work done, let alone acquire new skills. For a learning addict, it was crazy-making.

I don't want to give up on learning and growth completely, even with my new responsibilities. I don't have very much free time, but I'm willing to invest what I have as wisely as possible.

That's what prompted my interest in what I call rapid skill acquisition: methods of learning new skills quickly.

I want to continue to acquire new skills, but I don't want the process to take forever. I want to pick up the essentials quickly, so I can make noticeable progress without constantly feeling frustrated.

I'm sure you can relate. How much "free" time do you have each day, after all of your work and family obligations are complete? Do you feel like you'd need thirty-six or forty-eight hours in a day to finally sit down and learn something new?

There's an old cliché: "work smarter, not harder." As it turns out, the process of skill acquisition is not really about the raw hours you put in . . . it's what you put *into* those hours.

Damn You, Malcolm Gladwell

In 2008, Malcolm Gladwell wrote a book titled *Outliers: The Story of Success.* In it, he set about trying to explain what makes certain people more successful than others.

One of the ideas Gladwell mentions over and over again is what he calls the "10,000 hour rule." Based on research conducted by Dr. K. Anders Ericsson of Florida State University, expert-level performance takes, on average, ten thousand hours of deliberate practice to achieve.[1]

Ten thousand hours equals eight hours of deliberate practice every day for approximately three and a half years, with no breaks, no weekends, and no vacations. Assuming a standard 260 working days a year with no distractions, that's a full-time job for almost five years, assuming you spend 100 percent of that time exerting 100 percent of your energy and effort.

In practice, this level of focused attention is extremely taxing. Even world-class performers in ultracompetitive fields (like music performance and professional sports) can only muster the energy for approximately three and a half hours of deliberate practice every day. That means it can take a decade or more to develop a skill to mastery.

In essence, if you want to master a new skill, Dr. Ericsson's research indicates you're in for a very long haul. Being the best in the world at anything, even for a little while, requires years of relentless practice. If you're not willing to put in the time and effort, you'll be overshadowed by those who do.

Outliers shot straight to the top of the nonfiction bestseller lists, and stayed there for three months. Overnight, the "10,000 hour rule" was everywhere.

As if learning a new skill wasn't hard enough. Not only do you have to make time for practice . . . but you now also have to put in ten thousand hours? Most of us count ourselves lucky if we can set aside a few hours a week. Why bother at all if it takes so long to be good at something?

Look Upon My Works, Ye Mighty, and Despair!

Before you give up all hope, consider this.

There's an element of Dr. Ericsson's research that's very easy to overlook: it's a study of *expert-level performance*. If you're looking to become the next Tiger Woods, you'll probably need to spend at least ten thousand hours deliberately and systematically practicing every aspect of golf. Almost every single professional golfer began playing at a very young age and has been practicing nonstop for at least seven years. Developing world-class mastery takes time.

On the other hand, what if winning the PGA Tour isn't your goal? What if you just want to be good enough at golf that you're able to play decently, not embarrass yourself, have a good time, and maybe have a fighting chance to win your local country club tournament?

That's another matter entirely. World-class mastery may take ten thousand hours of focused effort, but developing the capacity to perform *well enough for your own purposes* usually requires far less of an investment.

That's not to discount the value of what Ericsson calls "deliberate practice": intentionally and systematically practicing in order to improve a skill. Deliberate practice is the core of skill acquisition. The question is how *much* deliberate practice is required to reach your goal. Usually, it's much less than you think.

Quality, Not Quantity

Embracing the idea of *sufficiency* is the key to rapid skill acquisition. In this book, we're going to discuss developing capacity, not world-class mastery. We're going to tackle the steep part of the learning curve and ascend it as quickly as possible.

Leave the ten thousand hours to the pros. We're going to start with twenty hours of concentrated, intelligent, focused effort.

We're shooting for the results we value with a fraction of the effort. You may never win a gold medal, but you'll reap the rewards you care about in far less time.

If you ultimately decide to master the skill, you'll have a better chance of success if you start with twenty hours of rapid skill acquisition. By knowing what you're getting into, learning the fundamentals, practicing intelligently, and developing a practice routine, you'll make progress more quickly and consistently, and you'll achieve expert status in record time.

What Is Rapid Skill Acquisition?

Rapid skill acquisition is a process—a way of breaking down the skill you're trying to acquire into the smallest possible parts, identifying which of those parts are most important, then deliberately practicing those elements first. It's as simple as that.

Rapid skill acquisition has four major steps:

- **Deconstructing** a skill into the smallest possible subskills;
- **Learning** enough about each subskill to be able to practice intelligently and self-correct during practice;
- **Removing** physical, mental, and emotional barriers that get in the way of practice;
- **Practicing** the most important subskills for at least twenty hours.

That's it. Rapid skill acquisition is not rocket science. You simply decide what to practice, figure out the best way to practice, make time to practice, then practice until you reach your target level of performance.

There's no magic to it—just smart, strategic effort invested in something you care about. With a little preparation, you'll acquire new skills rapidly, with less effort.

That's not to say that the results will be instant. The desire for instant gratification is one of the primary reasons people don't acquire new skills very quickly.

The "Matrix" Misconception

Remember the scene in *The Matrix* when Keanu Reeves opens his eyes, blinks a few times, and whispers "I know kung fu"?

Sorry to break it to you: rapid skill acquisition isn't *that* rapid.

Hollywood has done us a great disservice when it comes to skill acquisition. While it would certainly be nice to be able to learn how to pilot a Bell 212 helicopter in five seconds by uploading software directly into our brain, science is currently way behind science fiction.

Until brain uploads become a reality, "rapid" means taking considerably less time than it would typically take to learn a skill if you went about the process as most people do: blindly, haphazardly, and inconsistently.

One of the first professional skills I acquired was web development: being able to build useful, functioning websites. Beginning with a basic Angelfire.com website in 1996, I taught myself how to read and write HTML and CSS (the lingua franca of the web), use Adobe Photoshop to edit images, configure web servers, and maintain the systems that publish my work.

I didn't learn how to do these things in high school or college. Although I completed my undergraduate degree in business information systems, the overlap between what I learned in the classroom and what I do on a day-to-day basis is essentially nil.

I acquired the skill of web development by trying things at random and figuring it out as I went along. Every time I stumbled upon a new technique or tool that promised to enhance my website or reduce my workload, I experimented with it. Over a long period of time, my skills improved.

My haphazard approach to acquiring web development skills served the purpose: I got a job based on those skills, and I now publish information on the web for a living. Mission accomplished, from one perspective.

On the other hand, I learned everything the hard way. You could certainly reach my level of competence in these skills in much less than fifteen years if you approached the topic in a systematic way. If you went about practicing these skills intelligently, you could approach my general level of competence in a month.

That's what I mean by rapid skill acquisition. If you could learn most of what I know about web design in a single focused month versus fifteen years, that's a massive improvement. It's also well within the realm of possibility.

The amount of time it will take you to acquire a new skill is largely a matter of how much concentrated time you're willing to invest in deliberate practice and smart experimentation and how good you need to become to perform at the level you desire.

Don't expect overnight results. Do expect that your total time invested will be much, much less than it would otherwise be if you jumped into the process without a strategy.

Before we explore the method in detail, there's something you should know: rapid skill acquisition has nothing in common with how you "learned how to learn" in school. Academic learning and credentialing have almost zero overlap with skill acquisition, let alone achieving it quickly.

Skill Acquisition vs. Learning

Like many high school students in the United States, I studied a foreign language. Every school day for four years, I sat in a Spanish class. My marks were high: straight As.

Today, aside from saying *hola*, *cómo estás*, and *muy bien*, I can't hold a conversation with a native Spanish speaker to save my life. (I don't even know what to say if I'm *not* having a good day.)

On the other side of the spectrum, my friend, Carlos Miceli, grew up speaking Spanish in Argentina. In high school, Carlos decided he wanted to speak fluent English, so he made an effort to strike up as many conversations as possible with native-English speakers. In the process, he discovered Skype and set up his own website, so he could practice speaking and writing English regularly.

Carlos never took a class. He doesn't know the formal rules of English grammar. He can't even tell you *how* he knows English. That isn't really important. He can speak and write English fluently, which is what really matters.

Dr. Stephen Krashen, of the University of Southern California, is an expert in the area of second-language acquisition. One of Krashen's primary insights is that language *acquisition* is different from language *learning*.

In school, I learned a lot *about* Spanish. I learned thousands of vocabulary words, verb conjugation, and the rules of grammar. I learned all of these things well enough to pass the tests with flying colors.

Those tests, however, had nothing to do with my ability to exercise the skills of speaking Spanish intelligibly and understanding a native speaker talking at full speed. If my goal was to be able to speak Spanish fluently, a few weeks of trying to converse with people in Spanish would've produced better results than four years of schooling.

At that time, speaking Spanish fluently wasn't my goal. I just wanted to ace the final exam. Carlos, on the other hand, skipped the classroom and simply started practicing. Instead of doing verb conjugation drills, Carlos was practicing what really mattered: communicating with other people in English.

In terms of effectiveness and long-term value, Carlos's approach was far superior to mine. No contest.

The True Value of Learning

That's not to say learning about the skill you're acquiring isn't important. Learning can be extremely important, but not in the way you'd expect. Learning concepts related to a skill helps you *self-edit* or *self-correct* as you're practicing.

If you know how to conjugate verbs in Spanish, you're better able to self-correct your speech while talking to a native speaker. If you learn common vocabulary words, you're better able to understand what a native speaker is saying, as well as remember an appropriate word or phrase to use when you get stuck while speaking.

Dr. Krashen calls this the *monitor hypothesis*. Learning helps you plan, edit, and correct yourself as you practice. That's why learning is valuable. The trouble comes when we confuse learning with skill acquisition.

If you want to acquire a new skill, you must practice it in context. Learning enhances practice, but it doesn't replace it. If performance matters, learning alone is never enough.

Skill Acquisition vs. Training

There's also a huge difference between skill acquisition and training. *Training*, in this context, means improving a skill you've already acquired through repetition. It's what happens after you've acquired a basic skill if you want to keep improving.

Take running a marathon, for example. Most of us acquired the skill of running during childhood. Aside from putting one foot in front of the other and staying on your feet until you've covered 26.2 miles, there's not much in the way of new skills to acquire.

There is, however, a significant amount of necessary exertion required to strengthen your body and acclimate to the level of physical fitness it takes to complete a marathon. That exertion and strengthening process is training. The more you train, the stronger you become, and the faster you complete the marathon.

There's also an element of learning involved when running a marathon: how to sign up to participate in races, how to qualify for large events like the Boston Marathon, knowing what to expect as you run, pacing, useful equipment, et cetera.

For example, a small issue like friction between your shirt and your skin isn't a big deal if you're running a 5K, so most runners don't think about it. Unnecessary friction becomes a *huge* deal when you're running 26.2 miles.

Fail to prepare in advance and you're likely to experience the infamous "bleeding nipples" problem. It's painful, embarrassing . . . and entirely preventable. (Don't believe me? Google it.)

Training and learning will certainly make it easier to finish the race, but they're not skill acquisition. Without a certain amount of skill acquisition, training isn't possible or useful. Preparation and conditioning can make some forms of skill acquisition easier, but they can never replace practice.

Relearning how to run at a basic level, however, *is* skill acquisition. Techniques like ChiRunning[2] help the runner acquire the skill of moving in a way that minimizes effort and loss of forward momentum between strides. With a bit of practice, the runner can reacquire the core skill of running, which can then be reinforced in subsequent training.

Skill Acquisition vs. Education and Credentialing

Despite the high-minded efforts of teachers and professors around the world, modern methods of education and credentialing have almost nothing to do with skill acquisition.

Skill acquisition requires practicing the skill in question. It requires significant periods of sustained, focused concentration. It requires creativity, flexibility, and the freedom to set your own standard of success.

Unfortunately, most modern methods of education and credentialing require simple compliance. The primary (but unstated) goal isn't to acquire useful skills, it's to certify completion of a mostly arbitrary set of criteria, established by standards committees far removed from the student, for the purpose of validating certain qualities some third party appears to care about.

Creativity, flexibility, and freedom to experiment—the essential elements of rapid skill acquisition—are antithetical to the credentialing process. If the standards are too flexible, they're not really standards, are they?

Unfortunately, rigorous education and credentialing can actively *prevent* skill acquisition. The primary problem is opportunity cost: if the requirements to obtain the credential are so intense that they impair your ability to spend time practicing the skills in question, credentialing programs can do more harm than good.

Take a smart, motivated individual who is interested in starting a software company. Completing an undergraduate degree in computer science at a prestigious university usually takes at least four years.[3]

At the end of those four years, our newly minted graduate has spent thousands of hours learning algorithms and analyzing compilers well enough to pass dozens of examinations, but she is no closer to founding a software company than she was when she entered the university. Our unfortunate student has memorized many things about computer programming, at least temporarily, but she still doesn't know how to create a computer program that people find useful enough to purchase.

Starting a software company requires acquiring new skills: learning programming languages, setting up and maintaining computer systems, researching available tools and programs, creating prototypes, finding early users, obtaining any necessary funding or financing, and handling common business administrative tasks.

Is there some overlap between starting a startup and obtaining an educational credential? Sure. But notice the emphasis: most of the effort of obtaining a credential is devoted to the process of meeting the requirements. Whether or not those requirements actually help you acquire the skills you need to perform in the real world is a tertiary concern at best.

In my first book, *The Personal MBA: Master the Art of Business* (2010), I explained why I decided to skip graduate-level business education in favor of teaching myself the principles of modern business practice and starting my own company. By avoiding business school, and spending my time actually building businesses instead, I learned a ton, and saved over $150,000 in the process. Given what I wanted to accomplish, dedicating time to business skill acquisition on my own was better than business school in every respect.

If you want to get good at anything where real-life performance matters, you have to actually practice that skill in context. Study, by itself, is never enough.

The Neurophysiology of Skill: Brain Plasticity and Muscle Memory

One last thing before we jump into the nuts and bolts of rapid skill acquisition: you must fully appreciate the fact that you're capable of acquiring new skills.

That seems like an odd thing to say, but it's easy to believe your skills are fixed—that you're either good or talented or gifted at something . . . or you're not.

In *Mindset: The New Psychology of Success* (2007), psychologist Carol Dweck cites a wide body of research that indicates individuals commonly hold one of two views of how their minds work.

According to Dr. Dweck, people with a "fixed" mind-set assume that skills and talents are innate, that you're born with certain abilities that are what they are. If a person with a fixed mind-set is "not good at math," then extra effort practicing math is a waste. Why bother if you're never going to be good at it?

People with a "growth" mind-set, on the other hand, assume that skills and abilities grow with practice and persistence. If a person with a growth mind-set gets a few math problems wrong, it's not because they're not blessed with good-at-mathness; it's because they haven't practiced enough. With persistence and practice, it's only a matter of time before they will master the technique.

Here's the good news if you find yourself falling into the fixed mind-set trap: a wide (and growing) body of research indicates that all brains are capable of improving skills and capabilities with practice. Genetic predispositions exist, but they're very minor compared to the power of focused, intelligent practice. You can improve any skill, provided you're willing to practice.

The human brain is *plastic*—a term neuroscientists use to indicate that your brain physically changes in response to your environment, your actions, and the consequences of those actions. As you learn any new skill, physical or mental, the neurological wiring of your brain changes as you practice it.

In the words of Dr. Jon Medina (*Brain Rules*, 2009) "neurons that fire together wire together," forming unique new patterns in the physical circuitry of your brain. Over time, your neurons begin to fire in more efficient patterns in response to the feedback you receive from your environment as you practice.

If you're working on a *motor skill* (that is, a skill that involves physical movement), you're always relatively awkward and slow at first. You have to think about everything you're doing, and you often make frustrating mistakes. Learning the basics is a constant struggle.

As you practice, your muscle coordination becomes more automatic and synchronized with your mental processes. You gain the ability to pay more attention to the subtle elements of what you're doing, and you learn to adjust your approach to the feedback you get from the environment.

You start doing more of what works, and less of what doesn't. Eventually, you're able to perform without conscious attention to every detail.

In academic literature, this general process is called the "three-stage model" of skill acquisition,[4] and it applies to both physical and mental skills. The three stages are

1. **Cognitive (Early) Stage**—understanding what you're trying to do, researching, thinking about the process, and breaking the skill into manageable parts.

2. **Associative (Intermediate) Stage**—practicing the task, noticing environmental feedback, and adjusting your approach based on that feedback.

3. **Autonomous (Late) Stage**—performing the skill effectively and efficiently without thinking about it or paying unnecessary attention to the process.

This neurophysiological skill acquisition process is happening all the time, even while you're reading this sentence. There is no such thing as a mind in stasis. Your brain is learning, encoding, and consolidating new skills all the time.

As Dr. Dweck says in *Mindset*: "Your mind is like a muscle: the more you use it, the more it grows." The more you practice, the more efficient, effective, and automatic the skill becomes.

That's great news when it comes to rapid skill acquisition. If your mind and body are capable of learning to perform in new and better ways, we can figure out how to make that process *faster*.

2

Ten Principles of Rapid Skill Acquisition

> I realized that becoming a master of karate was not about learning 4,000
> moves but about doing just a handful of moves 4,000 times.
> —CHET HOLMES, AUTHOR OF *THE ULTIMATE SALES MACHINE*

■ ■ ■

Now that we're clear about what skill acquisition really means, let's examine how to do it quickly. The intent of this chapter is to give you a handy checklist for acquiring any new skill.

I find it useful to think of these principles as ways to cultivate a "temporary obsession." Rapid skill acquisition happens naturally when you become so curious and interested in something that other concerns fall away, at least temporarily.

Think of these principles as ways to identify a skill worthy of temporary obsession, focus on it, and remove distractions or barriers that distract you from effective practice.

Here are the ten major principles of rapid skill acquisition:

1. Choose a lovable project.

2. Focus your energy on one skill at a time.

3. Define your target performance level.

4. Deconstruct the skill into subskills.

5. Obtain critical tools.

6. Eliminate barriers to practice.

7. Make dedicated time for practice.

8. Create fast feedback loops.

9. Practice by the clock in short bursts.

10. Emphasize quantity and speed.

Many of these principles may strike you as common sense, and that's okay. Remember: simply knowing these principles is not enough. You must actually use them to reap the rewards.

1. Choose a lovable project.

Karl Popper was one of the greatest philosophers of the twentieth century. He's the guy who popularized the idea of *scientific falsifiability*. In layman's terms, if you can't potentially prove something wrong via observation or experiment, it's not actually science.

Popper said many wise things, but I think the following remark is among the wisest: "The best thing that can happen to a human being is to find a problem, to fall in love with that problem, and to live trying to solve that problem, unless another problem even more lovable appears."

If you want a formula for living a satisfying, productive life, you can't go wrong with that one.

Rapid skill acquisition requires choosing a lovable problem or project. The more excited you are about the skill you want to acquire, the more quickly you'll acquire it.

In practice, finding a lovable project is a very individual matter. For example, learning to speak and write Mandarin Chinese is not on my current list of skills to acquire because I have no urgent need to learn it at the moment, and I have a lot of other projects I'm more interested in tackling. If I decide to move to a Mandarin-speaking part of China in the future, it may become lovable, but I'm not there yet.

On the other hand, I'm intensely interested in learning how to play Go, the world's oldest strategic board game, which originated in China more than three thousand years ago. It's a beautiful game, and I've wanted to learn how to play since I stumbled across it years ago.

Learning to play Go requires study. The rules are simple, but accurately reading the evolving patterns of alternating black and white stones on the board is a challenge. Computers have dominated chess for years now, but even the best computers have a difficult time challenging an experienced human Go player.

You naturally learn things you care about faster than things you don't. I'm currently more interested in learning how to play Go, so I'm going to learn Go first, and save Mandarin for later.

If you focus on acquiring your *prime skill* (that is, your most lovable project) before anything else, you'll acquire it in far less time.

2. Focus your energy on one skill at a time.

One of the easiest mistakes to make when acquiring new skills is attempting to acquire too many skills at the same time.

It's a matter of simple math: acquiring new skills requires a critical mass of concentrated time and focused attention. If you only have an hour or two each day to devote to practice and learning, and you spread that time and energy across twenty different skills, no individual skill is going to receive enough time and energy to generate noticeable improvement.

Internalizing this principle is more difficult for some people than others. Personally, I've always had a "Renaissance man" sort of temperament: there are hundreds of things I want to learn at any given moment, in hundreds of different areas. Emotionally, it's difficult for me to decide to defer learning new things I discover or hear about.[1]

When I try to learn everything at once, however, I don't really learn anything. Instead of making progress, I spend too much time switching between different skills, getting frustrated, and moving on to something else. That's a recipe for extremely slow skill acquisition.

Pick one, and only one, new skill you wish to acquire. Put all of your spare focus and energy into acquiring that skill, and place other skills on temporary hold. David Allen, author of *Getting Things Done* (2002), recommends establishing what he calls a "someday/maybe" list: a list of things you may want to explore sometime in the future, but that aren't important enough to focus on right now. By adding an item to the list, you're temporarily absolving yourself of responsibility for acting or thinking about the idea until you decide to promote it to active status.

I can't emphasize this enough. Focusing on one prime skill at a time is absolutely necessary for rapid skill acquisition. You're not giving up on the other skills permanently, you're just saving them for later.

3. Define your target performance level.

A *target performance level* is a simple sentence that defines what "good enough" looks like. How well would you like to be able to perform the skill you're acquiring?

Your target performance level is a brief statement of what your desired level of skill looks like. Think of it as a single sentence description of what you're trying to achieve, and what you'll be able to do when you're done. The more specific your target performance level is, the better.

Defining your target performance level helps you imagine what it looks like to perform in a certain way. Once you determine exactly how good you want or need to be, it's easier to figure out how to get there. In the words of Charles Kettering, the inventor of the electric automobile ignition system: "A problem well stated is a problem half solved."

How you define your target performance level depends on why you chose to acquire the skill in the first place. If your intent is to have fun, your target is the point at which you stop feeling frustrated and start enjoying the practice itself. If your intent is to perform, what's the minimum level of performance you're willing to accept at first?

Once you reach your initial target performance level, you can always choose to keep going if you wish. The best target performance levels seem just out of reach, not out of the realm of possibility.

As a rule, the more relaxed your target performance level, the more rapidly you can acquire the associated skill. If you're operating under a world-class mastery mind-set, this may feel like cheating: you're just lowering the bar so you can "win" faster, right?

That's exactly what we're doing, and it's not cheating. Remember, world-class mastery is not the end point of rapid skill acquisition. We're shooting for capacity and sufficiency at maximum speed, not perfection.

It's important to note that some skills have safety considerations, which you should always include in your target performance level. Getting hurt (or killed) acquiring a new skill defeats the purpose.

4. Deconstruct the skill into subskills.

Most of the things we think of as skills are actually bundles of smaller subskills. Once you've identified a skill to focus on, the next step is to *de-construct* it—to break it down into the smallest possible parts. For example, playing golf is a skill that has many subcomponents: choosing the correct club, driving off the tee, hitting out of a bunker, putting, et cetera.

Once the skill is deconstructed sufficiently, it's much easier to identify which subskills appear to be most important. By focusing on the critical subskills first, you'll make more progress with less effort.

Deconstructing a skill also makes it easier to avoid feeling over-whelmed. You don't have to practice all parts of a skill at the same time. Instead, it's more effective to focus on the subskills that promise the most dramatic overall returns.

Deconstructing the skill before you begin also allows you to identify the parts of the skill that aren't important for beginning practitioners. By eliminating the noncritical subskills or techniques early in the process, you'll be able to invest more of your time and energy mastering the critical subskills first.

5. Obtain critical tools.

Most skills have prerequisites to practice and performance. It's difficult to play tennis if you don't have a tennis racquet, or learn how to pilot a heli-copter if you don't have access to one.

What tools, components, and environments do you need to have access to before you can practice efficiently? How can you obtain the very best tools you can find and afford?

Taking a moment to identify critical tools before you start practicing saves precious time. By ensuring you have the resources you need before you begin, you maximize your practice time.

6. Eliminate barriers to practice.

There are many things that can get in the way of practice, which makes it much more difficult to acquire any skill. These barriers can be anything from

- **Significant prepractice effort.** Such as misplacing your tools, not acquiring the correct tools before practicing, or skipping setup requirements.

- **Intermittent resource availability.** Such as using borrowed equipment or relying on a resource that has limited operating hours.

- **Environmental distractions.** Such as television, ringing phones, and incoming e-mail.

- **Emotional blocks.** Such as fear, doubt, and embarrassment.

Every single one of these elements makes it harder to start practicing, and therefore decreases your acquisition speed.

Relying on willpower to consistently overcome these barriers is a losing strategy. We only have so much willpower at our disposal each day, and it's best to use that willpower wisely.

The best way to invest willpower in support of skill acquisition is to use it to remove these soft barriers to practice. By rearranging your environment to make it as easy as possible to start practicing, you'll acquire the skill in far less time.

7. Make dedicated time for practice.

The time you spend acquiring a new skill must come from somewhere. Unfortunately, we tend to want to acquire new skills and keep doing many of the other activities we enjoy, like watching TV, playing video games, et cetera.

I'll get around to it, when I find the time, we say to ourselves.

Here's the truth: "finding" time is a myth.

No one ever "finds" time for *anything*, in the sense of miraculously discovering some bank of extra time, like finding a twenty-dollar bill you accidentally left in your coat pocket.

If you rely on finding time to do something, it will never be done. If you want to find time, you must *make* time.

You have 24 hours to invest each day: 1,440 minutes, no more or less. You will never have more time. If you sleep approximately 8 hours a day, you have 16 hours at your disposal. Some of those hours will be used to take care of yourself and your loved ones. Others will be used for work.

Whatever you have left over is the time you have for skill acquisition. If you want to improve your skills as quickly as possible, the larger the dedicated blocks of time you can set aside, the better.

The best approach to making time for skill acquisition is to identify low-value uses of time, then choose to eliminate them. As an experiment, I recommend keeping a simple log of how you spend your time for a few days. All you need is a notebook.

The results of this time log will surprise you: if you make a few tough choices to cut low-value uses of time, you'll have much more time for skill acquisition. The more time you have to devote each day, the less total time it will take to acquire new skills. I recommend making time for at least ninety minutes of practice each day by cutting low-value activities as much as possible.

I also recommend *precommitting* to completing at least twenty hours of practice. Once you start, you must keep practicing until you hit the twenty-hour mark. If you get stuck, keep pushing: you can't stop until you reach your target performance level or invest twenty hours. If you're not willing to invest at least twenty hours up front, choose another skill to acquire.

The reason for this is simple: the early parts of the skill acquisition process usually feel harder than they really are. You're often confused, and you'll run into unexpected problems and barriers. Instead of giving up when you experience the slightest difficulty, precommitting to twenty hours makes it easier to persist.

Think of this approach as an exercise in grit: you're not going to let some silly little issue stop you from doing what you've decided you really want to do. You'll either solve the problem, or do your best until you reach the twenty-hour mark. At that point, you'll be in a better position to decide how to proceed.

8. Create fast feedback loops.

"Fast feedback" means getting accurate information about how well you're performing as quickly as possible. The longer it takes to get accurate feedback, the longer it will take to acquire the skill.

Take the art of cheese making, for example. The subtle chemical processes that create fine cheeses often take months or years to complete, and there's no way to rush the process without ruining the result. If it takes six months to determine whether or not your cheese is any good, the delay in feedback makes it difficult to acquire the skill quickly.

Fast feedback naturally leads to rapid skill acquisition. If feedback arrives immediately, or with a very short delay, it's much easier to connect that information to your actions and make the appropriate adjustments.

The best forms of feedback are near instantaneous. That's why skills like programming can become mildly addictive: you make a change, and a few milliseconds later the computer tells you whether or not it worked. If you don't like the feedback ("my program crashed!"), make another change and try again.

There are many potential sources of useful feedback. As Atul Gawande, veteran surgeon and amateur tennis player, explained in an article in *The New Yorker*,[2] experienced coaches and mentors can give you immediate feedback on how you're performing and recommend necessary adjustments.

Coaches aren't the only source of fast feedback. Capture devices, like video cameras, can help you watch yourself as you perform. Tools like computer programs, training aides, and other devices can immediately indicate when you make a mistake or something is amiss.

The more sources of fast feedback you integrate into your practice, the faster you'll acquire the skill.

9. Practice by the clock in short bursts.

Our minds are built to learn—to notice patterns, simulate potential courses of action, and figure out what's probably going to happen next. They're not built to accurately estimate time—how long something will take, or how much time you've spent doing something.

In the early phases of practicing a new skill, it's very easy to overestimate how much time you've spent practicing. When you're no good (and you know it), time seems to slow to a crawl, and it feels like you've been practicing for a longer period of time than you actually have.

The solution for this is to practice by the clock. Buy a decent countdown timer[3] and set it for twenty minutes. There's only one rule: once you start the timer, you must practice until it goes off. No exceptions.

This simple technique will make it easier to complete longer periods of sustained practice, even when you get tired or frustrated.

The more periods of sustained practice you complete, the faster your skill acquisition. Set aside time for three to five practice sessions a day, and you'll see major progress in a very short period.

10. Emphasize quantity and speed.

When you begin to acquire a new skill, it's tempting to focus on practicing perfectly—a recipe for frustration. Your performance, of course, won't be anywhere close to perfection.

Instead of trying to be perfect, focus on practicing as much as you can as quickly as you can, while maintaining "good enough" form.

In *Art & Fear* (2001), authors David Bayles and Ted Orland share a very interesting anecdote on the value of volume:

> The ceramics teacher announced on opening day that he was dividing the class into two groups. All those on the left side of the studio, he said, would be graded solely on the quantity of work they produced, all those on the right solely on its quality.
>
> His procedure was simple: on the final day of class he would bring in his bathroom scales and weigh the work of the "quantity" group: fifty pounds of pots rated an A, forty pounds a B, and so on. Those being graded on "quality," however, needed to produce only one pot—albeit a perfect one—to get an A.
>
> Well, come grading time a curious fact emerged: the works of highest quality were all produced by the group being graded for quantity. It seems that while the "quantity" group was busily churning out piles of work and learning from their mistakes, the "quality" group had sat theorizing about perfection, and in the end had little more to show for their efforts than grandiose theories and a pile of dead clay.

Skill is the result of deliberate, consistent practice, and in early-stage practice, quantity and speed trump absolute quality. The faster and more often you practice, the more rapidly you'll acquire the skill.

That's not to say that you should ignore good form while practicing. Some skills, particularly skills that require physical actions or motions, require a certain quality of form to perform well. If you're practicing your painting technique, going Jackson Pollack on one hundred canvases in a day isn't going to help you if your aim is to paint lifelike portraits. Technique matters.

First, ensure you're practicing using form that's good enough to satisfy your target performance level. Once you're practicing in good form at least 80 to 90 percent of the time, crank up the speed for faster skill acquisition.

That's it: ten simple principles that will ensure you go about practicing your prime skill in the most efficient and effective way possible.

So Does it Work?

Will this method actually help you acquire skills more quickly? Research says absolutely.

In academic studies of cognitive and motor skill acquisition, researchers have noticed a common pattern: when study participants begin to practice a new skill, their performance always improves dramatically in a very short period of time. It doesn't take much practice at all to go from "very slow and grossly incompetent" to "reasonably fast and noticeably competent."

In the literature, this is referred to as the "power law of practice," and it appears over and over again. The effect has been widely known among skill acquisition researchers since at least 1926,[4] and it's been replicated many times since in studies of both physical and mental skills.[5] One study even went so far as to say "any theory of skill acquisition that does not accommodate the power law function for learning can be rejected immediately."[6]

Academic studies draw the "power law of practice" curve like this, with performance time on the y-axis and practice events on the x-axis:

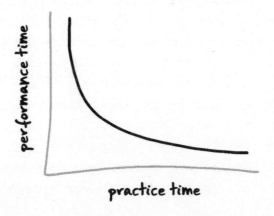

practice time

Since time is a quantity that increases, the curve slopes down. With practice, it takes less time to complete a given task.

It's interesting to note that if you relabel the y-axis as "how good you are" (that is, you define performance in more general terms versus a unit of time), you get the famous and widely known *learning curve*:

The general pattern of the learning curve looks like this: When you start, you're horrible, but you improve very quickly as you learn the most important parts of the skill. After reaching a certain level of skill very quickly, your rate of improvement declines, and subsequent improvement becomes much slower.

Contrary to popular usage, "steep learning curves" are good, not bad. The graph makes it clear why: Steep learning curves indicate a very fast rate of skill acquisition. The steeper the curve, the better you get per unit of time.

You can think of the checklist I just outlined as a way to intentionally make your personal learning curve steeper. The principles themselves are simple techniques that make the first two theoretical stages of the skill acquisition process (*cognition* and *association*) easier to do in practice.

Once you start practicing something new, your skills will naturally and noticeably improve in a very short period of time. The trick is to start practicing as quickly as possible. Not *thinking* about practicing or *worrying* about practicing, but *actually* practicing.

It's all too easy to feel like you're investing a lot of time in a skill without practicing very much at all. If you've wanted to learn something for a long time, you dream about being good at it, but you're hesitant to get started, you can spend *years* of mental and emotional energy without improving one bit. If you don't know where you're trying to go or don't have a solid strategy to get there, you can waste equal amounts of energy in unproductive wandering.

These ten principles are designed to help you eliminate this nonproductive thrashing and replace it with activities that are fundamental to the skill acquisition process. The more time and energy you spend moving through the first two phases of the skill acquisition process and the less time you spend doing things that don't help you, the more quickly you'll acquire the skill. Simple as that.

What About Immersion?

This isn't the only way to go about acquiring new skills, but it's certainly the most flexible. Other methods can produce similar results, but they require more significant tradeoffs.

The most well-known general method of rapid skill acquisition is *immersion*: completely changing your environment in a way that results in constant deliberate practice. If you want to learn to speak French, for example, learning through immersion would involve living in France for a few weeks or months.

In general, immersion works. If you move to France, you'll be forced to practice your speaking skills every moment of every day for as long as you're there. After a few frustrating days adapting to your new surroundings, you'll notice your skills improving at a rapid rate.

Immersion works because it ensures that you complete the crucial first hours of practice without fail: you can't escape your environment, so the practice happens automatically.

The downside of immersion is that it usually requires making the skill your primary focus for an extended period of time. If dropping all of your commitments, packing your bags, and moving to France is a workable option, learning French via immersion is a good strategy.

Unfortunately, most of us have commitments we can't (or don't want to) walk away from: family, work, mortgage payments, et cetera. In these cases, immersion can be difficult or impossible.

In the worst-case scenario, the idea of immersion becomes an active barrier: if you keep waiting for an immersion opportunity before committing to acquiring a new skill, you can waste years of valuable time.

Take the immersion opportunities as they come, but don't count on them. These techniques are designed to help you acquire new skills even if you only have an hour or two to spare each day.

Reactivating Old Skills

It's also important to note that these principles are useful even if the skill you're trying to acquire isn't completely new to you. It's entirely possible to use these techniques to reacquire old skills in record time.

For example, I learned to play the trumpet in high school, and I practiced enough that I was pretty good at it. Since graduating and going to college, I haven't played at all.

If I decided to pick up the trumpet again, it wouldn't take very much practice to reactivate the skill. I already know the required subskills, so I'd focus on embouchure (controlling the muscles around the lips while blowing into the mouthpiece), reading notes and recalling the related finger positions, and reviewing basic music theory (beats, tempo, dynamics, and expression).

It would only take a few hours of practice to reacquire the skill. Reactivation would mostly require making time, eliminating barriers to practice, and practicing by the clock.

Well Begun Is Half Done

Sometimes you'll want to give up the guitar. You'll hate the guitar. But if you stick with it, you're gonna be rewarded.
—JIMI HENDRIX, RENOWNED ELECTRIC-GUITAR PLAYER

You won't need to use every one of these principles for every skill you acquire, but you'll always find at least a handful of them essential.

I find it's useful to think of these principles as a checklist. Whenever you decide to learn something new, just go though the checklist and decide which principles apply to your particular project.

Here's the checklist for rapid skill acquisition:

1. Choose a lovable project.
2. Focus your energy on one skill at a time.
3. Define your target performance level.
4. Deconstruct the skill into subskills.
5. Obtain critical tools.
6. Eliminate barriers to practice.
7. Make dedicated time for practice.
8. Create fast feedback loops.
9. Practice by the clock in short bursts.
10. Emphasize quantity and speed.

That's it. Apply this checklist to your current prime skill, and your practice will be more effective and efficient, allowing you to acquire the skill more quickly.

As I said, this method isn't rocket science. It's common sense, strategy, and preparation applied to a skill you want to improve. Nothing more, nothing less.

Now, let's examine how learning and research can make your skill acquisition process even more effective.

3

Ten Principles of Effective Learning

No problem can withstand the assault of sustained thinking.
—VOLTAIRE

■ ■ ■

As we discussed in chapter 1, learning isn't the same thing as skill acquisition. That, however, doesn't mean learning is unimportant. Doing a bit of research before you jump into practice can save you precious time, energy, and emotional fortitude.

Learning makes your practice more efficient, which lets you spend more of your practice time working on the most important subskills first.

In that spirit, here are the ten major principles of effective learning:

1. Research the skill and related topics.

2. Jump in over your head.

3. Identify mental models and mental hooks.

4. Imagine the opposite of what you want.

5. Talk to practitioners to set expectations.

6. Eliminate distractions in your environment.

7. Use spaced repetition and reinforcement for memorization.

8. Create scaffolds and checklists.

9. Make and test predictions.

10. Honor your biology.

1. Research the skill and related topics.

Spend twenty minutes searching the web, browsing a bookstore, or scanning the stacks at your local library for books and resources related to the skill. The goal is to identify at least three books, instructional DVDs, courses, or other resources that appear to be connected to the skill you're trying to acquire.

Before you panic, understand that you don't have to spend hours memorizing these resources. On the contrary: time spent reading or watching is not time spent practicing.

You're not cramming for an exam. The intent of this early research is to identify the most important subskills, critical components, and required tools for practice as quickly as possible. The more you know in advance about the skill, the more intelligently you can prepare. The goal is to collect a wide body of knowledge about the skill as quickly as possible, creating an accurate overview of what the skill acquisition process will look like.

For rapid skill acquisition, skimming is better than deep reading. By noticing ideas and tools that come up over and over again in different texts, you can trust the accuracy of the patterns you notice and prepare your practice accordingly.

If you want to be able to bake the perfect croissant, pick up a few good books related to baking and pastries. Instead of reinventing the process, you'll find existing techniques that have been perfected over many years by the masters of the field. If you see the same technique or process described in multiple resources, chances are good it's important to know.

Once you've found what appear to be the most useful techniques, you can experiment with them in your own kitchen, saving you a ton of trial and error.

2. Jump in over your head.

Some of your early research will contain concepts, techniques, and ideas you don't understand. Often, something will appear particularly important, but you'll have no idea what it means. You'll read words you don't recognize, and see practitioners doing things you can't fathom.

Don't panic. Your initial confusion is completely normal. In fact, it's great. Move toward the confusion.

Early research is one of the best ways to identify critical subskills and ideas, but it's also very likely you won't know what they mean yet. The meaning comes later, once you've started practicing.

Dr. Stephen Krashen, the language acquisition expert I mentioned earlier, calls this *comprehensible input*. By default, the new information you're consuming isn't very comprehensible, since it's not connected to anything you know or have experienced. Over time, the same information will become comprehensible once you have some experience under your belt. In the words of renowned yoga teacher T. K. V. Desikachar: "The recognition of confusion is itself a form of clarity."

Noticing you're confused is valuable. Recognizing confusion can help you define exactly *what* you're confused about, which helps you figure out what you'll need to research or do next to resolve that confusion.

If you're not confused by at least half of your early research, you're not learning as quickly as you're capable of learning. If you start to feel intimidated or hesitant about the pace you're attempting, you're on the right track. Provided you're working on a lovable problem or project, the more confused you are at the outset, the more internal pressure you'll feel to figure things out, and the faster you'll learn.

Not being willing to jump in over your head is the single biggest emotional barrier to rapid skill acquisition. Feeling stupid isn't fun, but reminding yourself that you will understand with practice will help you move from confusion to clarity as quickly as possible.

3. Identify mental models and mental hooks.

As you conduct your research, you'll naturally begin to notice patterns: ideas and techniques that come up over and over again.

These concepts are called *mental models*, and they're very important. Mental models are the most basic unit of learning: a way of understanding and labeling an object or relationship that exists in the world. As you collect accurate mental models, it becomes easier to anticipate what will happen when you take a specific action. Mental models also make it much easier to discuss your experiences with others.

Here's an example: I was recently helping my father set up a website. As I went along, I tried to explain what I was doing. At first, it was frustrating for both of us: I kept using words like "server," and he had absolutely no idea what I was talking about.

Once Dad learned that a server is a special computer that delivers a web page to people who request it, and that the server was a *different* computer than the machine we were using, he found it much easier to understand what we were doing. In this case, server is a mental model—once you're familiar with the term, it's easier to understand the process of publishing a website.

You'll also notice a few things that look like something you're already familiar with. These are *mental hooks*: analogies and metaphors you can use to remember new concepts.

In the case of web servers, imagine a librarian. When you go to the library and request a specific book, a librarian will search shelves containing hundreds or thousands of books to find the exact book you're looking for. When the librarian finds the book, he or she brings it back for you. If the book can't be found, the librarian will tell you "I can't find the book you're looking for."

That's exactly how web servers work. When you request a specific web page, the server will search for that page in memory. If it finds the page, it will deliver it to you. If the server can't find the web page, it will return a message: "Error 404: Page Not Found." Thinking of the server software as a "computer librarian" is helpful when thinking about how the system works.

The more mental models and mental hooks you can identify in your early research, the easier it will be to use them while you're practicing.

4. Imagine the opposite of what you want.

A counterintuitive way to gain insight into a new skill is to contemplate disaster, not perfection.

What if you did everything wrong? What if you got the worst possible outcome?

This is a problem-solving technique called *inversion*, and it's helpful in learning the essentials of almost anything. By studying the opposite of what you want, you can identify important elements that aren't immediately obvious.

Take white-water kayaking. What would I need to know if I wanted to be able to kayak in a large, fast-moving, rock-strewn river?

Here's the inversion: What would it look like if everything went wrong?

- I'd flip upside down underwater, and not be able to get back up.
- I'd flood my kayak, causing it to sink or swamp, resulting in a total loss of the kayak.
- I'd lose my paddle, eliminating my maneuverability.
- I'd hit my head on a rock.
- I'd eject from my kayak, get stuck in a hydraulic (a point in the river where the river flows back on itself, creating a loop like a washing machine) and not be able to get out.

If I managed to do all of these things at once in the middle of a raging river, I'd probably die—the worst-case scenario.

This depressing line of thought is useful because it points to a few white-water kayaking skills that are probably very important:

- Learning to roll the kayak right side up if it flips, without ejecting.
- Learning how to prevent swamping the kayak if ejecting is necessary.
- Learning how to avoid losing my paddle in rough water.
- Learning and using safety precautions when rafting around large rocks.
- Scouting the river before the run to avoid dangerous river features entirely.

This mental simulation also gives me a shopping list: I'd need to invest in a flotation vest, helmet, and other safety gear.

Now, instead of (1) raft river (2) have fun (3) don't die, I have a concrete list of subskills to practice and actions to take to ensure I actually have fun, keep my gear, and survive the trip.

Inversion works.

5. Talk to practitioners to set expectations.

Early learning helps you set appropriate expectations: What does reasonable performance for a beginner actually look like?

When you jump into acquiring a new skill, it's very common to underestimate the complexity of the task, or the number of elements involved that are required to perform well. If the skill involves the possibility of social prestige, the associated mystique can also cloud early expectations.

Many wannabe rock stars have picked up an electric guitar, only to find it's extremely difficult to play well, sing on key, and look fabulous at the same time. Part of the problem is that "being a rock star" isn't a single skill. It's a bundle of many related subskills, each of which will require dedicated practice to develop.

Talking to people who have acquired the skill before you will help dispel myths and misconceptions before you invest your time and energy. By knowing what you can expect to see as you progress, you'll find it much easier to sustain your interest in practice, and avoid becoming discouraged early in the process.

6. Eliminate distractions in your environment.

Distractions are enemy number one of rapid skill acquisition. Distractions kill focused practice, and lack of focused practice leads to slow (or nonexistent) skill acquisition. You can preempt this by taking a few minutes to anticipate and eliminate (or reduce) as many distractions as possible before you start practicing.

The most significant sources of distraction come in two forms: electronic and biological.

Your television, phone, and Internet are electronic distractions. Turn them off, unplug them, block them, or otherwise remove them from your environment while you're practicing unless they're absolutely necessary for the practice itself.

Well-meaning family members, colleagues, and pets are biological distractions. You can't turn people off, but you can let them know in advance that you'll be unavailable while you're practicing, which makes it more likely they'll respect your practice time without interrupting.

The fewer distractions you have while practicing, the more quickly you'll acquire the skill.

7. Use spaced repetition and reinforcement for memorization.

To make use of material you've learned while practicing, you have to be able to recall related ideas quickly. Many skills require at least some level of memorization.

Here's the catch: your memory isn't perfect. Whenever you learn something new, you'll probably forget it unless you review the concept within a certain period of time. This repetition reinforces the idea, and helps your brain consolidate it into long-term memory.

Researchers have found that memory follows a *decay curve*: new concepts need to be reinforced regularly, but the longer you've known a concept, the less regularly you need to review it to maintain accurate recall.

Spaced repetition and reinforcement is a memorization technique that helps you systematically review important concepts and information on a regular basis. Ideas that are difficult to remember are reviewed often, while easier and older concepts are reviewed less often.

Flash card software programs like Anki,[1] SuperMemo,[2] and Smartr[3] make spaced repetition and reinforcement very simple. Spaced repetition systems rely on a "flash card" model of review, and you have to create the flash cards yourself. By creating flash cards as you're deconstructing the skill, you're killing two birds with one stone.

Once you've created your flash cards, it only takes a few minutes each day to review them. By systematizing the review process and tracking recall, these systems can help you learn new ideas, techniques, and processes in record time. If you review the decks consistently, you'll memorize necessary concepts and ideas extremely quickly.

It's important to note that skill acquisition is usually much more in-volved than academic learning. If you're primarily interested in memoriz-ing concepts, ideas, or vocabulary in order to pass an exam, you don't need much more than spaced repetition.[4]

The best use of this technique is in instances where fast recall of infor-mation is essential. If you're learning common vocabulary words in order to acquire a new language, spaced repetition and reinforcement is valu-able. In instances where fast recall isn't crucial, you're usually better off skipping the flash cards in favor of maximizing practice and experimenta-tion time.

8. Create scaffolds and checklists.

Many skills involve some sort of routine: setting up, preparing, main-taining, putting away, et cetera. Creating a simple system is the best way to ensure these important elements happen with as little additional effort as possible.

Checklists are handy for remembering things that must be done every time you practice. They're a way to systematize the process, which frees your attention to focus on more important matters.

Scaffolds are structures that ensure you approach the skill the same way every time. Think of the basketball player who establishes a pre–free throw routine. Wipe hands on pants, loosen the shoulders, catch the ball from the ref, bounce three times, pause for three seconds, and shoot. That's a scaffold.

Creating scaffolds and checklists makes your practice more efficient. They also make your practice easier to visualize, which helps you take ad-vantage of mental rehearsal, which can help with some forms of physical practice.

9. Make and test predictions.

Part of the skill acquisition process involves experimentation: trying new things to see if they work.

The true test of useful learning is prediction. Based on what you know, can you guess how a change or experiment will turn out before you do it?

Getting into the habit of making and testing predictions will help you acquire skills more rapidly. It's a variation on the scientific method, with four key elements:

- **Observations**—what are you currently observing?
- **Knowns**—what do you know about the topic already?
- **Hypotheses**—what do you think will improve your performance?
- **Tests**—what are you going to try next?

I recommend using a notebook or other reference tool to track your experiments and form hypotheses as you practice. By keeping track of your predictions and generating new ideas, you'll have more fruitful experiments to test.

10. Honor your biology.

Your brain and body are biological systems that have biological needs: food, water, exercise, rest, and sleep. It's very easy to push yourself too hard, which is counterproductive. Without the proper inputs, your body and mind won't produce useful output.

According to Tony Schwartz, author of *The Power of Full Engagement* (2004) and *Be Excellent at Anything* (2011), the optimal learning cycle appears to be approximately ninety minutes of focused concentration. Any more, and your mind and body will naturally need a break. Use that opportunity to exercise, rest, have a meal or snack, take a nap, or do something else.

This principle dovetails very nicely with practicing by the clock. By setting your timer for sixty to ninety minutes before you start practicing or researching, it will be easier to remember to take a break when you're done.

You can also split your practice into several smaller parts, with a short break in the middle if needed: twenty minutes of practice, ten-minute break, twenty minutes of practice, ten-minute break, et cetera.

Stacking the Deck

There ain't no rules around here. We're trying to accomplish something.
—THOMAS EDISON, INVENTOR

You won't need to use all of these principles for every skill you acquire, but you'll always find at least a few of them essential.

I find it's useful to think of these principles as a secondary checklist. Whenever you decide to acquire a new skill, just review this checklist and decide which principles apply to your project.

Here's the checklist for effective learning:

- Research the skill and related topics.
- Jump in over your head.
- Identify mental models and mental hooks.
- Imagine the opposite of what you want.
- Talk to practitioners to set expectations.
- Eliminate distractions in your environment.
- Use spaced repetition and reinforcement for memorization.
- Create scaffolds and checklists.
- Make and test predictions.
- Honor your biology.

That's it: apply this checklist to your current prime skill and you'll learn what you need to know to practice efficiently and effectively.

Putting Theory into Practice

How vain it is to sit down to write when you have not stood up to live.
—HENRY DAVID THOREAU

Enough theory: it's time for practice.

We've already covered the basics of rapid skill acquisition, but knowing how to do these things isn't nearly as important as actually doing them. Remember: no practice, no skill acquisition.

Instead of going on and on about the theory of skill acquisition, I'll show you how to actually do it. I'm going to use these principles to acquire several new skills, and you'll have a front row seat.

Here are the skills I intend to acquire:

- Yoga: developing a home asana practice.
- Programming: creating a functioning web application.
- Typing: relearning to touch-type with a nonstandard keyboard layout.
- Strategy: playing Go, the world's oldest and most complex board game.
- Music: playing the ukulele.
- Windsurfing: sailing and maneuvering on flat water.

I have no experience with any of these skills. Using the techniques and methods I just described, my goal is to acquire each of them in thirty days or less. My estimated time of acquiring each of these skills is approximately twenty hours, averaging sixty to ninety minutes of practice each day.

About These Examples

These particular skills are completely idiosyncratic. They're things I'm interested in learning for various reasons, which I'll explain later in detail. The skills *you* want to acquire may be quite different, but the core skill acquisition process will be largely the same.

My hope is that in showing you how I've used this process to acquire many different skills in many different areas, you'll come away with a more complete understanding of how to use these techniques to get better at the skills that matter to you.

If you're naturally more interested in one or two of these examples over the others, that's okay. Read those chapters first. If you start reading a chapter and find the skill boring or not applicable to your situation, feel free to skip it. I'm using the same core method for all of these examples, so you won't miss any crucial parts of the approach.

I'm writing these chapters in tutorial format, under the assumption you've never seen these skills before, so you don't have to have any experience or prior knowledge to follow along. In addition to illustrating the method, I hope you're also able to take away some valuable knowledge about six interesting skills that are worth practicing.

If you have a lot of experience in one of these subjects, it's likely you'll notice an error in my understanding, a mistake in my verbiage, or a disagreement with my method. That's totally fine. Remember, *I'm starting as a complete beginner, and I don't know what I'm doing.* (Yet.)

What you'll read is an overview of my learning process for each of these skills. I've made every attempt to ensure the information in this book is accurate and complete, but I'm bound to make mistakes. In all cases, the *method* of research and deliberate practice is what's most important.

First up: yoga.

4

Yoga

Lesson: Don't Make it Harder Than it Needs to Be

I do not measure my progress in Yoga by how far I can bend or twist, but by how I treat my wife and children.

—T. K. V. DESIKACHAR, RENOWNED YOGA TEACHER

■　■　■

For supplementary images, video, and commentary about this chapter, visit http://first20hours.com/yoga.

'm getting old.

To clarify: relatively speaking, I'm still a young man, but I'm beginning to notice a few things about my body that concern me.

When I wake up in the morning, I often have a dull ache in the middle of my back. After a long day in front of the computer, my neck and shoulders feel tight and sore. It's not a pleasant sensation.

Up to this point, I haven't thought much about my body. It just worked. After leaving high school, and with it, organized sports, I haven't exercised at all. Once I started college, I began treating my body as a vehicle whose only purpose was to transport my brain from one class to the next.

Since graduation that hasn't changed, and up to this point I've felt okay. Now, those years of physical neglect are catching up with me.

I'm crunchy, and I know it.

"You Should Really Look into Yoga . . ."

Kelsey, my wife, has been doing yoga since college. Every day or so, she'd walk down the street to the local studio and spend an hour or more contorting herself into various positions in a very warm room. She loved it, and always came home happy and relaxed.

Every week, Kelsey would tell me "You should really try yoga. It's great. You'd really like it."

I hesitated. Yoga, to me, just wasn't very appealing.

It wasn't the stretching. I ran track in high school, so stretching wasn't a big deal. My favorite event was the 110-meter hurdles, which required a significant level of flexibility.[1]

Training for hurdles involved a lot of stretching, and I've maintained a lot of the flexibility I developed during those years, particularly in my hamstrings. Even now, over a decade later, I can place my palms on the floor without bending my knees.

My hesitation in practicing yoga was, to put it bluntly, how *weird* it seemed.

Chakras, Auras, and Kundalinis, Oh My!

Sh!t Yogis Say,[2] a video produced by lululemon,[3] one of the most profitable athletic apparel retailers in the world, is a tongue-in-cheek, over-the-top example of how yoga can sound to the uninitiated. Here are a few highlights:

- "I'm concerned about your aura . . ."
- "How do you say that in Sanskrit?"
- "My chakras are *so* aligned."
- "Want to see where I can put my leg?"

The video has been viewed over 2 million times since it was released on YouTube in December 2011, so it clearly struck a chord.

I'm a pretty rational, down-to-earth guy. I'm prepared to believe that stretching on a regular basis is good for you. Learning a sequence of stretches seems perfectly reasonable.

All of this talk about auras, chakras, and esoteric spiritual devotionals, however, is a huge turnoff. I don't know what any of that has to do with exercise, and frankly, the hippie mysticism makes yoga sound like some weird cult.

That's not all. The practice of yoga in America has evolved into a lifestyle at the center of an 8 billion dollar fitness and clothing industry. Showing off how yogic you are has become a trendy social status signal, the obnoxious earth-child equivalent of carrying the latest handbag from Louis Vuitton.

No thanks. My "chakras" are fine, thank you very much.

"Relax Your Face"

Eventually, Kelsey convinced me to try yoga as a New Year's resolution. I was working from home, so she pitched it as a good way to get out of the apartment and meet people. I was still skeptical, but I decided to humor her.

We secured memberships at Pure Yoga, a brand new high-end studio on New York's Upper East Side. Many of the classes were taught by Marco Rojas, Kelsey's favorite teacher and one of the top-rated instructors in the city.

Imagine a younger, leaner version of Antonio Banderas in yoga pants, and you have Marco. He's handsome, charismatic, and has a killer voice with a Spanish accent. Marco's classes are *packed*, both because he's a genuinely great teacher, and because 99 percent of the yoginis in the city have a serious crush on him. (And who can blame them?)

Since I was brand new to yoga, I tried my best to follow along as Marco taught. I didn't know the poses, or what each pose was called, so I just watched what everyone else was doing and tried to imitate. It took a lot of concentration. I could keep up, but it was a struggle. Some poses, like headstands, were way beyond my ability.

I tried to stay toward the back of the room, so I could watch what everyone else was doing, and also reduce collateral damage in case I fell, which happened more often than I'd like to admit.

I enjoyed Marco's classes, but I didn't really grok what was going on. Every now and again, Marco would stop by my mat and adjust me, helping me do the pose correctly.

On one memorable occasion, Marco braced my feet with his own, so they were perpendicular to the floor. Then, he grabbed my hands and pulled. Hard.

"Engage your quadriceps . . . pivot at the hips. Good. Now . . . relax your face."

I was grimacing, and for good reason: my wrists were touching my toes. I relaxed my face.

The "Householder" Dilemma

As much as I enjoyed Marco's courses, it was hard to make time for them. Each class was an hour and a half, not including the time it took to walk to the studio, change, shower afterward, and walk home.

Even though the studio was only a few blocks away, it was still a solid two-hour commitment. I was working from home at a demanding job for a Fortune 500 company at the time, and I often had meetings that overlapped with the scheduled class times. It didn't help that the classes were in the middle of the morning and afternoon, which meant I'd have to skip out on work to attend. Generally speaking, my work arrangements were flexible, so it was mostly a psychological problem: it was hard to convince myself it was acceptable to go twist my body into knots for two hours when there was work to be done.

In the end, I attended maybe fifteen classes that year. Even though I felt great after each class, I just couldn't justify the time commitment.

In addition, I wasn't practicing at home. I didn't know how. During class, I was mimicking other students. I could roll a mat on the floor at home and stretch, but in my mind, that wasn't really yoga.

When the Student Is Ready, the Teacher Appears

After we moved to Colorado, Kelsey mentioned to me one evening that she missed New York. She missed going to Marco's classes, and she missed Leslie Kaminoff's yoga anatomy course, which she took after completing her yoga teacher certification. Leslie is the coauthor of *Yoga Anatomy* (first edition, 2007; second edition, 2011), one of the bestselling yoga books of all time, and his material is used in yoga teacher training programs all over the world. Unfortunately, to take Leslie's course, you had to live in New York City, so Kelsey had to stop when we moved.

"Someone should really put Leslie's course online," she said.

Here's the irony. A few weeks earlier, Kelsey had helped me launch my first online course, so she knew how to do it. She was also right about Leslie's course: since it was only available for students who lived in New York City, but students from all over the world wanted to participate, it would make a lot of sense to publish the course online.

I pointed out the obvious: Kelsey was fully capable of creating the course if Leslie was willing to let her produce it. That night, she sent Leslie a proposal.

Two days later, Kelsey and Leslie agreed to move forward, and Kelsey founded her first business, an online yoga course production company.

Since we were both working from home, I suddenly started hearing a *lot* more about yoga. Part of the production process involves watching raw footage from each class, then making detailed notes for the video editor and transcriptionists. As a result, I ended up listening to bits and pieces of Leslie's course as Kelsey was producing it.

The Moment I Decided to Get Serious About Yoga

One of the first things that piqued my interest was Leslie's tone. He didn't sound anything like a woo-woo hippie, which is what I expected. On the contrary, he has three decades of hands-on experience in anatomy, physiology, and sports medicine, and has very little tolerance for fluffy terminology.

From Leslie's perspective, yoga is valuable primarily because it's useful. Yoga, as a practice, is very good at building strength, increasing flexibility, and maintaining range of motion.

Yoga is even more effective when you focus on the breathing aspect of the practice. Most people think of yoga practice as an odd combination of aerobics, gymnastics, and contortion, but that's not an accurate picture. What makes yoga *yoga* is combining breathing, movement, and a mindful mental state.

Leslie also explains some of the oddities in yogic terminology. Early practitioners were experimenting with the body and mind. They were trying to do science before modern disciplines like anatomy, biology, and cognitive psychology were formalized.

As a result, when these early practitioners found something interesting, their only option was to explain what they found in terms of story or metaphor. For example, when yogic practitioners discovered that specific poses and breathing techniques tended to provoke certain emotional responses, they explained what they noticed in the best way they could.

That's the origin of concepts like *chakras*: scientifically, there are no hidden pools of energy in your bowels, sacrum, solar plexus, heart, throat, forehead, and crown. As metaphors, however, they helped early practitioners talk about something they were experiencing internally. The metaphors were useful enough that they stuck around.

The last straw came in the form of a YouTube video Leslie presented during one of his first online classes. In the video, Gil Hedley,[4] a human anatomy teacher, is leading an educational autopsy of a human cadaver for a group of students.[5] At one point in the video, Gil highlights an interesting feature of muscular fascia, the layers of fibrous tissue that encase our muscles.

Just like ligaments and tendons, fascia is connective tissue: it binds our bodies together. By encasing muscle groups, our fascia helps us move by allowing our muscles to slide over each other more easily.

There is, however, a drawback: when these layers of fascia are at rest, "fuzzy" strands of connective tissue, which have roughly the appearance and consistency of cotton candy, begin to grow *between* the fascia.

Normally, that's not a big deal. Individual strands are very thin, so the sliding of muscles over each other breaks them easily. The trouble comes when you don't move enough.

If you don't move your muscles for a certain period of time, the "fuzz" stays there and gradually builds up over time. When the fuzz gets thick enough, it can solidify, limiting your normal range of motion.

I *know* I'm not moving enough, so this video got my attention. Is the "crunchiness" I've been feeling my body's way of telling me my muscles are fuzzing over? (That's creepy!)

That's one potential explanation, but it's not the only possibility. According to Leslie, back and neck pain can also be caused by a lack of oxygen flowing to the muscles in question, a situation called *ischemia*. Lack of movement can cause a shortage of blood flow to the muscles. When a muscle runs short of oxygen, its pain receptors begin to fire, creating that persistent, dull ache. The longer the condition persists, the more pain you'll experience.

Chronic stress and suppressed breathing patterns also contribute to ischemia. These causes often go together: it's common for people to hold their breath when they are experiencing stress. If you help your muscles get more oxygen by moving, breathing, and reducing your general level of stress, the muscle aches go away.[6]

Regardless, frequent movement and oxygen intake are important in relieving muscle pain and maintaining range of motion. Yoga combines movement, breathing, and meditation, so it's typically very effective in reducing or eliminating chronic muscle pain.

That's enough evidence for me. I'm going to learn how to do yoga.

Now . . . how do I start?

What Is "Yoga," Really?

If I'm going to do yoga, I'll need to have some fundamental understanding of what it is I'm doing. If yoga only consisted of stretching, people would just call it "stretching."

As it turns out, the key to identifying the essence of yoga is understanding where it comes from and how it became what we call "yoga" today.[7]

Yoga has existed in various forms for thousands of years. The earliest recognizable evidence of yoga comes from artifacts recovered from archeological sites related to the Indus Valley civilization, which was located in present-day Pakistan and northwest India from 3300 to 1300 BCE.

Yoga, as a philosophy and practice, was a set of nonreligious techniques that were intertwined with the religious and philosophical traditions of the region. Ancient Vedic priests completed elaborate physical rituals to connect the physical world to the divine in search of Brahma, the "ultimate ground of all being." The word "yoga" comes from the ancient Sanskrit word for *yoke*. In the same sense that an ox is attached to a plow to work a field, through their rituals, the priests were trying to tie the spiritual world to the physical world.

Over time, Vedic tradition waned. Priests began to explore the idea of *atman*, the essence of the human self. External physical ritual turned to introspective meditation, and spiritual practitioners began to renounce the material world and complex ritual in favor of roaming the forests, practicing meditation, and taking vows of poverty and asceticism in search of ultimate truth.

Yājñavalkya, a sage who lived in what's now called the Upanishadic period, proposed that the grasping human ego prevents us from knowing our real selves. By destroying the ego, we can become one with our atman, our "soul" or essential self. Yājñavalkya also introduced the idea of *karma*, which he defined as actions taken to achieve liberation from the ego. By separating the body from the atman, it was possible to attain what the Buddha would later call enlightenment.

Enter the Asanas

Yājñavalkya's philosophical insight led to the development of what most practitioners consider the core of contemporary yoga practice: physical postures combined with controlled breathing and meditation. As religious historical scholar Karen Armstrong explains in *The Great Transformation*:[8]

Yoga is one of India's greatest achievements and, in its most evolved form, almost certainly was first designed [by practitioners] to release the *purusha* [essential self] from the entanglement of nature.

This classical yoga was very different from the version of yoga that is often taught in the West today. It was not an aerobic exercise, and it did not help people to feel better about their lives—quite the contrary. Yoga was a systematic assault on the ego, an exacting regimen that over a long period of time taught the aspirant to abolish his normal consciousness with its errors and delusions, and replace it with the ecstatic discovery of his *purusha*.

Yoga was a full-time job. It wasn't for the dabbler or the faint of heart: it was a demanding, exacting spiritual discipline, the exclusive domain of monks and gurus. Classical yogis didn't practice to get stronger or more flexible. They strove to sever the link between their body and their atman. Heavy stuff.

The Codification of Yoga

In the second century BCE, a scholar named Patañjali began compiling and curating the yoga philosophies and practices of the time. Patañjali's summary of the best (*raja*, or "kingly") practices became *The Yoga Sutras of Patañjali*, a collection of aphorisms that went on to become the foundational text of yoga practitioners.

In *The Yoga Sutras*, Patañjali outlined eight fundamental aspects, or "limbs" of *raja* yoga practice:

- **Yama**—morality
- **Niyama**—self-purification
- **Asana**—posture
- **Pranayama**—breath control
- **Pratyahara**—sense control
- **Dharana**—intention
- **Dhyana**—meditation
- **Samadhi**—absorption/contemplation

Patañjali called this system "ashtanga," or "eight-limbed" yoga. By diligently practicing all eight limbs of yoga, the practitioner would experience *kaivalya*: a perfect detachment of the practitioner's soul from the material world, leading to eternal happiness.

What most people think of when they hear the word "yoga"—bending yourself into strange postures—is only one limb, *asana*. Asana is typically practiced with specific breathing techniques called *pranayama*. The intent of practice is to prepare for meditation (*dhyana*).

Patañjali's system focused on yoga as a philosophy, not as a system of exercise. Asana was mostly limited to static seated poses—a far cry from the gymnastic contortions modern practitioners are familiar with.

That's not to say intense poses didn't exist. *Hatha* (forceful) yoga poses had been around since Yājñavalkya, but athleticism wasn't the primary concern.

The most famous compilation of hatha yoga practices is the *Hatha Yoga Pradipika* by Maharishi Swatmarama, a fifteenth-century sage. Swatmarama considered hatha yoga the ideal way to attain Patañjali's *raja* yoga. By purifying the body through exercise, practicing pranayama, and ritually inhaling smoke while doing a headstand, Swatmarama believed hatha practitioners could achieve higher states of consciousness.

Early forms of hatha yoga never really caught on. Intense physical posture practice remained an obscure offshoot of *raja* yoga until a Brahman from Mysore, India, revolutionized the practice four centuries later.

The Man Who "Invented" Modern Yoga

Tirumalai Krishnamacharya was born in 1888, the eldest son of Sri Tatacharya, a well-known Brahman priest.[9] Krishnamacharya was introduced to hatha practice by his father at the age of five, and continued strict hatha practice throughout his formal education. In 1919, he arranged to travel to Mount Kailash in Tibet to study under one of the last remaining masters of hatha yoga, Sri Ramamohana Brahmachari.

Krishnamacharya studied under Brahmachari for seven and a half years, memorizing the *Yoga Sutras* of Patañjali and practicing asana. He also, as the story goes, picked up a few attention-grabbing feats of skill, like slowing his respiration and stopping his pulse for extended periods of time. Krishnamacharya would later use these skills to great effect, demonstrating them in public as a way of popularizing hatha practice.

The Guru's Request

The guru/student relationship has a long and established history in India. At the end of a student's tenure with his or her guru, it's customary for the student to offer a payment to the guru, a practice called *guru dakshina*, as a gesture of thanks and deep respect for the guru's teaching. Often, the payment consisted of money or material goods, but sometimes the guru requested completion of a special task. When Krishnamacharya's studies were complete, Brahmachari's request was simple: Krishnamacharya was to marry, have children, and teach the yoga he had learned at Mount Kailash.

Brahmachari's request was *shocking*. Krishnamacharya had already been appointed to several high-status religious and educational positions, under the expectation he'd eventually assume his great-grandfather's position as the primary religious leader of South India. To get a sense of the status shock, imagine being appointed as the CEO of a prestigious company, only to be told you're duty-bound to work as a janitor instead. Brahmachari's *dakshina* was a permanent sentence of hardship and low status.

Krishnamacharya honored his guru's request and returned to Mysore, living in abject poverty and looking for opportunities to teach hatha yoga.

In 1931, Krishnamacharya was invited to teach hatha at the Sanskrit College in Mysore. There, he was introduced to Krishna Raja Wadiyar IV, the ruling maharaja of Mysore. Impressed with Krishnamacharya's abilities and scholarship, and thankful for Krishnamacharya's help in managing his diabetes, the maharaja invited Krishnamacharya to open a yoga school in the palace under his patronage.

Since most of the students at the *yoga shala* in Mysore were energetic young boys, Krishnamacharya developed a new form of hatha yoga practice that emphasized building strength and increasing flexibility. He combined traditional hatha asanas and pranayama with movements from British gymnastics, adapting and modifying the sequence for each individual student.[10]

A New Yoga

That was the genesis of what is known today as ashtanga vinyasa yoga. If you go to a yoga class in a gym or pick up any book that contains the words *ashtanga*, *vinyasa*, "Power," "Flow," "Core," *viniyoga*, or Iyengar, you're practicing in the tradition of Krishnamacharya.

Krishnamacharya adapted his teaching to the needs of his students. Ashtanga yoga was popularized by one of Krishnamacharya's first devotees, K. Pattabhi Jois, who studied with him in Mysore. Ashtanga primarily focuses on six vigorous sequences of poses, starting with the "Primary Series," which Krishnamacharya taught at the *yoga shala*. Present-day ashtanga practice retains this emphasis on sequence and athleticism.

When instructing his brother-in-law, B. K. S. Iyengar, Krishnamacharya emphasized the alignment of the body in asana, given Iyengar's fragile health at the time. Iyengar went on to develop this approach into the alignment-oriented style of yoga practiced today.

Later in life, when Krishnamacharya was spending most of his time working as a healer, he taught his son, T. K. V. Desikachar, the therapeutic aspects of asana practice. Today, Desikachar's students emphasize yoga as a tool for wellness, and are exploring a wide range of potential health applications, from physical therapy to anxiety relief. As a result, pretty much every major form of modern yoga has been heavily influenced by Krishnamacharya's teachings.

What didn't change was the emphasis on normal people with everyday responsibilities. Krishnamacharya's yoga was not for the monk or ascetic: his focus on personalized practice for everyday people made asana accessible for millions of busy people around the world. In the words of T. K. V. Desikachar: "You do yoga so you can live your life, not the other way around."

Yoga = Breathing + Movement + Meditation

Back to the present. What does any of this history have to do with modern yoga?

Here's what surprised me: modern asana practice, historically speaking, is a *recent* invention. Sure, the philosophical bits of yoga have been around for a few thousand years, but the actual practice of spending time assuming postures while breathing and meditating is, historically speaking, practically brand new.

The emphasis on strength and flexibility in yoga practice is also new. Very few of us are actively trying to forcibly dissociate our soul from our body in search of our atman. Most modern yoga practitioners aren't ascetics or renunciates. In general, present-day yoga practitioners are primarily concerned with staying fit, improving flexibility, and shedding some stress.

At the core, it's clear that modern yoga practice consists of combining movement, breathing, and meditation. The poses themselves aren't magical. They've changed a lot over the centuries, and Krishnamacharya wasn't shy about adding new elements or modifying the practice to fit the student.

It's also clear that yoga isn't about flashy moves. There's a philosophical bent to the practice: a recognition that you're spending time in this way in the service of becoming a better person. Even though modern asana is relatively new, yoga philosophy has been around for thousands of years, and it's interesting in its own right. Yoga is deep in ways that the latest fitness fads aren't.

There's also no need to go out of your way to practice crazy poses. Being a "real" yogi doesn't mean being able to assume Gumby-like positions: it's practicing in a way that helps you live a better life. Can't do a pose because you're not flexible enough, strong enough, or have an injury? No problem: adjust the pose, or do a different one. As long as you're focusing on your breath as you move, and you pay attention to what your body is telling you, you're doing it right.

At the core, modern yoga practice is about integrating breathing, movement, and mindfulness meditation. It's not about gymnastics, acrobatics, or becoming super flexible. Being super flexible or acrobatic does not make you a better yogi.

Clearing up Misconceptions

Here are a few more common misconceptions about yoga:

- You don't need to know thousands of poses to do yoga. Knowing lots of poses does not make you a better yogi. Krishnamacharya himself started with twenty-four.

- You don't need to know the Sanskrit names of the poses, or even the English names of the poses. Knowing a lot of poses or their names does not make you a better yogi.

- Some yoga practitioners adhere to religions like Hinduism, but religious belief is not necessary to benefit from asana practice.

- Some yoga practitioners adopt diets like vegetarianism, veganism, or practice Ayurveda, but a special diet isn't a prerequisite for asana practice.

- Some yoga practitioners are also interested in alternative medicine, astrology, and other similar topics, but these interests are not prerequisites for asana practice.

All of these things are misconceptions I had when I first heard about yoga. A little time spent learning what yoga practice *actually is* was enough to alleviate my initial concerns, as well as prevent me from wasting time on things that aren't important.

Is Yoga Dangerous?

There's one last thing I'm concerned about: Can I hurt myself doing yoga?

Around the time I was researching asana, an inflammatory article about yoga practice was published in the *New York Times*. The article, titled "How Yoga Can Wreck Your Body,"[11] was written by the *Times'* staff science journalist, William J. Broad. The essay was essentially an excerpt from Broad's book, *The Science of Yoga: The Risks and the Rewards* (2012), which was slated for release a few weeks after the article was published.

The article prompted a lot of hand-wringing in the yoga world. Broad cited quite a few scientific studies about the benefits of asana practice, mostly related to range of motion and emotional balance. He then went on the attack, suggesting yoga practice is responsible for a wide range of serious injuries, from sprains to strokes. In a few cases, Broad suggested yoga was responsible for practitioners lapsing into a coma.

This topic is an example of a useful *inversion*. What does it look like to do yoga incorrectly, and what are the most significant risks of asana practice?

The yoga teaching community's response to Broad's article and book was swift and fierce: Given the evidence, Broad sensationalized. Yoga, like any physical activity, has risks, but those risks aren't likely to seriously harm you if you practice in a safe way.

While it is indeed possible to injure yourself doing yoga, major health issues like strokes and comas are extremely rare, and there's no evidence that suggests asana practice increases the risk of major injury. Compared to other physical activities, even noncontact sports like golf, yoga is statistically very safe.

As for muscle sprains, strains, and tears, those types of injuries are certainly possible if you force your body into poses, ignoring pain and discomfort. If you believe that "real" yogis should be able to touch their noses to their knees, and you force your body into that position, you run the risk of spraining ligaments or tearing your hamstrings. Likewise, if a yoga teacher forcefully adjusts you in a way that exceeds your body's limits, you're likely to sustain an injury.

One significant potential area for injury is the cervical spine. Some poses, like headstands, put pressure on the head and neck, and if you fall in the wrong way while doing them, it's possible to seriously injure your neck or spine.

Based on this information, as long as I listen to my body, don't force myself into poses, and avoid unnecessary weight on my cervical spine, I can reap the benefits of practice without significant risk of injury. That's great to know.

Minimum Viable Asana

I'm all set to start practicing . . . so where do I begin?

It's clear that there are many types, forms, and philosophies of what yoga "should" look like. That's all well and good, but I need to take a step back and decide what the purpose of yoga is for *me*.

Why am I doing this?

I want to be more physically active, and my body is making it clear that I need to move more. My doctor has recommended range-of-motion exercise, and mentioned yoga as an option. I've read about the benefits of both exercise and meditation, and I like that yoga combines both. I don't have time to go to a studio for long classes, so I'd like to be able to practice at home in a way that's effective and safe.

That's enough detail for a useful target performance level. Here's mine:

1. Learn a sequence of physical postures I can practice to increase my daily level of physical exertion, strength, and general flexibility.

2. Combine exercise with breathing and meditation, reaping several major physical and mental benefits in a single period of time.

3. Practice safely from memory for twenty to thirty minutes, adjusting for duration, strength, flexibility, and general level of energy.

Yoga Equipment

Before I start practicing, I'll need some basic equipment. First and foremost is a mat, which provides some cushioning and prevents hands and feet from slipping out of position. Yoga practice can be sweaty, and if you slip, it can lead to an injury, so getting a good mat is important.

When I practiced at Pure Yoga, they supplied the mats, which was nice. I noticed, however, that the mats were a bit too short for me. I'd often find myself slipping off the edge, and I'd have to stop and adjust. It's probably best if I can find a longer mat.

After a bit of research, I settled on an eighty-five inch Manduka PRO mat.[12] It's extra long, super grippy, very durable, and happens to be a nice green color. Works for me.

In addition, I picked up a mat bag and a few hand towels, just in case my hands get sweaty. I already have shorts and T-shirts, as well as a few pairs of yoga pants, so I'm set in terms of clothing. Asana is practiced barefoot, so I don't need special shoes.

At Kelsey's suggestion, I purchased a long cotton strap and a bamboo block, which she says can help when modifying certain poses.

That's all the equipment I need, which is nice. You don't need a lot of stuff to do yoga.

Learning the Poses

Here's my initial strategy: Kelsey is a trained yoga teacher, so it makes sense to start with her instruction. We set aside ninety minutes one afternoon to cover the basics.

If I didn't have a yoga teacher in the family, I'd book a private tutorial with a local instructor. One-on-one coaching for this type of learning is very helpful, since movement is difficult to learn from a book.

That doesn't mean I'm skipping the books. I've already picked up a few resources:

- *Yoga Anatomy* by Leslie Kaminoff and Amy Matthews (2011)
- *Yoga for Wellness* by Gary Kraftsow (1999)
- *Ashtanga Yoga: Practice and Philosophy* by Gregor Maehle (2007)
- *Breath-Centered Yoga with Leslie Kaminoff* (DVD) by Leslie Kaminoff (2010)

I'm using these resources primarily as references. They contain photographs and illustrations of poses, as well as detailed instructions on how to do each pose properly, so I'll look up information as necessary. I'll know more about what I need to learn after I start practicing.

Kelsey and I roll out our mats and begin. First up: Sun Salutations.

The Sun Salutation Sequence

Sun Salutations are a sequence of postures designed to help you warm up your body, so most asana practices begin with a few rounds.

A quick note if you decide to try these yourself: Everyone is different, and the "right" way to do each pose depends on your body's unique limits. If you pay attention to what your body is telling you, avoid overextending, and adjust each pose to your personal limits, you'll be able to practice asana safely.

Here's how it goes:

1. Inhale. Stand straight at the front of the mat, arms relaxed at your sides, knees soft.

2. Exhale. Bring your hands up into the universal "prayer" position in front of your chest.

3. Inhale while bringing your arms up and out to the side until they are fully extended above your head. Then, look up at your hands. (If that feels uncomfortable, just look straight ahead.)

4. Exhale and fold forward, hinging at your hips to bring your hands down to the floor to touch your toes. Go as far as you can without overextending; it's okay to bend your knees. Relax your shoulders and neck.

5. Inhale and look at the wall in front of you while your hands maintain contact with the floor. (Alternatively, try to straighten your legs while keeping your head and neck relaxed.)

6. Exhale as you return to the forward bend.

7. Inhale as you step your feet back to "push-up position," so your body is fully extended with your arms and the bottom of your toes supporting your weight. You can either walk your feet back or jump, as you prefer. (This pose is called Plank.)

8. Exhale and lower yourself toward the ground, as if you're doing a push-up. Don't rest on the ground; stop an inch or two from the

mat and pause. Be sure to keep ninety-degree angles in your shoulders, elbows, and wrists to prevent injury. If this is too strenuous at first, it's okay to bring your knees to the floor. (This pose is called Chaturanga Dandasana, usually shortened to Chaturanga.)

9. Inhale as you push forward, arching your back while you push up until your torso is upright. At the same time, "roll" your feet so that the top of each foot is touching the ground, and your legs are an inch or so off the mat. (This pose is called Upward-Facing Dog, since it resembles a dog stretching.)

10. Exhale and roll your feet back, so the bottoms are touching the mat. At the same time, move your tailbone up and back until your body is in an inverted V shape. Relax your neck and shoulders. If you feel a stretching sensation in your hamstrings, it can help to imagine yourself "breathing" into them. Stay in this position for three to five breaths. (This pose is often called Downward-Facing Dog.)

11. Inhale, then exhale as you walk or jump your feet forward, until your feet are beneath your shoulders.

12. Repeat steps 5 and 6.

13. Inhale while bringing your arms up and out to the side until they are fully extended above your head, as in step 3.

14. Bring your arms down in front of you until your hands are in the universal "prayer" position in front of your chest, as in step 2.

You'll notice the sequence ends in the same position as it begins. Once you've completed the sequence, you can repeat it as many times as you like, or easily move into a different standing pose.

Also, notice how each step begins with "inhale" or "exhale"? That's intentional: each movement corresponds with a breath. Focusing on the breath is what makes yoga different from aerobics.

You can think of the Sun Salutation sequence as "minimum viable asana": if you really wanted to, your entire practice could consist of doing Sun Salutations over and over again. The sequence hits all of the body's major muscle groups, requires a good mix of strength and flexibility, and is challenging without being complicated. Krishnamacharya really knew what he was doing.

In traditional ashtanga practice, a Sun Salutation (also called a *vinyasa*) is done in between every individual pose. That means you spend the majority of the two-hour Primary Series doing this simple sequence. It's a good example of the power law in action: a minority of poses makes up the majority of the practice.

Still, the human body is prone to repetitive stress injury: if you overdo Sun Salutations, it's possible to hurt yourself.[13] That's why it's a good idea to do a few sets of Sun Salutations to warm up, then move on to different poses.

Remember to Breathe Like Darth Vader

While practicing asana, it's common to use a special breathing technique called *ujjayi*. This is the simplest of the breathing techniques (pranayama) used in yoga practice, and it's designed to make it easier to focus on the breath.

In the back of your throat there's a small fleshy structure called the *glottis*, in roughly the same area as your tonsils and vocal chords. If you focus on that area for a moment, you can consciously contract the glottis very slightly, which constricts the air flowing into and out of your lungs.

The effect of this constriction is noticeable: you can hear (and feel) cold air rushing into your lungs when you inhale, and warm air flowing out when you exhale.

The *Yoga Sutras* describe the sound of ujjayi as "like the ocean," but I prefer a modern analogy: ujjayi sounds like Darth Vader from *Star Wars*. If you imitate the Dark Lord of the Sith's infamous respiration pattern, then close your mouth, you'll be doing ujjayi.

Ancient yoga texts ascribe mystical qualities to ujjayi, as well as other pranayama techniques. Regardless of whether or not ujjayi "builds heat in the body" or "encourages the flow of prana [the universal life force]," it certainly makes it easier to pay attention to your breathing.

The primary purpose of ujjayi is to help keep your breathing calm, relaxed, and regular. By maintaining ujjayi as you practice, it's much easier to keep your mind focused on your breathing, which keeps your attention from wandering. If you follow your breath to the exclusion of everything else, you're meditating without really trying.

I've learned the most frequently used sequence in asana, as well as the primary breathing pattern, in about twenty minutes. So far, so good!

Now, let's learn some common standing poses.

Standing Poses

Warrior 1

Warrior poses are a staple of ashtanga and vinyasa classes. The poses often appear after (or in the middle of) a Sun Salutation sequence, and can be done as a small sequence in themselves.

Here's how the first Warrior posture works: stand facing forward. Inhale and take a step back with one leg, letting the toes of your back foot point approximately forty-five degrees to the side. Raise your arms above your head, parallel to each other. The front leg should be bent at the knee, foot flat, with the front shin approximately perpendicular to the floor. The back foot should be flat on the ground. Hold the pose for three to five breaths.

Warrior 2

From Warrior 1, open your arms and hips to face the side of your mat. (If your right foot is back, open to the right, and vice versa.) Keep your arms parallel to the ground, "broadening" through the chest. Hold the pose for three to five breaths.

Warrior 3

Warrior 3 could easily be called the Superman pose. The goal this time is to move your torso forward while balancing on one foot, with the rest of your body parallel to the floor.

From a neutral standing position (regular standing or Warrior 1), raise your arms above your head, then lift one foot slightly off the floor. Move that foot backward in space while leaning forward with your torso, hinging at the hip until you're in Superman position. Focus on balancing with the muscles in your foot, and keep your bottom knee solid, but not locked.

Hold the pose for three to five breaths, then return to a neutral standing position.

The Kaminoff Spiral

From a neutral standing position, inhale and let your arms spiral out and up, just like at the beginning of a Sun Salutation. From there, exhale and let your arms spiral back in and down, while hinging forward at the hips until your chest is close to your knees. Repeat a few times, inhaling as you spiral up, and exhaling as you fold down.

This is my favorite standing pose: it feels *so good* after getting out of bed, or after a few hours at the computer. The benefit of this variation is that it doesn't put any weight on the hands or arms, which is good if you suffer from carpal tunnel syndrome, are recovering from injuries, or need to build strength and flexibility before trying more challenging poses.

Forward Bend

From a neutral standing position, hinge at the hips and fold forward, letting your knees bend if you need to. Relax your neck and shoulders, and let your head hang down as you try to touch the floor with your fingers. Play with bending and straightening your knees, and notice where you begin to feel a stretching sensation. (If your hamstrings are very flexible, you may be able to touch the floor with your palms, but don't overextend yourself.) After three to five breaths, return to standing.

Wide Forward Bend

From a neutral standing position, move your legs apart to each side, creating a nice wide V-shaped stance. Then, hinge at the hips and fold forward. Relax your neck and shoulders and let your head hang down as you try to touch the floor with your palms. After three to five breaths, return to standing.

Triangle

From a neutral standing position, move your legs apart to each side, creating a wide V-shaped stance, feet pointing forward. Then, rotate at the hip so one of your feet points to the side of the mat. Bend that knee and let your elbow come to rest on it. Reach your free hand up toward the ceiling. Finally, straighten your bent knee, and let your bottom hand fall to your leg or the floor. Hold the pose for three to five breaths, return to a wide stance, then repeat on the other side.

Extended Side Angle

From a neutral standing position, move your legs apart to each side, creating a wide V-shaped stance, feet pointing forward. Then, rotate at the hip so one of your feet points to the side of the mat. Bend that knee and let your elbow come to rest on it. Reach your free hand up toward the ceiling, then (if it's comfortable), bring your bottom palm to the floor. Your arms should be perpendicular to the floor, forming a straight line.

There's a variation of Extended Side Angle that I really like: you can bring your hands together in the universal "prayer" position instead of extending your arms to the floor and ceiling. After holding the pose for three to five breaths, come back to the wide forward stance, then repeat on the other side.

Chair

Stand straight, legs together and arms at your side. Inhale and raise your arms straight above your head. Then exhale and bend your knees, keeping your legs together, until you're in roughly a seated position, like you're sitting in an imaginary chair. (This is difficult, and gets more difficult the longer you hold the pose.)

Hold the pose for three to five breaths, then straighten to standing.

Tree

Stand straight, legs together and arms at your sides. Lift one foot off the ground, bend at the knee, and grab your ankle with the corresponding hand. Balancing on the other foot, guide the free foot to the inside of your upper thigh, pointing your knee to the side. You'll probably notice the muscles in your grounded foot activating like crazy until you find your balance.

Once your leg is in position, let go of your ankle and put your palms to-gether in front of your chest in the universal "prayer" position. Hold the pose for three to five breaths, then repeat with the other foot.

Floor Poses

Cat/Cow

Get down on your hands and knees, arms shoulder width apart, and legs hip width apart. Keep your neck and shoulders relaxed, and look down at the ground.

Exhale as you arch your back, pulling your belly toward your spine. You'll find yourself looking back toward your legs. This is the Cat position.

Next, inhale as you flatten your back and return to neutral, then arch in the opposite direction, pulling your belly toward the floor, as you did at the beginning of the Sun Salutation. You'll find yourself looking forward, and your back will be concave. This is the Cow position.

Breathe and move back and forth between these positions at least five times.

Seated Forward Bend

Sit on the mat, legs extended straight in front of you. Keep your feet flexed, perpendicular to the floor. With-out bending your legs, pivot from your hips as you en-gage your quadriceps (the muscles on the front of your thighs), then reach forward with your hands toward your feet. Reach as far as you can without pain or major discomfort. Hold the pose for three to five breaths.

One-Legged Forward Bend

Think of this pose as a combination of Tree and Forward Bend. Bring one foot up, bend at the knee, then rotate your leg to the side. Place your foot on the inside of your thigh, then hinge forward at the hip, just like in Forward Bend. Reach as far as you can without pain or major discomfort, then hold the pose for three to five breaths.

Staff

This pose is harder than it looks. Sit on the mat, legs extended straight in front of you. Keep your feet flexed, perpendicular to the floor. Place your hands flat on the floor, then push your hands into the floor, lifting your body off the floor slightly as you try to keep your feet pointing straight up. Hold the pose for three to five breaths.

Bound Angle

Sit on the floor, and bring your knees up against your chest. Then, let your knees open to the side until they're close to the floor, and the soles of your feet are touching. Hold your feet with your hands, and maintain this position for three to five breaths.

Seated Spinal Twist

Sit on the mat, legs extended straight in front of you. Bring one knee up to your chest, until your foot is close to your opposite knee. Then, pick up your foot with your hands and place it on the other side of your extended leg. Place your hands palms-down on the ground by your hips, just like in Staff pose.

Once you're in position, move the opposite arm across your body until your elbow is touching the outside of your knee. (If your right leg is bent, you'll be moving your left arm.) Bend the arm at the elbow, and keep your fingers pointing to the ceiling. Continue the twist by pushing your arm gently against your leg. Complete the twist all the way up your spine by rotating your head in the same direction as you're twisting.

The neat thing about this position is that you can really notice the differences in rotation in the various parts of your spine. According to Leslie Kaminoff, the lumbar spine has only five degrees of rotation. The thoracic spine has thirty-five degrees, and the cervical spine has eighty to ninety degrees, so when you're fully rotated, you should be able to look behind you.

Hold the twist for three to five breaths, release, then repeat on the opposite side.

Boat

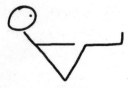

This is a hard one. Sit on the mat, legs extended straight out in front of you. Bend your knees so you're balancing on your seat, and your toes lightly touch the floor. Extend your arms straight in front of you, then keep your legs together as you lift them off the floor. Keep your shins together and back straight, and adjust as necessary to keep your balance. Hold for three to five breaths, then release.

Crow

Squat on the mat, with your palms flat on the floor. Position your elbows on the inside of each corresponding knee, then lean forward until your center of gravity shifts forward, and your feet leave the ground. Balance on your arms as long as you can, keeping your breathing steady.

Wheel

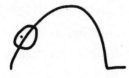

Lay on the mat on your back. Bring your knees up until your feet are flat, just below your hips. At the same time, place your hands palms-down on the ground by your ears. As you inhale, pull strongly with your legs and push strongly with your hands so that your body arches off the mat. Hold the pose for three to five breaths, then release, bringing your torso down slowly to rest on the floor.

Adjusting the Difficulty

Notice how these poses usually end by being held for three to five breaths? That's intentional. Breathing is what makes yoga unique, so it's an important part of every pose. Three to five ujjayi breaths is a good start as a beginner.

Advanced asana practitioners don't necessarily do more complicated poses, or a larger quantity of poses: they do the poses more slowly, with more control, and hold each pose longer. As I get better with practice, I'll hold each pose for a few more breaths.

Shavasana

Shavasana is, in yogic tradition, the ultimate purpose of all of this bending and breathing. Remember, the early purpose of asana was to prepare for meditation. That tradition has continued into modern practice, and for good reason: it's quite nice.

Shavasana is a complete release of all muscular tension combined with deep meditation. It's often referred to as the Corpse pose, but don't let that morbid label put you off. The pose itself is simple: lay flat on the mat, legs extended straight, arms at your sides. Close your eyes and release all tension from your body. Your muscles shouldn't be working at all.

Scan your body from head to toe, and wherever you notice any muscles contracting, release them. This includes muscle groups we're not used to paying attention to, like your neck and even your tongue. At this point, you also stop maintaining ujjayi, and start breathing normally.

The sensation feels like you're melting into the floor. After so much time keeping your muscles in constant motion, shavasana is a relief. Exhausting your body seems to allow you to relax your mind, so it's easier to meditate when you reach shavasana.

Stay in shavasana for five minutes or so, then get up. Your asana practice is complete.

Reviewing the Method

At this point, I've accomplished my target performance threshold. After a total of three hours of instruction, I'm capable of practicing asana at home in a safe, effective manner.

Let's review the core of the method I used to learn yoga:

- I acquired the necessary equipment: a mat, strap, and block.
- I spent a few hours with an experienced instructor to learn the basics and correct major misconceptions.
- I learned that yoga asana practice involves moving through poses while focusing on the breath and maintaining a mindful mental state.
- I learned a basic vinyasa sequence of poses (the Sun Salutation), ten common standing poses, and ten common seated/reclining poses.
- I learned basic breathing techniques (pranayama) that make it easier to stay focused on the breath while practicing.
- I learned to prevent injury by paying attention to my body, modifying poses as necessary, avoiding overextension, and avoiding unnecessary weight on the cervical spine.
- I practiced until I was able to complete the sequence from memory, which takes around twenty-five minutes.

Where I'm Going from Here

At the moment, I'm happy with my asana practice. After three hours of research and instruction, I'm able to practice yoga whenever I want or need to, and I don't have to rely on going to a structured class at a studio. Twenty-five minutes in the morning or evening, and I'm set.

I like that yoga combines exercise with meditation. After I practice, it's apparent how much better my body feels, as well as how I feel emotionally. Continuing to practice will ensure I reap the benefits of both meditation and range-of-motion exercise.

That's the trick: I need to practice on a regular basis to reap the rewards. Setting aside time in the morning and evening to practice is key. Instead of starting the day by hopping online to check my e-mail or getting right to work, I'm changing my schedule so I can practice before I do anything else.

Taking care of my body needs to become my first priority, not my last. Yoga will help keep me in good condition for decades to come.

I don't have to become a monk or a contortionist to enjoy the benefits of yoga. I don't have to know every pose, or be able to stick my leg behind my head. I just need to practice the basics, which weren't at all difficult to learn.

Even better: I learned what I wanted to learn in only three hours, which is way better than I anticipated. I started this project expecting to study a long series of complicated postures but, as it turns out, that wasn't necessary at all. I could achieve what I wanted to achieve by simplifying, which allowed me to get the results I wanted in less time.

When it comes to learning something new, there's no sense in making it more difficult than it really needs to be.

5

Programming

Lesson: Complex Things Are Simple When You Break Them Down

If debugging is the process of removing software bugs, then programming
must be the process of putting them in.
—EDSGER DIJKSTRA, RENOWNED COMPUTER SCIENTIST

■ ■ ■

**For supplementary images, video, and commentary about this
chapter, visit http://first20hours.com/programming.**

I've been making my living on the web since 2007, when I quit my full-
time job as a marketing manager at Procter & Gamble in favor of starting
my own publishing and consulting company.

My primary website, PersonalMBA.com, is my livelihood: I'm effectively a business professor, but I don't work at a university. Each year, I update my list of the best business books available for readers who want to
teach themselves business fundamentals.[1]

The Personal MBA recommended reading list has been a perennial
reader favorite since the first edition was published in 2005, and updates
to the list are met with tidal waves of visitors from around the world. Since
2005, PersonalMBA.com has been visited by over 2 million readers.

My first book, *The Personal MBA: Master the Art of Business* (2010), was a natural extension of PersonalMBA.com, and went on to become an international bestseller. Part of the process of writing a book is figuring out how to spread the word, so over the years I've worked hard to attract new readers.

As a result, *The Personal MBA* has been featured in the *New York Times*, *Wall Street Journal*, *Fortune*, *Forbes*, and *FastCompany*, and on many popular websites and blogs. Each time my book or website is featured, thousands of readers visit PersonalMBA.com in a very short period of time.

The Price of Progress

Having thousands of simultaneous visitors to your website is a great thing, provided those visitors can actually reach the site. That was my problem: whenever my website received any significant amount of traffic, it would go down in a blaze of glory, leaving visitors with only a cryptic error message.

Here's a typical example: Lifehacker.com, a popular productivity blog, has featured *The Personal MBA* three times in the past seven years. Each time, thousands of people would try to visit PersonalMBA.com at the same time, overwhelming my web server (the computer that delivers a web page when it's requested by a visitor). Instead of delivering the requested information, my server would return an "Error establishing database connection" or "Error 503" message, the digital equivalent of the server pleading for mercy.

Each time my server crashed under the heavy load, a little piece of my soul died with it. All of the time spent marketing my website was wasted. Thousands of curious readers were finally interested in learning what I had to offer, but with my server down, they were all walking away disappointed and empty-handed. My marketing was working too well, and my systems couldn't cope with the sudden demand.

Examining the Problem

At first, my approach was to beef up the server by adding more processing power and more memory. That helped, but only to a point. Beyond that point, my site would crash and burn, which happened to coincide with pretty much every major marketing victory.

At the time, PersonalMBA.com was running on a popular website management system called WordPress.[2] WordPress is optimized for easy installation and use, not performance under heavy loads. Under the default WordPress configuration, every web page request kicks off a cascade of server activity, generating hundreds of hidden requests in order to deliver each web page to the reader.

That makes each individual web page request "expensive." That is, each request requires a significant amount of memory and processing power to complete. If a single visitor views five pages on the website, that user generates five expensive requests. If a thousand visitors request the exact same page at the exact same time, the server will attempt to kick off a thousand identical expensive processes all at once.

The System Is Down

In this situation, the poor beleaguered server will attempt to return every request, but since each request demands a lot of resources, the server will run out of memory before every request is fulfilled. At that point, the server raises the white flag of surrender, and visitors are out of luck.

To combat this issue, I switched web-hosting companies five times and spent hundreds of hours learning how to configure WordPress servers to stay online under a heavy load. Each new server configuration increased in complexity, and each new installation required more and more ongoing maintenance.

Eventually I was building my own custom server configurations, invoking a long series of arcane system commands to install, configure, and modify complex server applications I barely understood. Every error or issue I experienced in setup or maintenance devolved into hours of research and troubleshooting.

If that wasn't enough, WordPress's popularity and relative insecurity make it a popular target for hackers and spammers. Every week or so, a shady programmer finds some new vulnerability, then uses it to take over user accounts or fill millions of WordPress blog archives with spam.

Securing a WordPress installation and keeping on top of software updates can be a full-time job in itself, particularly if you maintain multiple websites. (I was maintaining twelve websites at the time and failing miserably.)

At a certain point, I realized that I was spending more time keeping my sites online than I was researching and writing for my readers. That made no sense. Not only was I wasting productive capacity, I wasn't really learning how to program. I was learning a bunch of situation-specific hacks and workarounds that only applied to running WordPress. Not cool.[3]

I decided to look for another way to maintain my websites, and it didn't take long to find a promising alternative.

A Potential Solution

One day, I stumbled upon an essay about Jekyll,[4] a website management program created by Tom Preston-Werner, best known as the founder of the open source code repository GitHub.[5] Jekyll is designed to replace systems like WordPress by making it easy to run websites that don't rely on expensive requests.

Imagine you have hundreds of word processing documents that contain important information and you need to make them all look the same— same font, same heading style, et cetera. If you wrote a program that could apply a given page design you choose to every file automatically (versus updating every file by hand), it'd save you a lot of time.

That's essentially what Jekyll does for web pages. Run a single command and Jekyll produces a complete website using the files on your computer that contain your website information and design template. If you make a change to the design or page content, you just run Jekyll again, and the entire site will be updated with the changes automatically, saving you hours of effort.

Jekyll presented a promising opportunity. In theory, I could replace WordPress with a simple folder of text files on my computer. My website would be blazing fast, ultra stable, and I'd save myself over one hundred hours of server maintenance every year.

There was, however, a catch: Jekyll is written in Ruby, a programming language I don't know. I don't have any idea how to write code in Ruby or run Ruby applications that serve real users. Some of the things I need to do to run PersonalMBA.com require more than simple formatting.

To run my websites using Jekyll, I'd have to learn how to program and deploy Ruby web applications.

Looks like I've found a "lovable problem."

Learning to Code

I've wanted to learn how to program for quite a while, but other projects have always taken priority. If I can learn to code, my publishing and business opportunities will expand considerably, since everything I do to build my business runs on the web.

It's important to note that everything I've been doing to date is not programming. HTML and CSS, the languages I use to build web pages, are called "markup" languages. HTML and CSS code isn't smart in any way: it simply tells the computer to show the user a text file in a specific way (i.e., "make this text bold" or "this section is a heading with a 24-point font size").

The same is true for my crazy server setup. Even though I was putting together software, I wasn't really programming. Instead, I was installing prewritten programs, then changing a few settings. Programmers wrote the applications I was using, but I didn't need any knowledge of programming to use them. Server configuration and administration is a useful skill, but it's not programming.

So What Is "Programming"?

My first thought is that programming is telling a computer to do things, but that isn't very specific or helpful. Do what? What "things"?

Ten years ago, I took two basic programming courses in college, so not being able to come up with a useful definition is a bit embarrassing, frankly. I remember a few basic terms, like *variable, loop, input, output, function, object orientation*, and something called a *bubble sort*, but not a whole lot else.

The course assignments required learning a programming language called C++, and I remember being frustrated when it took hours to find a missing semicolon that kept crashing my program. I remember my professor saying things like "you'll never use a bubble sort for a real application, but we're going to learn it anyway."

I wrote a few basic programs for the course because I had to: the goal was to pass the class with a good grade, and I did. Unfortunately, the programs we were writing had no real use outside of the classroom, and I haven't used these concepts in a long time. Even though I remember a few words, I'll have to start over in terms of understanding the key ideas.

Since I'm not able to specifically define what I'm trying to do when I say I want to "learn programming," I'm going to have trouble defining a useful target performance level. "Create a computer program" is a bit more specific, but still not very useful.

Time to unpack what I currently know about programming:

- I know programmers "write" programs, which suggests that it's a creative exercise that can be done in many ways.

- Programs are often called "applications," and the words are used interchangeably.

- When computer programs are "run" or "executed," they do the thing they were written to do, whatever that happens to be.

- "Input" and "output" are easy to remember, since they're in common usage. Input is information or data the program uses, and output is what you get when the program is done running.

- A "variable" is basically a placeholder for something that changes. You can create as many variables as you want, and make those variables stand for whatever you want.

- The "program" itself is essentially a detailed set of instructions and rules that tells the computer exactly what to do to (or with) the input. When the program is done running, it gives you the output.

- Programs "crash" or display an error message when something goes wrong or the computer can't figure out what to do next.

Now we're getting somewhere. This is a very basic deconstruction: instead of "programming," we now have three subconcepts to work with:

- **Input**—information you use to execute a process.
- **Process**—a series of steps the program takes, given the input.
- **Output**—the end result of the program.

This breakdown is much more useful. "Writing a computer program" means defining what information you're starting with, defining a series of steps that describes exactly what the computer will do with that input, and defining the output the computer will return when the program is finished running.

Think of a flowchart, which appears to be a useful mental hook for how programs work. You start the process with certain inputs. Along the way, you take certain actions when specific conditions are true or false. The process ends when you reach the end of the flowchart, and you're left with the output: the end result of the complete process the flowchart describes.

Creating a computer program seems to be a different way of doing the same kind of thinking you do when you create a flowchart. You ask the same sorts of questions:

- What am I starting with?
- What happens at the beginning of the process?
- What happens after that? After that?
- When does the process end?
- What do I have when the process is done?

Flowcharts describe the answers to these questions in a visual format, and programs describe them using text, but the thought process is the same.

The flowchart analogy is also useful because it provides a few clues about other concepts that are probably important.

Conditionals are statements like:

- "If X is true/false then do Y"
- "If X is/isn't Y then do Z"

- "When X is true/false then do Y"
- "When X is Y then do Z"
- "While X is true/false then do Y"
- "While X is Y then do Z"

X, Y, and Z in this case are *variables*, which can stand for anything. Variables may stand for numbers, like in basic algebra, or they may stand for words. Sometimes variables are single letters or symbols, and sometimes they're words. Either way, they represent whatever we're working with.

Conditionals (the IF, THEN, WHEN, and WHILE parts) are like the arrows with questions on a flowchart. Think of driving a car: IF the traffic light is red, THEN stop. WHEN the traffic light turns green, THEN go. WHEN the traffic light is yellow, slow down and prepare to stop.

It's worth digging into these conditional statements a bit more, since there are a few common patterns. True/false appears a lot, and WHILE seems to imply we keep doing something instead of taking a single action.

In all cases, the conditional contains some statement that defines whether or not to take action. This statement is called a *condition*, and it can take many forms. Sometimes the condition is a basic true/false (Is the light red?) comparison, sometimes it's a mathematical comparison (Is X greater than 100?), and sometimes it contains logic (Is the stoplight NOT red?).

The purpose of the condition is to define whether or not the associated process should happen. If the condition is true or valid, the program processes the instruction. If it's not, the associated instruction is skipped, and the program goes to the next instruction.

True/false variables are called *Boolean variables*, which is a fancy phrase for something that only has two options. Yes/no and on/off are also Boolean variables. Boolean variables are pretty important in computer programs, since they're the basic unit of both simple processes (like the true/false in a flowchart) and the on/off flipping of the tiny electronic switches at the core of the computer.

WHILE, in this case, is a special type of conditional called a *loop*. Loops cause the process in question to repeat until the condition is met. Going back to the driving analogy: WHILE the traffic light is red, don't move.

Pretty easy, right? If we think of writing a computer program like drawing a flowchart, the basic process is easier to visualize.

There's one last wrinkle: what if the computer gets stuck, doesn't know what to do, or the instructions the computer tries at some point don't work or make sense? What happens?

The program "crashes"—the program stops completely, and often outputs an error message instead of the desired result. We've all experienced the dreaded Windows "blue screen of death" or an "Error 404: Web Page Not Found" error while browsing the web. Something unexpected occurs, the computer freaks out, and the program crashes.

As a computer programmer, your job is to prevent crashes and errors from happening. The best way to do that is to ensure the program always has the information it needs to complete the process as planned, but that's not always possible. In cases where uncertainty is unavoidable, it's useful to have a way to recover when the program fails while trying to complete a process.

These error-recovery statements are called *exceptions*, and they're very handy. You can think of them as error-specific conditionals: IF the program is about to crash in X way, THEN do Y instead of crashing.

Exceptions are a bit like adding a backup generator to a hospital building. Most of the time, the generator just sits there doing nothing. If the electricity goes out, however, the generator fires up, and the hospital uses power from the generator instead of going completely dark. That's a very good thing if there are patients in the hospital on life-support machines that require electricity. Complete failures are dangerous, so backup plans are critical.

That's basic programming, really. Defining inputs. Setting variables. Creating processes that lead to the desired outputs. Thinking through those processes like a flowchart, adding conditionals and exceptions as necessary. If all goes well, you supply the inputs, run the program, and get the desired output.

This is a massive oversimplification of a very complex activity, but it's detailed enough to be useful for someone new to programming. By deconstructing programming in this way, it's easier to know where to start.

Programming Languages

Here's the tricky part: computers don't speak languages in the same way humans do. At the core, computers work by flipping tiny electronic switches on and off in very specific ways. Unless the computer has some way of translating our human-language commands into electronic switch-flipping, the computer won't be able to do what we command.

That's what programming languages do: they give a human programmer a specific way to tell the computer when to start, what to do, and when to stop. They also allow the programmer to define what the inputs, processes, and outputs look like, and what to do when the program is done running.

Each programming language has a specific way of writing commands, called a *syntax*. The language's syntax contains the rules the computer uses to translate the program commands into tiny electronic switch-flips.

Pretty much every language has a way of defining variables, conditionals, and exceptions. The details vary, but the core concepts are the same.

Thinking Like a Programmer

Programmers often think through problems in what's called *pseudocode*: language that looks or sounds like code, but isn't specific enough for a computer to actually execute. Think of it as a form of sketching. Pseudocode helps you think through the process of solving a problem.

The driving example I've been using is an example of pseudocode. If I got in my car and said, "IF I turn the key, THEN start the engine" out loud, nothing would happen. That doesn't mean the statement is useless. The statement is just a way of thinking through the steps required to solve a problem or get a desired result.

You can use the basic programming concepts we've just discussed to sketch out some simple programs for common tasks.

Here's a fun way of trying this yourself. Find a friend, and ask them to help you complete a simple task like "make a sandwich." The only rule is that your friend can only do exactly what you tell him, nothing more, nothing less. He is not allowed to assume knowledge of anything, and has to take every request literally.

In minutes, you'll find yourself having a conversation like this:

You: Pick up the bread.
Friend: I don't understand "pick up."
You: Move your hand to where I say and grasp it.
Friend: I don't understand "hand."
You: (Sigh) This thing right here. [You point to the friend's hand.]
Friend: Understood.
You: Move your hand to where I say and grasp it.
Friend: I don't understand "grasp."
You: Flex your fingers like this. [You demonstrate, flexing and releasing your fingers.]
Friend: Understood.
You: Move your hand to the bread and grasp it.
Friend: I don't understand "bread."
You: This thing right here! [You point to the bread.]
Friend: Understood.
You: Move your hand to the bread and grasp it.
Friend: [Moves hand to bread, flexes fingers, and releases. The bread doesn't move.]
You: THIS IS A STUPID GAME!!!

It's a silly example, but it's very close to what programming looks and feels like, particularly at the beginning.

The computer, like your friend, can't understand anything you don't explicitly define. Any complex process you try to define needs to be specified completely and unambiguously.

That's what makes programming difficult: a single ambiguity or stray command can cause the entire program to fail. Programming is an unforgiving craft in this respect: your code is either correct or incorrect, and must be expressed in exacting detail.

Computers are not impressed by charm or wit. If your code is incomplete or ill formed, your application will crash, you'll lose data, and/or you'll create a *bug*: a bit of rogue code that produces unexpected or unforeseen consequences. Like math, the logic either works or it doesn't. There is no A for effort.

That said, in programming there's no single universal solution to a given problem, as there is in math. There are thousands of ways to produce your desired output given the specified inputs. As a programmer, you get to choose your approach based on the tools you have at your disposal.

Once you get used to the fact that the computer can't read your mind, you learn to start giving commands the system can understand, in the same way you learned to explicitly define terms and demonstrate basic actions to your friend in the "Sandwich Game" before giving complex commands.

What Makes Web Application Programming Different?

We now have a working definition of programming. It's very simplified, but it provides a good enough understanding of what we're trying to do for now.

I'm not interested in every type of programming, though: I want to write programs that run on websites. If you've ever used a web-based e-mail program like Gmail, Hotmail, Yahoo Mail, or the like, you know what I'm talking about. These programs run in your Internet browser. You don't have to download a software program to your computer to use them. You just point your browser to the website, log in, and you're ready to go.

This distinction between software that runs *locally* and software that runs *remotely* on a web server is an important one. To develop a web application, you first have to write the application and then test it to see if it works. All of the development and testing happens on your own computer.

Once the program works, you then send it to the "production" web server so other people can access it. People on the Internet can't log into your personal computer from the web, so uploading the software to a publicly accessible web server is necessary for other people to use your program.

That means the development process has two major phases: local programming and testing, and pushing the finished program to a remote production server for actual use. I'll have to figure out how both of these phases work.

Here's something else I know from my previous experience with HTML and CSS: they're "dumb," in that you can't ask a basic web page to store any information.

Say you have a web page file that says, "Hello, World!"[6] and you want to replace "World" with the name of the person visiting the page. It's a nice thought, but basic web pages don't have any way of storing information for later recall. They just display the text in the file, and the file isn't allowed to update itself.

The technical term for this is *state*. Basic web pages built using HTML and CSS have no state, so they're referred to as "stateless" resources. You can add a small form to a web page that asks for the user's name with a Save button next to it, but the button won't actually save any information unless you create a separate place for that information to go.

That's why web applications use two common approaches to saving data for later: *databases* and *cookies*.

The best way to understand what a database does is to imagine a stack of index cards. Let's say you're trying to create an address book, and you want to capture the name, phone number, e-mail address, gender, and age of each of your friends.

Each friend gets their own index card, and their information is recorded on that card. If one of your friends changes their e-mail address, for example, you can erase the old information and update the card with the new information. When you look at a particular friend's card, you can see all of their information at once.

You can think of the entire stack of index cards as a database. Each card in the stack is called a *record*. You can have as many records in the database as you like, but at some point, the stack becomes hard to manage. It often makes sense to split the stack into a few smaller substacks: friends and family in one stack, colleagues from work in another, for example.

Clear so far? Here's where it gets cool: imagine your stack of index cards is now a magic stack of index cards. You can talk to the magic stack and command it to show you cards that fit certain conditions, such as

- "Show me John Smith's card."

- "Show me all of the cards where gender is female."

- "Show me all of the cards where age is greater than fifty."

Pretty useful, right? In essence, that's what databases do: they give you a way to store structured information, as well as a way to retrieve that information however you want.

Each of the pieces of data we put on the card is called a *field*. The more fields you have in your database, the more ways you can potentially retrieve the data when you want it.

Databases are the most common way to store data in a web application. If you want to store information like a user's name, e-mail address, and other information, using a database is a natural fit. Once John Smith logs in to your application, you can have your application retrieve the name from John's database record, then display "Hello, John Smith!"

The other common way to store information in a web application is by using a cookie: a very small text file that's saved on the user's computer. Cookies are useful for storing small amounts of data that don't need to exist for very long.

In the case of our address book program, it'd be appropriate to store a cookie when John Smith logs in. John's cookie file would contain information like username = johnsmith and loggedin = true. If Smith left the application, but came back later, the application would recognize the cookie and grant him access without requiring another login. Cookies can be set to expire in a set period of time, which makes them handy for this sort of programming. (If you've ever seen a "Remember this password" feature on a website, this is how it works.)

What we're doing here is basic deconstruction. This isn't an exhaustive list of what makes web programming unique, but it's complete enough to provide a simple framework of what I'll need to learn: variables, conditionals, exceptions, local/production environments, databases, and cookies.

See how this breakdown is useful? I started with a very vague idea of what I wanted to do, and now I have a specific list of key subskills that are important to learn.

I'm not ready to jump in yet, though. Remember I mentioned that computers can't understand human language? I need to choose a programming language to write my program's instructions, which will require a bit more research.

Choosing a Language for Web Application Programming

There are thousands of different programming languages available, and new languages are being invented every day. Each language's syntax is different, and is heavily influenced by what the language is designed to accomplish. Some languages are more optimized for certain tasks than others.

Before jumping in, I decided to take an hour to poke around a few major programming websites to see which language working web application developers recommend. This early research will help me decide what language to learn and which early skills I need to practice.

Two of the most popular destinations for programmers are Stack Overflow[7] and Hacker News,[8] so I begin by browsing for advice on the best language to learn.

Stack Overflow is a question-and-answer website: a place to ask "How do I do X?" sorts of questions. More knowledgeable and experienced coders usually respond to questions with specific suggestions, approaches, or bug fixes, making Stack Overflow the best destination for getting help on tricky programming problems.

Hacker News is a social news website: a collection of links with associated discussions. The topics on Hacker News change minute to minute, but usually revolve around new developments in programming, technology, and business, making Hacker News an ideal place to browse for at least semi-informed opinions on new developments in programming.

New languages, libraries, and techniques are created by programmers around the world every day. Some combinations of technologies and approaches are useful for some problems, and others aren't. Often, you can't tell until you try them.

"Best," in programming terms, is relative to the problem you're trying to solve and your particular priorities. In general, the advice is to (1) choose tools that allow you to solve the problem efficiently and (2) if you have a choice, choose tools you enjoy using. Fair enough.

Browsing the archives of Stack Overflow and Hacker News gave me a huge case of information overload: there's too much information to process at once, particularly if you're not familiar with the terminology. I needed to reduce the noise if I wanted to find more specific advice.

Here's a tactical research trick that most people don't know: popular search engines allow you to limit your search to a specific website instead of the entire web. The code to do this in Google looks like this:

```
"search phrase" site:example.com
```

Replace "search phrase" with the term you're searching for, and "example.com" with the website you want to search. The quotation marks mean to search for exact matches of the search phrase. Without the quotation marks, Google will return pages that contain all of the words in the phrase, but not necessarily in that order.

Using this technique, I searched several variations of the phrases "web application programming," "learn to code," and "programming for beginners," then spent another hour or so reading the results.

Here's what I found: experienced web developers currently recommend beginning with one of two common languages: Ruby or Python. Ruby and Python, by reputation, are relatively easy to learn, powerful, and give you a good foundation in important programming concepts. Ruby is a bit more popular with programmers who focus on web applications, while Python is more popular with scientists and mathematicians due to its wide variety of science, math, and graphing libraries.

Ruby and Python each have active communities of developers, loads of free available resources and well-written books, and pre-existing programs and tools that make important features easier to implement. Choosing which language to work with appears to be mostly a matter of preference.

After reading a few examples of code written in each of these languages, I decided to learn Ruby. To my untrained eye, Ruby code looks clean, readable, and seems relatively easy to understand. Since the major ideas and techniques I learn using Ruby will transfer to the other languages

I may decide to learn later, I might as well make the learning process enjoyable at the beginning.

In addition, there are a number of programs and tools I'd like to use that support or require Ruby. In particular, Jekyll is written in Ruby, so learning Ruby will help me solve a pressing problem. Similar tools exist for Python, but look more complicated to use.

Choosing a Framework

In addition to advice on programming languages, working web application programmers have strong opinions on *frameworks*: libraries of code that make it easier to do things that most applications need to do.

Libraries are important because computers do exactly what you tell them to do. Nothing more, nothing less.

That's tricky, because the code you provide is all that exists as far as a computer program is concerned. It's like the quotation by Carl Sagan, the famous physicist: "If you wish to make an apple pie from scratch, you must first invent the universe."

Your program's "universe" is defined by (1) the instructions and commands in the codebase, (2) the libraries your program imports, and (3) the system the program is running on. If the code that's necessary to complete a given operation doesn't exist somewhere in the system, your program will crash or return an error.

Most programming languages contain many common libraries that most programs need, but few specialized tools. That's where frameworks come in. Instead of coding everything from scratch, which would take a very long time, using a framework lets you import and use tested, reliable libraries for specialized tasks, allowing you to focus on the core of your application instead of reinventing the universe.

Frameworks can be large or small. Some frameworks include many functions and commands in an attempt to save the programmer effort, and others are more minimal, covering only a few essential functions.

At the moment, Ruby boasts several major web application development frameworks, of which two are the most popular: Ruby on Rails[9] and Sinatra.[10]

Ruby on Rails (often abbreviated to Rails) is one of the first major web application frameworks developed for Ruby. Created by David Heinemeier Hansson in 2004, Rails is easily the most popular Ruby framework and was used to develop several successful applications at 37signals,[11] a privately held web application company where Hansson is a partner. To date, thousands of businesses have developed large business-critical web applications using Rails.

Rails relies heavily on "generators": built-in programs that create large amounts of boilerplate code with a single command. The boilerplate is then modified based on the programmer's unique requirements. Instead of spending hours creating an application from scratch, Rails helps developers create a functioning app without a lot of effort, provided they know what they're doing.

Sinatra, on the other hand, is a minimal framework designed and developed by Blake Mizerany. Instead of relying on generators, Sinatra focuses on giving the developer a few simple common functions that most web applications need, then getting out of the way.

Sinatra applications look and feel simple compared to Rails applications. A single command in Rails can generate ten or more folders and twenty or more files. In contrast, it's not uncommon for a Sinatra application to be fully contained in a single file. Instead of generating a ton of code that may need to be removed, Sinatra development rewards keeping the project simple and adding just enough code to do the job.

Like choosing a language, choosing a framework is mostly a matter of preference and selecting the best tool for the job. Rails tends to be preferred for large projects with multiple programmers, and Sinatra is generally better suited for small projects. There are many overlapping features, so a recent analysis on RubySource.com concludes that it's ultimately a subjective choice.[12]

GitHub is an open source code repository many programmers use to release and maintain their projects. It's easy to find examples of applications written in Rails and Sinatra to get a feel for each framework, so I spent another hour browsing public projects.

There's a nontrivial risk here: in order to make progress in programming, you have to commit to something. Once you've chosen a language and a framework, it's much easier to begin learning everything you need to know to write a program. If you resist making a choice, however, you can spend years trying to find the "perfect" programming environment.

It's better to pick a language and framework that appeals to you, commit to exploring it for a while, and accept the inevitable tradeoffs than to spend years "researching" and making zero progress. Browsing Stack Overflow and Hacker News all day is *not* programming.

In the end, I decided to start with Sinatra. Even though Rails generators can save a lot of time if you know what you're doing, I *don't* know what I'm doing.

My intuition tells me that Sinatra is the best choice at this point. The syntax is clear, simple, and easy to understand. The only code that exists in a Sinatra app is code the developer adds. The framework is well documented, and it's easy to find examples of working applications on GitHub, as well as help on Stack Overflow.

I may experiment with Rails at some point in the future. For now, I'm starting with Sinatra.

Deconstructing the End Result

Approximately five hours of preliminary research has yielded everything I need to get started: a deconstruction of web programming, a language, a framework, and a specific project. Time to get to work.

"Code a Sinatra application that serves a Jekyll website" represents a decent target performance level, but I need to deconstruct what goes into that statement to figure out what to do next. What do I have to be able to do?

One more hour of research determines the following:

1. Running Jekyll creates the finished website from local static files. I'll need to create an HTML template for the website with special formatting tags, and export my archive of posts from PersonalMBA.com, which is described in a tutorial created by Paul Stamatiou.[13]

2. The Sinatra application handles requests from website visitors, delivering the requested files. I'll need to write this application from scratch.

3. Both the finished Jekyll website and Sinatra server application need to be uploaded to a website host.

4. To complete all of these tasks, I need to figure out how to install the latest version of Ruby on my machine, as well as Sinatra and other programs I need.

This last requirement is a good example of obtaining critical tools. If I can't figure out how to install Ruby on my machine, I can't do any of the subsequent steps, so it's the best place to begin.

It's important to note that web technology changes daily. It's very likely that the specific series of commands in this section will be obsolete by the time you read this. Don't worry: the method is what's important, not the commands.

Likewise, you're going to be tempted to gloss over the code sections of this chapter. It's a natural impulse: it looks complicated, and you won't immediately recognize what it means.

I encourage you to fight this impulse. These names, commands, and symbols are as unfamiliar to me as they are to you. This chapter is about the process of figuring out what this stuff means and how to use it. If you try to read the code, you'll get a lot more from this chapter.

Onward!

Upgrading Ruby

I already have a computer, which is a start: you can't program without one.

At present, I'm using an Apple MacBook Air that's running the Mac

OS X 10.6 operating system. A quick search indicates that the operating system comes with Ruby version 1.8.7 preinstalled, which is good news: theoretically, I can start running Ruby programs on my own computer right away.

The trouble is that Ruby 1.8.7 isn't the latest version of Ruby. When I try to install Jekyll, the system tells me the program requires at least version 1.9.1, which means I'll have to figure out how to upgrade. Back to Google I go.

Some basic searching turned up two programs that are designed to make managing Ruby installations easier: rbenv and ruby-build. Both programs are maintained by Sam Stephenson, a Ruby developer at 37signals. Together, these programs help you install new versions of Ruby and tell your computer which version of Ruby to use.

There's a tutorial on the rbenv documentation page[14] that shows how to install the programs on your machine. Here's what the installation commands looks like:

```
$ cd ~
$ git clone git://github.com/sstephenson/ruby-build.git
$ cd ruby-build
$ sudo ./install.sh
$ cd ..
$ git clone git://github.com/sstephenson/rbenv.git .rbenv
$ mkdir -p ~/.rbenv/plugins
$ cd ~/.rbenv/plugins
$ git clone git://github.com/sstephenson/ruby-build.git
$ echo 'export PATH="$HOME/.rbenv/bin:$PATH"' >> ~/.bashprofile
$ echo 'eval "$(rbenv init -)"' >> ~/.bashprofile
$ exec $SHELL
$ rbenv install 1.9.3-p125
$ rbenv rehash
$ rbenv global 1.9.3-p125
```

This looks intimidating, but it's just a list of commands. Let's break it down.

These commands are entered into a program called Terminal, which comes preinstalled on Apple computers. If you've ever seen hackers in movies typing frantically into computers that are displaying long lines of text, those computers are running a Terminal program.[15]

I open Terminal and enter the first command:

```
$ cd ~
```

This command is easy to understand. $ is what Terminal displays when it's ready for a new command, so it's already there. cd is an abbreviation of "change directory," which is another term for folder. A quick search tells me ~ is an abbreviation for "user's home folder," the folder in my computer where my user profile is stored.

I type the command and press the Enter key. Now, Terminal displays this:

```
joshkaufman $
```

That's good news: I'm in my home directory. So far, so good. I type the second command:

```
$ git clone git://github.com/sstephenson/ruby-build.git
```

The computer returns:

```
git: command not found
```

Looks like the program git isn't installed on my machine. I'll have to figure out how to install it.

What's a "Git"?

After searching for instructions on how to install git on Mac OS X, I find the Heroku Toolbelt.[16] Heroku[17] is a web application server hosting company, so they have a vested interest in making it easy for developers to create web applications.

The Heroku Toolbelt is a program that installs a few common software development tools programmers need to develop applications on Heroku. git[18] is one of those programs.

I download the installer package, run it, and receive a confirmation that everything is set up correctly. Time to try the command again:

```
$ git clone git://github.com/sstephenson/ruby-build.git
```

I get this output:

```
Cloning into ruby-build . . .
remote: Counting objects: 1004, done.
remote: Compressing objects: 100% (453/453), done.
remote: Total 1004 (delta 490), reused 937 (delta 431)
Receiving objects: 100% (1004/1004), 108.77 KiB, done.
Resolving deltas: 100% (490/490), done.
```

Success! "Done" is a good sign, and I didn't get an error message. Onward.

I continue with the rest of the commands. Based on the information in the installation tutorial, all I'm doing is downloading the necessary files, using a command called echo to automatically add a bit of text to my computer's configuration files, then restarting a program on my computer called SHELL to save the changes. Once the SHELL reboots, rbenv and ruby-build are installed. Yay!

Now it's time to install the latest version of Ruby:

```
$ rbenv install 1.9.3-p125
```

The program automatically downloads the Ruby source code and builds it, spitting out an impressive amount of scrolling information in the Terminal program in the process. (Now I'm starting to feel like a proper Hollywood programmer.)[19]

```
$ rbenv rehash
```

This command, from the documentation, helps the computer recognize there's a new version of Ruby installed.

```
$ rbenv global 1.9.3-p125
```

This command sets version 1.9.3-p125 as the default version of Ruby on this computer. The tutorial tells me to run this command to make sure my computer is using the new version:

```
$ ruby -v
```

Here's what I get:

```
ruby 1.9.3p125 (2012-02-16 revision 34643) [x8664-darwin11.3.0]
```

Success! That's what it's supposed to say, based on the tutorial.

According to the documentation, if I want to install a new version of Ruby on this computer, all I have to do is run rbenv install, rbenv rehash, and rbenv global again. Easy enough.

Even though the commands looked intimidating at first, they're actually quite simple. What looks like gibberish is just abbreviation. Once you know what the abbreviations stand for, the commands themselves are easy to understand.

Remember, no one is born knowing this stuff. Most of the time, all you need to do is spend a few minutes reading the documentation, then try what it tells you.[20]

Installing Ruby Libraries (Gems)

Now that the latest version of Ruby is installed, it's time to figure out how to install the libraries I need, including Sinatra.

Ruby libraries are called *gems*, and it turns out they're very easy to install. Here's the command that installs the Sinatra gem:

```
$ gem install sinatra
```

To update Sinatra, here's the command:

```
$ gem update sinatra
```

It doesn't get any easier than that!

Before I install too many libraries, however, I want to make sure the gem program is up-to-date. Since my computer shipped with an old version of Ruby, it seems likely the related software will need an update as well.

After a bit of searching, I find the command to update the Ruby gem program:

```
$ gem update--system
```

Easy enough.

As I run the gem install command, I notice that the command also installs additional gems, like rack, rack-protection, and tilt. These extra libraries are called *dependencies*. Sinatra relies on them to run, so the gem install command installs them automatically.

Hitting the Books

Now that I'm ready to run Ruby applications, I decided to pick up two general Ruby reference books that came highly recommended on Stack Overflow: *The Well-Grounded Rubyist* (2009) by David A. Black and *Eloquent Ruby* (2011) by Russ Olsen. Both books are introductory primers designed to introduce the reader to common Ruby concepts and techniques, as well as basic reference texts.

I also purchased *Sinatra: Up and Running* (2011) by Alan Harris and Konstantin Hasse. This book is designed to be a basic introduction to the Sinatra framework. Even though Sinatra is very well documented online, the book contains a lot of examples, which will make it easier to figure out how to use Sinatra for common tasks.

While browsing for books, I also found several reference websites that cover basic Ruby syntax:

- The Official Beginner's Guide to Ruby[21]
- The Ruby Refresher[22]
- Ruby Security Reviewer's Guide[23]

That's plenty of reference material to start with, so I set aside ninety minutes to do a quick preview of everything I've collected so far.

I sat down with each book, and did a quick scan of the table of contents and index, noting terms and ideas that look important. I also captured concepts that came up over and over again, as well as the order of introduction. I read the headlines and sidebars. Once I was done with the books, I did the same thing with the websites.

Here's what I learned. In addition to variables, conditionals, exceptions, and the other basics of programming, Ruby is built around two core ideas: *objects* and *methods*.

Objects are the nouns of the programming world: they're things we can do something to (or with). Let's say I want to create a new variable in Ruby called `firstname`, and I want it to contain my name. In Ruby, that command looks like this:

```
firstname = "Josh"
```

Simple enough. By putting "Josh" in quotation marks, I'm telling Ruby that `firstname` is a *string*: a sequence of alphanumeric characters. That makes `firstname` an object in the "string" class. (A class is just a specific type of object with certain characteristics.)

Strings aren't the only class of objects. Here's an object that's in the integer class:

```
million = 1000000
```

If objects are nouns in programming, methods are the verbs: they're things we can do to (or with) an object.

Let's say I have two string objects that contain my first and last name:

```
firstname = "Josh"
lastname = "Kaufman"
```

I can use a plus sign (+) to *concatenate* these strings, which is a fancy term for "putting them together":

```
fullname = firstname + lastname
```

Pop quiz: what does `fullname` contain? If you guessed "Josh Kaufman," you're wrong.

Remember, the computer will only do exactly what you tell it to. We didn't tell the computer to add a space between "Josh" and "Kaufman," so it didn't. `fullname` equals "JoshKaufman."

If we want to correct this little bug, we have to change the code to add a space:

```
fullname = firstname + " " + lastname
```

The + is a method, and how the method works depends on the objects we use it on. If we use it on integers instead of strings, it performs addition instead of concatenation:

```
sum = million + million
```

What does sum equal? "2000000"

Ruby's built-in methods can help you do a lot of cool things right away. Let's say I want to see what my full name looks like backward. Instead of figuring it out by hand or writing my own little program to reverse the letters, I can just use the reverse method available for every string object:

```
fullname.reverse
```

Here's the output: namfuaKhsoJ

I can also use more than one method at a time. If I want to reverse the letters in my name *and* convert all of the characters to lowercase at the same time, I can run this:

```
fullname.reverse.downcase
```

Output: namfuakhsoj. Neat!

A large part of learning to code in Ruby appears to involve using, creating, and manipulating objects, classes, and methods. The language has a lot of them built in, and Ruby allows you to create, modify, or remove objects, classes, and methods pretty much however you want, which gives the language a lot of power and flexibility.[24]

Ruby's official documentation[25] contains the canonical list of all of the objects and methods available for use. A quick glance is overwhelming, but it helps to realize that you don't have to use them all. On the contrary, most of them are safe to ignore for now. They're options, ready to use when you need them.

The documentation serves another purpose: when you try to do something that Ruby can't understand, the resulting error message will tell you where the program broke.

Let's say we try to run a program like this:

```
animal = "Zebra"
number = 7
puts animal + number
```

The command puts is another way of saying print. We just want the program to display what it thinks animal + number means.

Here's what I get when I try to run the program:

```
TypeError: can't convert Fixnum into String from program.
rb:3:in '+'
```

In noncomputer speak: you can't use arithmetic to add a number to a word in a way that makes sense, so the computer displays an error. It's like trying to divide by zero: you just can't do it, so the program stops.

To fix the program, we either need to convert the number to a string so the + method will concatenate the two variables instead of trying to use arithmetic, or modify the program to do something else.

Here's a revised program:

```
animal = "Zebra"
number = 7.to_s
puts animal + number
```

When we run the program, we get the output "Zebra7." The built-in method .to_s converts the number 7 into a string, so Ruby can use concatenation.

We could also do something completely different, like this:

```
animal = "Zebra"
number = 7
number.times { puts "#{animal}" }
```

Here's the output:

```
Zebra
Zebra
Zebra
Zebra
Zebra
Zebra
Zebra
```

We just used a basic conditional loop, which is built into Ruby: number. times means "do this X times, where X equals the value of the number variable." If we change the value of animal or number, we'll change the output. (Yes, you can modify this program to print "wombat" a billion times if you really want to.)

Commenting and Debugging

As I read, I also picked up another basic feature in Ruby: *commenting*. Any time you begin a line of a program with # (often called a "pound sign" or, less often, an "octothorpe"), Ruby interprets that line as a comment and skips it.

Adding comments to a program makes it much easier to follow, since you can explain in plain language what you're trying to do. Here's how comments would look in my "Animal Print" program:

```
# Assign variables
animal = "Wombat"
number = 1000000000
# Print loop
number.times { puts "#{animal}" }
```

Commenting is also a basic troubleshooting technique: you can comment out a few lines of code at a time to isolate issues or bugs. Combined with well-placed print or puts statements, you can follow a program's execution step by step to make sure everything is working as expected.

After a total of eight hours of research and installation, I'm now running the latest version of Ruby, I can install any library I need, and I have a basic understanding of how Ruby programs work.

It's important to note that I haven't actually programmed anything of substance yet. The time so far has been spent doing research, installing Ruby, and getting a feel for what it looks like to write a Ruby program.

Let's explore more complicated programs.

Kicking the Tires with IRB

In my Stack Overflow research, I found an online Ruby tutorial called *Learn Ruby the Hard Way*[26] by Rob Sobers and Zed Shaw. The tutorial illustrates how Ruby works by giving you examples of simple Ruby programs and asking you to modify and run them to produce specific results. If you don't get the correct result, your job is to experiment by modifying the program until you get the intended result.

This "code, test, run, debug" method is a good example of a *fast feedback loop*. When you run a program, the computer will let you know in milliseconds whether or not it worked. If there's a bug in your code, you can change it and run the program again, testing several variations in the space of a minute.

The first chapters of *Learn Ruby the Hard Way* involve setting up Ruby, installing a basic text editing program, and learning how to use IRB: a program that runs Ruby programs on your own computer.

Here's how it works. You type your program into a text editor and save it in a file. (Let's assume the file's name is program.rb.) When you're ready to run the program, you type this into Terminal:

```
$ irb program.rb
```

IRB will run the program and give you the result. It will also show you the steps the computer took to get to that result, which is useful for debugging. If the program isn't correct, IRB will spit out a detailed error message.

Learn Ruby the Hard Way begins with assigning variables, doing basic arithmetic, manipulating strings, and setting up basic conditional statements, similar to the examples I just mentioned. It's a very structured, logical approach to learning the basics.

My original plan was to read *Eloquent Ruby* and *The Well-Grounded Rubyist*, then complete all of the exercises in *Learn Ruby the Hard Way* before attempting to write my first "real" program. Around lesson 10, however, I noticed something important: I'm getting restless and losing interest.

Here's the core of the issue: I'm copying programs someone else created and solving problems someone else defined. These programs are sometimes interesting, but they don't solve my problems. Programming is starting to feel like an academic exercise instead of a useful skill. I need to get out of research mode and into implementation mode.

I don't need to read all of the books, courses, tutorials, and other resources I've discovered before I start programming. I need to start writing real programs immediately, then refer to my resources if and when I get stuck.

Time to get my hands dirty. . . .

Application #1: A Static Website in Sinatra

I already have an idea for my first web application: a Sinatra application that serves a basic HTML website. Here's my target performance level for this application:

1. Create a basic working Sinatra application capable of delivering a simple website to an end user (a reader).

2. Test the application on my computer to make sure it works.

3. Deploy that application to production on Heroku, making it "live" so real readers can use it.

That's it. No fancy features, just a very simple Sinatra program running on a public server.

So where should I start? Let's review my practice checklist:

1. Choose a lovable project.

2. Focus your energy on one skill at a time.

3. Define your target performance level.

4. Deconstruct the skill into subskills.

5. Obtain critical tools.

6. Eliminate barriers to practice.

7. Make dedicated time for practice.

8. Create fast feedback loops.

9. Practice by the clock in short bursts.

10. Emphasize quantity and speed.

I have a single, well-defined project. I've deconstructed the skill, and I know what this program will look like when I'm done. That brings me to critical tools: Is there anything I need to complete this project that I don't already have?

As it turns out, yes: I don't yet have a Heroku account. That's easy to fix: I visit Heroku.com, click the Sign Up button, verify my e-mail address, and create a password.

Since I've already downloaded the Heroku Toolbelt (the program I used to install git), the Heroku gem is already on my computer, so I'm set there as well.

Based on the instructions, there's one last thing I need to do to allow my computer to talk to Heroku: generate something called an "SSH key," a special file that appears to serve as a password. Once I have a key, I'm supposed to upload it to Heroku so the system can recognize my computer and grant it access.

Fortunately, Heroku has a tutorial about how to do this.[27] I run this command to generate the key:

```
$ ssh-keygen -t rsa
```

. . . this command to log in to Heroku:

```
$ heroku login
```

. . . and this command to add the key to my Heroku account:

```
$ heroku keys:add
```

Great: I'm in. Now how do I start writing the application?

Creating the Basic App

Time to browse Heroku's documentation. Great: there are two guides that look useful:

- "Getting Started with Ruby on Heroku"[28]
- "Deploying Rack-Based Apps"[29]

Based on these guides, it looks like I need to:

1. Create the program files on my computer.
2. Add them to a "git repository." (Whatever that is . . .)

3. Use the git push heroku master command to send the finished application to Heroku.

Fortunately, the tutorial includes an example, and it's a Sinatra application! This'll be easier than I thought. . . .

I create a new folder on my computer. This folder is called the "root" folder, and every file in the program will be stored here.

Next, I open up my text editor (I'm using TextMate[30]) and create three files, following the instructions:

```
application.rb
config.ru
Gemfile
```

The core of the program will go in application.rb. Ruby applications always end in .rb.

config.ru is where Rack configuration settings go. Remember, Sinatra is built on top of Rack, so it makes sense that it has a separate configuration file. "Rackup" files end in .ru.

Gemfile is the place to specify which gems the program will use. Your program will only ever have one Gemfile, so it's always called "Gemfile." Seems simple enough.

After creating the files, the Heroku documentation suggests writing a basic "Hello, World!" program to test the setup. Here's what goes in application.rb:

```
require 'sinatra'
get '/' do
  "Hello World!"
end
```

Here's what goes in config.ru:

```
require './application.rb'
run Sinatra::Application
```

And here's what goes in the Gemfile:

```
source 'http://rubygems.org'
gem 'sinatra'
```

That's not a lot of code, and it's pretty easy to understand.

- The Gemfile tells the server to include the Sinatra gem, which is required to run the application. The gem will be downloaded from RubyGems.org.
- The config.ru file sets up the main application, then executes the program.
- Once the program is running, the program will display "Hello, World!" whenever someone visits "/", which is a shorthand way of referring to the home page of a website.

Can it really be this easy?

The tutorial tells me there's one more thing to do: store the files in a git repository (sometimes abbreviated to "repo"). I'm not exactly sure what that means, but I know git is already installed, and they supply the commands:

```
$ git init .
$ git add -A
$ git commit -m "Initial Commit"
```

The first command creates a new git repo in the current root folder. The add -A command adds all of the files in the folder to the repo. The command commit -m" commits the files to the repo, alongside a message from the programmer that details what's being committed. (I'm not clear on the difference between "add" and "commit" quite yet, so I'm making a note to explore this later.)

After entering these commands, the computer tells me:

```
[master (root-commit) 8ed1099] Initial commit
3 files changed, 9 insertions(+), 0 deletions(-)
```

```
create mode 100644 Gemfile
create mode 100644 application.rb
create mode 100644 config.ru
```

Looks like it worked! There's only one more thing to do: create a new empty server in Heroku, then "push" my program to that server.

I run this command to create the server:

```
$ heroku create
```

And I get this response:

```
    Creating shielded-springs-2049 . . . done, stack is stack
is bamboo-ree-1.8.7
    http://shielded-springs-2049.heroku.com/ | git@heroku.
com:shielded-springs-2049.git
    Git remote heroku added
```

Success! The "stack" details the software the server is running, and the message gives me the public URL of the server.

Here's the final command:

```
$ git push heroku master
```

If all goes well, I'll have officially pushed my first application to production on Heroku.

Here's what I get:

```
Heroku receiving push
Ruby/Sinatra app detected
Gemfile detected, running Bundler version 1.0.7
Unresolved dependencies detected; Installing . . .
Using—without development:test
! Gemfile.lock will soon be required
! Check Gemfile.lock into git with `git add Gemfile.lock`
! See http://devcenter.heroku.com/articles/bundler
```

```
Fetching source index for http://rubygems.org/
Installing rack (1.4.1)
Installing rack-protection (1.2.0)
Installing tilt (1.3.3)
Installing sinatra (1.3.3)
Using bundler (1.0.7)
Your bundle is complete! It was installed into ./.bundle/gems/
Compiled slug size: 500K
Launching . . . done, v4
http://shielded-springs-2049.heroku.com deployed to Heroku
```

Now, the moment of truth . . . I open a web browser, navigate to http://shielded-springs–2049.heroku.com, and this is what I see:

```
"Hello, World!"
```

VICTORY!

Warning, Warning!

The program worked, but I also got a warning message. What is `Gemfile.lock`?

Heroku's Ruby documentation shows that the system uses a library called bundler[31] to install gems on Heroku. It's a gem, so I can install it locally by running:

```
$ gem install bundler
```

Bundler is necessary because Heroku doesn't install any gems in your application by default. For security reasons, Heroku doesn't give me the same level of computer access as I have on my machine, so there's no way I can run `gem install sinatra` directly in my account.

Instead of giving me (or any other user) dangerous levels of system access, Heroku uses bundler to install gems specified in `Gemfile`. Once you've identified which gems you want to install in your application, you run this command on your computer:

```
$ bundle install
```

This command creates a new file called Gemfile.lock in your program. When you upload your files to Heroku, the system looks at Gemfile and Gemfile.lock, verifies they're the same for security, downloads the gems, then installs them for you.

If you look at the output when I pushed the program to Heroku, you can see that the system installed bundler automatically as a dependency. Instead of displaying an error message, Heroku's engineers added an exception to the program to install the program automatically and display a warning instead of crashing.

The system worked this time, but in the future, I'll have to add Gemfile. lock to the git repository before I push the application. Good to know!

Sinatra Takes the Stage

Now that my simple application is up and running, I can finally begin learning how Sinatra works. Sinatra's documentation[32] is very comprehensive, and full of examples, so that's where I decided to start.

The core of Sinatra applications is called a *route*. The best way to understand this idea is by example.

Our basic Sinatra application has a single route, which contains the "root" of our little website. Internet users usually refer to the website root as the home page of a website.

If you visit google.com or yahoo.com, your web browser sends a request to Google or Yahoo's servers. This request is called a GET request, and it asks the server to show you whatever is in the website's root directory. The *protocol*, or format the computer uses to send the request, is called HTTP, which stands for "hypertext transfer protocol." That's what the "http://" you often see at the beginning of web addresses means.

GET is the most common type of HTTP request, but it's not the only type. There are three additional HTTP "verbs":

- POST—send a resource to the server
- PUT—update a resource on the server
- DELETE—remove a resource on the server

If you've ever posted a public comment on a website, your witty remarks were sent to the server using a POST command. If you made a mistake and edited the comment, your update was sent via a PUT command. If you decided the comment was dumb and chose to remove it, the browser sent a DELETE command.

Routes that contain GET, POST, PUT, and DELETE commands are the core of how Sinatra applications work. Each route you create is a conditional: "Do X if a GET/POST/PUT/DELETE command is received on route Y."

Sinatra routes can also contain variables, which are called *parameters*. Sinatra applications usually use parameters as inputs for the process contained in each route.

Let's modify our simple Sinatra "Hello, World!" application to greet our user by name. Here's a route that will do it:

```
get '/hello/:name' do
  "Hello, #{params[:name]}!"
end
```

You can see this in action at http://first20hours.com/hello/name. Feel free to replace "name" with your name. It works!

This application works by allowing the server to look at whatever is in the "name" part of the route, then use it in the application. The command in the route is a simple instruction to display the "name" parameter to the user.

Sinatra allows you to name parameters (like :name), but it also has a "wildcard" parameter (also called a "splat") that can contain anything. Here's how we'd use it in our modified "Hello" application:

```
get '/hello/*' do
  "Hello, #{params[:splat]}!"
end
```

That's pretty cool. Between named parameters and wildcards, you can create some very smart routes. The routes you create determine how your Sinatra application works.

That's enough detail to figure out how to write a program that satisfies my target performance level. Since Jekyll is creating the actual files the application will be delivering in response to user GET requests, all I need to do is write a few routes that accept these requests, find the correct file in the system, and deliver it to the reader.

Based on Jekyll's documentation, the program places the finished web pages in a folder called "site" in the root directory. The route to that page is automatically generated by Jekyll. If we want our website's About page to be available at http://example.com/about, we set a route of /about in our Jekyll files, and the program will create the file in _site/about/index.html in our website's root folder.

That means I have to create a new route in Sinatra to read a file in response to the user's GET request. Here's what that looks like:

```
# Index handler
get '/?' do
## File.read("_site/index.html")
end

# Post handler
get '/*/?' do
## File.read("_site/#{params[:splat]}/index.html")
end
```

File.read("") is a command that's built into Ruby. File is an object, and .read is a method. The usage is pretty straightforward: what goes in the ("") part is the location of the file you want the program to read, relative to the application's root folder. Easy.

What if the file doesn't exist? That calls for an exception, and Sinatra has two basic error routes built in: not_found and error. Let's make both routes return the same error page:

```
not_found do
## File.read("_site/error/index.html")
end
```

```
error do
  File.read("_site/error/index.html")
end
```

Everything else stays the same. I'm not going to make any changes to config.ru or our Gemfile. I'm just adding the new routes to the program's Git repository, committing the changes, then pushing the updated program to Heroku. Done.

Want to see what our updated program looks like in action? Visit PersonalMBA.com: the site is now running Jekyll instead of WordPress using this exact program. Using a load-testing program called seige, my website is now able to serve over two thousand concurrent readers without breaking a sweat. Most page requests are delivered in eighteen to twenty-five milliseconds, so my site is now fully protected from crashing due to heavy traffic.

My first working web application is complete. It took me about an hour to figure out how to do these steps, and another hour to figure out how to transfer my website information and design out of WordPress and into Jekyll.

Total time to completion: around ten hours, which includes my research and programming concept review. Not bad!

Application #2: Codex, a Personal Notes Database

My first application works, and it works well. It's simple, but that's a major benefit in this case. Fewer moving parts means fewer ways for the program to break.

Let's look at something a bit more complex.

Remember our database discussion earlier? Basic web pages can't update themselves, so they can't store information. The first application only works because the files are static: they don't change. Any changes to the files are made via Jekyll, which is a separate program. The application is fast and stable because it doesn't rely on a database.

What about applications that use databases? Databases are a big part of web applications in general, so I need to understand how they work. To learn how they work, I need to start working on a project that relies on a database.

One of the applications I use on a daily basis is Backpack,[33] which was developed by 37signals. The primary benefit of Backpack is creating "pages" that can contain pretty much anything: text, lists, images, files, et cetera. When you save information in a page in Backpack, you can access it later from any computer, since all of the information is stored in the application's database.

I wonder: Can I create something similar myself? Worth a try . . . but how do I start?

While researching Jekyll, I read an essay by Tom Preston-Werner, the programmer who created Jekyll, called "Readme Driven Development."[34] The gist of the essay is that contrary to the waves of project management fads that sweep the software industry every few years, the best way to create an application is to write a Readme document before you do anything else.

A Readme is a file that programmers include in the application's root folder alongside the code. The file contains information on how to set up, configure, and use the program.

Readme files are important because many programs aren't self-explanatory. Without a bit of documentation, it's usually very difficult to figure out how to use a program. Digging into the code to figure it out yourself isn't as efficient as reading a detailed explanation written by the original programmer.

Tom argues that it's best to write your program's Readme file first, before you begin coding. Most programmers code first, then (maybe) write the Readme. That's a missed opportunity: writing the documentation first helps you figure out exactly how the program will work. The Readme can be a design tool as much as a documentation tool.

That makes sense to me. One of the product development techniques I learned in the process of working on *The Personal MBA* was writing sales copy before creating an offer, not after it's done. By figuring out what potential purchasers want and incorporating that into your sales copy, you gain a more complete understanding of what the product needs to be in order to attract customers. The marketing research informs the development of the offer itself.

I took out a notebook and wrote a list of things I wanted the application to do, as well as qualities I wanted the application to have:

- The program is a simple reference and note-taking application.

- The application is designed for a single user.

- The application uses Sinatra and a database to create, save, update, and delete page records.

- The application allows the user to create pages that have fancy formatting like bold, italics, headlines, et cetera.

- The application requires a password to access it, and keeps the information in the database as secure as possible.

- The application looks nice.

- The application can be easily deployed to Heroku or another similar host.

I'm going to call this application Codex, an old term for "book," since the application will be useful primarily for reference information, lists, and the like.

The web programming term of art for this sort of application is "CRUD," which stands for *Create, Read, Update, Delete*. It's worth mentioning that these functions are basically the same thing as GET, POST, PUT, DELETE, so building this sort of application is certainly possible using Sinatra routes. The big difference is the introduction of a database.

What sort of database options are available on Heroku? I don't know: back to the documentation.

By default, Heroku uses a database called Postgres.[35] Every new application is assigned a small development database by default. That works for me, but how do I use it, and what do I use to test the program on my own computer?

Enter DataMapper

To answer these questions, I decided to search Stack Overflow. The consensus is that using a library called DataMapper[36] makes this sort of development much easier.

DataMapper is a type of program called an "object relational mapper," usually abbreviated to ORM.[37] ORMs solve a pressing issue for programmers: databases often use their own language, which is different from the language the programmer uses to create the application. The most common database language is called SQL,[38] but there are hundreds of others.

Let's assume we're a programmer for Amazon.com, and we want to display a list of books by J. K. Rowling, author of the Harry Potter series. Here's what the SQL command might look like:

```
SELECT * FROM Book WHERE author = "J.K. Rowling" ORDER BY
title;
```

This command retrieves all records from the Book database that have an author field that contains "J.K. Rowling" and returns them in alphabetical order by title.

Unfortunately, getting SQL or any other database query language to play nicely with languages like Ruby can be tricky. It's hard enough to program in one language, let alone several at the same time.

That's where ORMs come in: they allow the programmer to write code in one language, which the ORM then translates into the database's language. Much easier.

DataMapper, then, is a library that makes it much easier to communicate with databases using Ruby. By default, DataMapper provides a lot of useful features for creating, reading, updating, and deleting database records. Since DataMapper has been around for a while and has been tested thoroughly, in most cases it's more reliable than trying to write your own database code.

DataMapper is available as a gem, which is installed like this:

```
$ gem install data_mapper
```

Since DataMapper is such a big library, it's also possible to install piece by piece. This is a concept called "modularity," and it's a hallmark of good programming. Here's a command that installs all of the individual gems:

```
$ gem install dm-core dm-aggregates dm-constraints dm-
migrations dm-transactions dm-serializer dm-timestamps dm-
validations dm-types
```

Instead of installing the entire library, you can install only the parts your program will use, which is much more efficient.

Using DataMapper

Now that DataMapper is installed, I have to figure out how to use it to (1) talk to a database, and (2) set up the database to store and retrieve the information I want.

Based on Heroku's Postgres documentation, the following command will allow my Sinatra application to talk to the database:

```
DataMapper.setup(:default, ENV['DATABASE_URL'] ||
"sqlite3://#{Dir.pwd}/database.db")
```

In this case, the || is another way of saying "or." ENV['DATABASEURL'] is a variable that Heroku uses to stand for your application's database. If that database is not available, it will use the second option, a database called Sqlite.[39]

Sqlite is installed on Mac computers by default, so it's ready to go. DataMapper can talk to both Postgres and Sqlite if I install these two gems:

```
$ gem install dm-sqlite-adapter dm-postgres-adapter
```

This means that my application will use Postgres when it's running on Heroku, but Sqlite when it's running on my computer. In either case, my code will be the same, even though the databases speak different languages. That's really cool.

Speaking of running this application on my computer . . . how do I do that?

Pow!

I searched Stack Overflow and Hacker News for information on how to run this sort of application locally on my machine. Fortunately, there are a few options. It appears I can install libraries (like Foreman or Shotgun) that will run the application when I enter a command into Terminal, or I can install a program that keeps the program running all the time.

A program that takes the second approach is Pow,[40] a "a zero-configuration Rack server for Mac OS X." The site promises to make it easy to set up local development hosting on my computer in less than a minute. Sounds great to me!

Installing Pow takes about ten seconds: it requires a single Terminal command to download and install the application. Once installed, you run a command to link your program to Pow, and Pow will allow you to run it on your machine.

There's a Ruby gem called Powder[41] that makes this process even easier:

```
$ gem install powder
```

Once the gem is installed, you run this to install Pow:

```
$ powder install
```

Then, you go to the root directory of your application, and enter this command:

```
$ powder link
```

That's it. My root directory is called "codex," so my application is now running on my private machine at http://codex.dev, and I can test my work.

If I make a change, this command restarts the program:

```
$ powder restart
```

Easy. I'm now ready to start building. I set aside an hour and a half every evening to code, and I'll keep going until it's done.

Code, Test, Revise

At this point, I'm going to describe what I'm doing versus how I'm doing it. You can see the full code at https://github.com/first20hours/codex if you want to follow along.

Here's what I want the application to look like when I'm done:

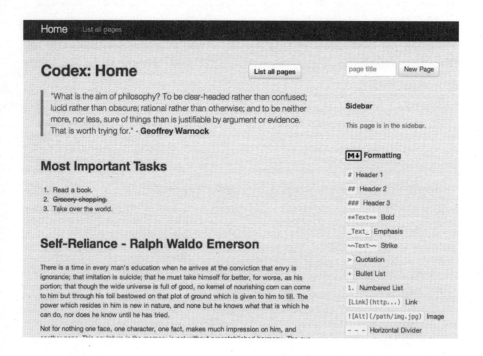

You'll notice this design has three parts: a top navigation bar, a main content area, and a sidebar. I put together this basic design using Bootstrap,[42] which was created by Mark Otto and Jacob Thornton, both developers at Twitter.

Instead of creating a web design from scratch, Bootstrap is a library of prewritten HTML and CSS that's free to use. Using Bootstrap saves a ton of time: you can put together a basic prototype of what you want an application to look like in minutes instead of days.

The basic unit of this application is a "Page," which displays a record stored in the database. The Page information goes in the main content area. There's a button that leads to a screen that lists all Pages in the database, and two buttons at the bottom. The first button allows you to edit the current Page, and the second lets you delete it.

The sidebar contains three main features. At the top, there's a form that allows you to create a new Page, which requires a title. Second, there's a list of Pages the user has added to the sidebar, which acts as a quick reference section. Third, there's a formatting reference, which helps the user remember how to use common formatting features.

The navigation bar at the top is pretty simple. It contains a link to the home page, as well as a secondary link to the "List all pages" screen. I can add additional items to the navigation bar later if I like, but that's all I really need for now.

Every web application has a home page, so I need to decide what I want to have on that page. In this case, I just want to display the Home record in the database.

So what's in a Page? Since each Page is a database record, and records have fields that contain the actual information, I need to tell DataMapper which fields to set up. Here's the code:

```
class Page
    include DataMapper::Resource
    property :id, Serial
    property :title, String
    property :content, Text
    property :lastupdated, DateTime
end
```

```
DataMapper.finalize
```

This code uses DataMapper to create a new type of object called a Page. Ruby can now use a Page like any other object, and I can create and use methods that build, modify, and delete Pages. When I make a change to a Page, that change is stored in the database via DataMapper.

The `Datamapper.finalize` command tells the application to set up these fields in the actual database if they don't already exist.

Now that I have the database set up, it's time to figure out which routes Sinatra should expect to serve. Here's my list, based on what I know so far:

```
# Show home page
get '/'
```

```
# Creates new note from "new page" form
post '/'
```

```
# Displays requested note
get '/:url/'
```

```
# Edits requested note
get '/:url/edit'
```

```
# Saves user edits to note
post '/:url/edit'
```

```
# Deletes specified note
delete '/:url/'
```

```
# List all pages in database
get '/all/'
```

```
# Error handling
not_found
error
```

That's a pretty good list. My application will revolve around what commands I create for each route.

Slugs, Slugs Everywhere!

Remember when I mentioned that databases are a bit like a stack of magic index cards, and you can search them any way you want? We need a way to search for specific page records, which is why you see :url in these routes. The content of the url parameter will tell the database which record to retrieve.

We could use the page title as the parameter, but there's a problem with that: web browsers don't like things like spaces, capital letters, and special characters (like $ and %) in web addresses. Page titles may very well include those things, so you need to have a way to strip them out.

A string that uniquely identifies a website page is called a *slug*.[43] My page slug will be based on the page title, with the following rules to make it web-address friendly:

1. All characters will be lowercase.

2. No special characters—alphanumeric only.

3. No spaces—all spaces should be replaced with a dash.

The way to do this is by creating a method that accepts the page title, then converts it to slug format. The tricky substitutions are taken care of by a type of programming called *regular expressions*, which transform or find text within strings based on given rules.[44]

Regular expressions can be very arcane, but this is a common use, so I was able to find a boilerplate example. Here's my method:

```
# Converts page name into post slug
def slugify(content)
  content.downcase.gsub(/ /, '-').gsub(/[^a-z0-9-]/, '').squeeze('-')
end
```

Now, I can use the slugify method to transform a string like "Page Title" into "page-title," making it appropriate to use in a web address.

In addition, if we store the slug alongside the page's title, we can use it to retrieve the page record using the :url parameter.

I added this field to the DataMapper class:

```
property :slug, String
```

Now, whenever we create a page, we can "slugify" the page's title, store it in the database, and use it to show the page again when we want to retrieve it. That's how the application will know which page to show.

Creating Pages

I start by working down my list of necessary routes. The "home" route is easy: I redirect it to the /home/ slug, since I want the home page to show the home record.

The "create Page" route is linked to the little form at the top of the sidebar. The user enters the page title in the form, then clicks the button. The system captures the page title, slugifies it, then saves the title, slug, and time of creation in the database. It then sends a GET request containing the slug, displaying the new page.

There's a tiny detail in the "create Page" route that's very important: what if the Page already exists? I don't want to overwrite the Page if it already contains data. Accidental data loss is unacceptable.

Fortunately, DataMapper solves this particular issue with the built-in method .first_or_create. Before creating the Page, DataMapper will check whether it already exists. If the page exists, DataMapper won't overwrite it, and Sinatra will redirect the browser to the existing page instead. Problem solved.

The "display Page" route reads the slug in the URL, retrieves the record from the database, then displays the information in the main content area. Later, I'll add some fancy formatting, but for now, I just want it to work.

Editing Pages

Editing a Page involves two separate routes. The first route GETs the Page that the user wants to edit, then displays the contents of the page record in forms the user can edit.

To display these pages, the application relies on a template syntax called ERB, which is basically HTML + Ruby commands. ERB allows programmers to write HTML that includes elements that can change. Since ERB processes the page before it's displayed to the user, it can change the text on the page every time the page is loaded, based on the Ruby commands in the template.

The Save button on the editing screen sends a POST request to the application that updates the Page record.

Deleting Pages

Deleting Pages requires some caution: remember, accidental data loss is unacceptable. If you're going to delete a Page, you want to be absolutely certain the user actually intends to delete that Page.

The wrong way to do this would be to link a delete button directly to a DELETE route in the application. That approach would delete the Page even if the user clicked the button accidentally.

A better strategy is to use a two-phase process. Clicking the Delete button on a page takes the user to a confirmation screen that displays the title of the Page the user wants to delete. If the user wants to proceed, they can click on a confirmation button that sends the DELETE request. If the user clicked the Delete button by accident, they can hit the Cancel or the Back button on their browser.

Listing All Pages

"List all Pages" redirects the user to the /all/ slug, which is different from regular pages.

Instead of retrieving a single record, DataMapper retrieves all of the

Page records in the database. The ERB template for the Page contains a conditional loop that creates a list item for every Page retrieved. Each item contains the title of the Page, which is displayed as a link that contains that Page's associated slug. Clicking on the link takes the user to the individual Page record.

Launching the Application the First Time

I have the basic features in place, but I'm having a problem: when I test the application by visiting the home page, I immediately get an error message. The program is trying to find the Home record in the database, but it doesn't exist, because I just started the application!

The solution for this is to create a "one-time administrative process" using a program called Rake. Rake programs are stored in a Rakefile, which is located in the root folder of the application.

Rakefiles work just like regular Ruby applications, with one exception: they exist outside of your core program, and you have to run the commands manually.

That makes Rake very useful for doing things like adding default information to the database before we officially run the actual program. I copy the important bits of application.rb into the Rakefile, then create a command that creates a new "Home" Page in the database. Then, all I need to do is run this command once:

```
$ rake setup
```

Rake creates the "Home" Page record, and my application stops showing errors on startup. When I push this application to Heroku, I'll run the Rake command remotely to set up the database before I try to use the application.

At this point, we have all of the major features in place. Now, it's time to add some fun things.

Adding Sidebar Support

I just realized that I didn't include a way to add pages to the sidebar, like I originally intended. This sort of feature requires a Boolean, since it only has two values: the page is supposed to be displayed in the sidebar, or it's not.

I added this to the DataMapper class:

```
property :sidebar, Boolean, :default => false
```

I also add a checkbox to the "edit" screen alongside "Include in sidebar?" which I link to the sidebar field in the database. I then write a simple loop to find records in the database where :sidebar = true, then display them as a list, similar to the "List all" page.

I restart the application, edit a record, and the whole application crashes. Yikes!

I try and try to figure out what's going wrong, but I'm having no luck. After combing the DataMapper documentation and searching Stack Overflow, I find that using Boolean variables in this way doesn't mesh well with HTML forms. Another approach is needed:

```
property :sidebar, Enum[ :yes, :no ], :default => :no
```

This is another way to do basically the same thing. Enum, which stands for "enumerate," creates a list of options, and the form sets which option to save in the database.

Adding Markdown Support

Now I want to make sure my pages can contain fancy formatting, like italics, bold text, and headlines.

I've chosen Markdown as the formatting syntax, which is a popular and very useful little markup language created by John Gruber.[45] I'm already familiar with how Markdown works as a user, since a few applications I use on my computer include it. I'll have to figure out how to make my program understand it, though.

A bit of searching tells me there are several Markdown gems available. I choose the rdiscount library, which I include in application.rb:

```
require 'rdiscount'
```

Rdiscount transforms text that's written in Markdown format into HTML: the user's web browser then displays that text with the proper formatting. Markdown files aren't anything special in themselves: they're just text files that are written in a certain way.

That means that I don't need to transform my page information to Markdown before I add it to the database. It's just text, after all. All I need to do is call rdiscount whenever I want to show the fancy formatted text.

Here's the command that does the work, which I added to the ERB templates responsible for showing pages:

```
<% markdown(@page.content) %>
```

The method sucks in the Page content field, transforms it to HTML, then displays the end result to the user. Easy.

Adding Security

What about login information? If I put this application up on Heroku without requiring a username and password, anyone will be able to see what I've stored in the database.

As it turns out, modern web browsers support a security protocol called HTTP Basic Authentication,[46] which is a simple way to require the user to enter a username and password before they can proceed. If the user can't supply the access credentials, they're redirected to an error page.

Here's the code that enables basic authentication in Sinatra:

```
use Rack::Auth::Basic, "Restricted Area" do |username, password|
    [username, password] == [ENV['ADMIN_USER'], ENV['ADMIN_PASS']]
end
```

In this case, I'm storing the actual username and password in Heroku as *environment variables*, which I can set with a Terminal command. That allows me to use the same code for different applications, as well as show you this code without also giving you my passwords!

This is also a good example of why it's important to know that Sinatra is built on top of Rack. There are many libraries like Rack::Auth::Basic available, and I can use any of them with Sinatra. The less I have to reinvent the wheel, the better.

There's one more piece of security I want to add: encryption. I'm going to add SSL encryption—the same type of security banks use to ensure their online banking sessions are private—to my application with the rack-ssl-enforcer gem:

```
require 'rack-ssl-enforcer'
use Rack::SslEnforcer
```

This library forces the web browser to use a secure SSL connection to access the site. Heroku allows applications hosting on Heroku domains to use SSL by default, so there's nothing more to set up.[47]

Adding "Flash" Messages

There's one last feature I'd like to add: I've seen websites that show you little messages like "Your page has been created/edited/deleted" after you do something. How do you do that?

I poke around a bit, and find a library called sinatra-flash that handles this.[48] These messages are called "flash" messages, and they work by storing a little bit of text in the user's browser cookie before going to the next page. When the next page loads, the application reads the cookie and displays the message to the user.

I added the library to the Gemfile and application.rb, set the messages I wanted to show in the appropriate routes, then added a little code to actually display those messages in my ERB templates, and I was done. My app is now complete.

Code Complete

Here's the beginning of the final Codex Readme file:

Codex is a simple single-user reference web application written in Ruby. Codex uses Sinatra and DataMapper to create, save, update, and delete page records from a simple Postgres database. The application is ready for immediate deployment on Heroku.

Markdown formatting is enabled for all pages, which makes it easy to write complex pages with simple markup. HTTP authentication and forced SSL for all traffic keeps your information secure. Bootstrap styling makes your pages look clean and attractive.

The Readme continues with detailed instructions on how to set up the application on Heroku. "Readme Driven Development" was a very good approach.

In total, Codex took me ten hours to build. That brings my total investment in learning programming to twenty hours. (It took me longer to write this chapter than to write the actual application.)

After creating Codex, I attended a local Ruby programmers meetup, and volunteered to explain how the program worked. The feedback was very positive, and I was complimented on how clean, compact, and understandable the code was. One of the participants remarked that the code quality was better than projects he'd seen that were written by professional programmers.

Mission accomplished.

Rage Against the Machine

I want to clarify something: the process I described sounds very linear and straightforward. That's because, up to now, I've been describing what worked, not what didn't.

Coding a useful, working web application is a bit like putting together a puzzle with a few extra challenges: you don't know which pieces exist, you have to create some of the pieces yourself, and if you make a mistake, the puzzle explodes.

Here's what my programming process actually looked like: I'd come up with an idea for how I thought part of the program would work. I wrote some code, tested it, and it broke the program. I'd try to modify it. Sometimes my change would fix the program, sometimes it wouldn't, and sometimes it would break even more things. If I got seriously stuck, I'd search for the error message or library on Stack Overflow or Google.

When you're still learning what everything does, your application is broken way more often than it's working. You also learn about the value of things like version control, which lets you roll back your code to a previous working version.

Remember when I mentioned I didn't really grok what git was for? It's for this: if you're editing files and something breaks, you may not be able to find what's broken. Rolling back to a previous version that works is a godsend and a relief. If you can't, you panic.

Around the point where I started coding the Add to Sidebar feature, I broke the application. I tried to find what I did wrong, but I couldn't figure it out. If I had hair on my head, I would've torn it out.

That's when you learn the value of git branch and git merge: you can create experimental copies of your program, then make your modifications. If your code works, you can merge it back into the master copy. If you screw things up, you can delete your experimental branch without losing all of your previous work.

Programming is hard, and there are millions of ways to screw it up. The computer is unforgiving, and doesn't suffer ill-formed commands. Likewise, it's easy to overlook little details that produce unexpected results. I was having a terrible time with a bug that was saving a bunch of blank records to the database, which showed up on the "List all" page.

Every time I viewed the page, more phantom pages would appear in the list, and I couldn't figure out where they were coming from. It ended up being a bug in the "list all" route: I was using an incorrect command to retrieve the records from the database.

Every time I broke something, I learned something. That's one of the hidden benefits of programming. The computer is the fastest of all feed-back loops. If you do something wrong, you know it right away. If you do it right, you get to see the results of your work immediately. If you can avoid the impulse to throw your computer across the room, the instant feedback can make programming quite addictive.

At the beginning of this experiment, I couldn't program at all. Now, I can. All it took was spending the time necessary to beat some code into submission, and pushing through or doing a little research whenever I got stuck.

What did I gain for my efforts? A ton. I learned what programming is, what it looks like, and why it's useful. I learned how to create real working web applications in Ruby from scratch, then push them to production servers. I learned the basics of Sinatra, Heroku, Jekyll, DataMapper, Rake, and other versatile tools I can use to create useful new applications. I learned how to troubleshoot errors and find bugs, then fix them.

Reviewing the Method

Let's review the core of the method I used to learn programming:

- I spent some time learning what programming and web applications are in general, then deconstructed these skills into smaller subskills that are easier to understand and practice.

- I set my target performance level by choosing two specific projects I wanted to create, then defined what those projects would look like when finished.

- I deconstructed those projects into smaller substeps then identified which substeps seemed most important.

- I made sure I had the tools I needed to work (like the latest version of Ruby), and that I was able to find and use any additional tools I needed.

- I found a few reliable sources of programming information, but I skipped canned tutorials in favor of jumping in and writing the actual programs.

- I worked on the most important substeps first, like figuring out how to test programs on my computer, push the finished application to production, et cetera.

- I used reference examples to get started and build confidence, then tested various approaches to figure out how to program the features I wanted.

- When I made an error, the program crashed and gave me an error message, creating a fast feedback loop.

- After getting an error, I experimented with several ways to fix it. If I couldn't fix the problem myself, I searched for help.

- I kept using the build/test/fix approach until my programs were complete.

Total time elapsed: approximately twenty hours. Ten of those hours were research, and the remaining ten were programming the two applications, which are now finished and in production.

Where I'm Going from Here

I've continued to program web applications since completing these basic projects, focusing on programs that make running my business easier.

I'm proud to say that my entire business now runs on software I've created myself. My applications are capable of charging credit cards, setting up subscriptions, sending e-mail, and managing website access for my customers. By learning to code, I now have my own little robot army that's programmed to do my bidding.

How long did it take to write all of these programs? About ninety hours in total, including the twenty I've detailed in this chapter.

Here's an added benefit: whenever I find an area of my business that's repetitive or frustrating, I start thinking in code. How would a program that solves this problem work? More often than not, there's a way to systematize the process in a way that makes my day-to-day life easier.

I'm also picking up new tricks, like customizing my computer to make programming faster. I'm learning keyboard shortcuts in my text editor to save time, and I've upgraded Terminal to iTerm2 and Z-Shell to make coding a bit easier.

I'm still practicing, and I'm not an expert by any standard. I have to research everything, and it takes me a while to solve problems, errors, and bugs. It's often frustrating.

Still, I'm creating programs that solve real problems in a straightforward, reliable way. That's what really counts.

I fight the computer, and I win.

6

Touch Typing

Lesson: Old Habits Don't Necessarily Die Hard

Anything worth doing well is worth doing poorly at first.
—RAY CONGDON

■ ■ ■

For supplementary images, video, and commentary about this chapter, visit http://first20hours.com/typing.

Up to this point, I've been learning new skills in areas where I have little previous experience. That lack of experience is certainly a barrier at first, but at least my mind isn't actively *interfering* with the learning process.

What happens when you're practicing something new *and* your brain is rebelling at the same time?

There are certainly dramatic examples of reacquiring a skill. Tiger Woods has famously retrained his already high-performing golf swing three times.[1] Sometimes it's worth learning how to do something important in a new and better way, even if it's at the cost of short-term inefficiency or frustration.

The pace of modern technology makes relearning very common: What happens if a software program you rely on to do your job changes, or a new program becomes the most efficient way to complete a task? What if you get a new job that requires working with new tools? Relearning skills quickly is often just as important as learning something new.

I'm curious: What does it feel like to retrain yourself to do something that really matters?

I started listing things I already knew how to do, then combed the list looking for skills that (1) I was already good at doing, and (2) that had several methods for accomplishing the same result. It didn't take long to find a promising candidate.

The skill? Touch typing.

A Life Behind the Keyboard

According to David Allen, author of the productivity uber–bestseller *Getting Things Done* (2002), if your work requires using any sort of computer, learning how to touch-type is the single most significant thing you can do to improve your productivity.

The critical threshold seems to be about sixty words per minute (abbreviated WPM). If you can't touch-type at least sixty WPM with a low error rate, you're seriously crippling your ability to do productive work. The less effort you need to put into typing, the more time and energy you have to do higher-value tasks.

I've been touch typing for at least seventeen years, probably longer. In school, every student was required to take a typing course in seventh grade, and I remember being bored. I already knew how to touch-type, so I finished the assignments in a few minutes, then spent the rest of the class time figuring out how to make the word processor spit out strange-looking characters, like pilcrows (¶), section marks (§), and interrobangs (‽).

I learned how to touch-type mostly by spending a lot of time working with computers in my spare time. My typing practice was ambient, not deliberate: I didn't consciously work on improving my speed or accuracy. I just used the computer, and in the process, I learned how to type.

That's not to say my technique was great. My hands flew all over the keyboard instead of spending most of the time on the *home row*, the keys in the middle of the keyboard. My method wasn't textbook correct, but it got the job done, which was all I cared about.

Even though my typing form isn't great, it's functional. In my line of work, I'm at the computer a lot, and my typing speed and accuracy get the job done.

Every now and again, however, I come across an article about alternative keyboard layouts: arrangements of keys that are different from QWERTY, the so-called universal default layout that graces the vast majority of English-language keyboards produced each year:[2]

QWERTY, the argument goes, is grossly inefficient—a horrible design. There are other ways to arrange the keys on a keyboard that help the user type more quickly, accurately, and with less effort.

Cumulative effort is a very big deal: repetitive stress injury (RSI) and carpal tunnel syndrome are common hand and wrist disorders that can be caused or exacerbated by typing. Although I haven't experienced noticeable symptoms yet, I have several close friends who have, and it's not fun. I want to avoid dealing with these disorders if I can.

I'm planning on writing and programming for many years to come, and unless speech recognition or thought-to-text becomes the primary method of computer use, I'll be typing for the foreseeable future. It's probably in my best interest to learn how to type in the most efficient way possible, even if that involves short-term confusion or discomfort.

Goodbye QWERTY: I'm going to relearn how to touch-type.

How the QWERTY Layout Became
the "Universal" Standard

Contrary to popular belief, the QWERTY keyboard format wasn't designed to slow typists down: it was a solution to a mechanical engineering problem.

In the olden days, before word processors and computers, mechanical typewriters made characters appear on pages by swinging a small metal key, called a *typebar*, toward a piece of paper, which was wrapped tightly around a cylinder. An inked ribbon lay between the paper and the key. The key struck the ribbon, which made contact with the paper, leaving a character on the page. The "Return" key rotated the cylinder, moving the paper up and allowing the typist to continue to type on a new line.

C. L. Sholes, who is credited with the invention of the QWERTY typewriter layout, built his first prototype in 1868. Sholes wasn't the first person to create a typewriter: there were at least fifty-one other inventors who tried before he did, and Sholes studied their work, incorporating many of their features into his design.[3]

The keys on Sholes's first prototype were arranged in alphabetical order, which made sense. At the time, no one imagined that people would (or could) learn to touch-type with all ten fingers. Putting the keys in alphabetical order ensured that untrained users could find the appropriate letters as they pecked with two index fingers.

There was a major problem with the prototype, however: the typebars had a nasty habit of sticking together when adjacent letters were pressed in quick succession. Consider the most commonly used letters in English words: the vowels AOEUI, and the consonants DHTNS. On an alphabetical mechanical keyboard, S and T sit right next to each other. If one typebar was going up while the other was going down, they would jam, requiring the typist to stop and untangle the typebars manually.

To correct this chronic annoyance, Sholes enlisted the help of Amos Densmore, a teacher. Densmore conducted a quick-and-dirty study of letter frequency in the English language, which Sholes then used to put common letter combinations, like TH, on opposite sides of the bank of typebars, preventing collisions.

This strategy didn't completely solve the issue, but it improved it so much that Sholes filed for a patent on the design in 1872.[4] E. Remington & Sons, a company that was then primarily known for manufacturing firearms, purchased Sholes's patent in 1873.

After making a few additional mechanical improvements, like adding a Shift key to allow typists to switch between capital and lowercase letters, Remington began mass-producing typewriters that featured the QWERTY layout, with the intent of selling them to the business market, in 1874.

Remington wasn't the only company selling typewriters. Others, like Hammond and Blickensderfer, were offering competing devices, which each had their own distinct keyboard layouts.

At the time, businesses relied primarily on written memos for records and correspondence. Typewriters could potentially save a lot of manual effort, but only if the operators knew how to use them. In order to land a sale, companies had to overcome the necessity of training typists to use the odd contraptions.

That led to an interesting market dynamic: the typewriter companies recruited and trained typists themselves, effectively operating placement agencies. If a businessperson wanted to hire someone who could type, they called Remington, who would sell the business both the typewriter and the services of someone who could use it.

Over time, as more and more businesses adopted typewriters, QWERTY began to emerge as a standard. There was no defining moment, no law or bureaucratic standards-setting committee, just a subtle market movement toward a single good-enough solution.

Businesses needed typists and typewriters; Remington was good at supplying both. And when a business needed a new typewriter or a new typist, it was most efficient to buy a new QWERTY machine and hire a typist who knew QWERTY. Over a period of sixty years, QWERTY became the de facto standard, and competing layouts slowly disappeared. As the decades passed, QWERTY quietly took over the world.

Competition Appears: Dvorak

In 1932, August Dvorak, a professor at the University of Washington, was given a $130,000 grant by the Carnegie Commission for Education to research keyboard design. One of the motivating factors of this research was the realization that QWERTY was designed to solve a mechanical engineering problem that no longer really existed. Was there a better way to design a keyboard?

Four years later, in 1936, Dvorak filed a patent for the Dvorak Simplified Keyboard, which he claimed was far superior to other layouts. The basis for this claim was simple: Dvorak's layout placed the most commonly used characters directly under the user's fingers on the home row.

The most common consonants were placed on the right side of the home row, and all five vowels were placed on the left side. This split between vowels and consonants balanced the typing load evenly between a typist's left and right hands, theoretically reducing fatigue and improving speed.

Dvorak also claimed the layout was easier to learn, and pursued research studies with organizations that trained a significant number of typists, most notably, those in the U.S. military. Outcomes were mixed: since Dr. Dvorak ran these studies himself, many of the favorable results were cast into doubt, given his obvious financial stake in the results.

An independent controlled study by the General Services Admission, which was responsible for training U.S. government typists, found that it took QWERTY trained typists over one hundred hours to regain their previous typing speed if they retrained on Dvorak. That was too long. Hence, the study recommended standardizing government typists on QWERTY. Typewriter manufacturers and businesses followed suit.

Dvorak, as a layout, continued to exist as a fringe option, but as a standard, it was a failure. Even though it had many valid claims to efficiency over QWERTY, it wasn't able to replace the status quo. Dvorak languished for decades, a very distant number two.

A New Challenger Appears: Colemak

QWERTY and Dvorak aren't the only two English keyboard layouts in existence. Although the vast majority of typists learn QWERTY, inventors and hobbyists have pursued innovations in keyboard design for decades. Most of these alternative layouts never gain wide traction, but in 2006, a brand new keyboard layout began to attract the attention of adventurous typists, thanks in large part to the Internet.

Here's the story. Shai Coleman, a computer programmer, decided to try his hand at keyboard design. His goal was simple: to create a layout that had the relative efficiency of Dvorak, but was easier to learn.

One of the major problems with Dvorak was that it changed *everything*: every single letter key is different in Dvorak versus QWERTY. If you originally learned how to type on QWERTY, the magnitude of the change makes learning Dvorak an absolute nightmare.

Even worse, now that computers are the primary typing tools, it's common to rely on keyboard shortcuts to accomplish repetitive tasks, like saving a file, cutting and pasting text, et cetera. If you're used to certain keyboard combinations working in a certain way, Dvorak is particularly jarring: not only do all of the letters move, but all of the shortcuts are different as well.

Coleman's strategy was to combine computer analysis of a very large dataset of English documents with the idea of preserving as many keys as possible to keep the same keyboard shortcuts. The left side of the keyboard, as well as most of the bottom row, was left mostly as is. Only the most significant keys were changed. Coleman's algorithm recommended most of the changes, leaving only a few ambiguous keys that required a judgment call.

In the end, Coleman's new layout, which he named Colemak, changed seventeen keys compared to the standard QWERTY layout. Based on the numbers, it was *way* more efficient than QWERTY, and slightly more efficient than Dvorak. Even more promising, since Colemak switched fewer keys, it was likely to be easier for QWERTY users to learn.

Coleman created a website, colemak.com, that contained details about the new layout, as well as instructions about how to install and learn it. Compared to Dvorak's expensive efforts to popularize his layout in face-to-face meetings with large organizations, the Internet made spreading the word of Colemak's existence downright cheap.

As a result, Colemak is now the third most popular English keyboard layout, behind QWERTY and Dvorak. The layout now comes bundled in most new computer operating systems by default and has thousands of users all over the world. Not bad at all for a layout developed by a single hobbyist that's existed less than a decade.

When in Doubt, Test

With all of these alternative keyboard layouts flying around, how do you decide which one is best?

Simple: you test them.

Modern programming technology has made it much easier to collect hard data on various approaches to keyboard design. Instead of testing and collecting data manually, it's possible to use a program that analyzes keyboard layouts for you. One such program is called carpalx,[5] the creation of Martin Krzywinski, a programmer who works for the British Columbia Genome Sciences Centre.

Carpalx is designed to "perform a stochastic simulation to find a layout that minimizes the effort score for a given set of model parameters." In other words, carpalx can automatically test the efficiency of various keyboard layouts by running them against sample texts.

Kyrzwinski used carpalx to design his own layout, but he also used it to compare Colemak with QWERTY and Dvorak, producing a very large and thorough set of comparative data. Here's what he found:[6]

QWERTY comes out as the big loser here, with a huge increase over Colemak in the base effort (+193 percent), a large stroke path increase (+36 percent) and a significant penalty increase (+16 percent). Dvorak is already an improvement over QWERTY, so the difference between it and Colemak is smaller.

Colemak makes even greater use of the home row (74 percent) than Dvorak (71 percent). This leaves QWERTY's 34 percent far behind. And Colemak's bottom row use is low at 9 percent, like Dvorak.

Colemak is more balanced in hand use, with a 6 percent preference for the right hand (Dvorak has 14 percent for the right and QWERTY has 15 percent for the left).

Colemak is very good at maintaining hand alternation for both hands. Both Colemak and Dvorak make greater use of the pinkie. Colemak uses the pinkie 16 percent of the time (18 percent for Dvorak and 10 percent for QWERTY). Colemak does a good job at loading the stronger fingers (index and middle) and uses them 67 percent of the time. This is better than Dvorak, which uses these fingers 60 percent of the time, but not as good as QWERTY, which uses them 69 percent of the time.

Based on Krzywinski's data, it takes almost twice as much physical effort to type on a QWERTY keyboard, compared to a Colemak keyboard. Colemak also beats Dvorak slightly, which is impressive, given Colemak only changes seventeen keys on the standard QWERTY layout, versus Dvorak's twenty-four.

Given the data, I'm going to learn Colemak. I like that it saves effort without completely rearranging common keyboard shortcuts, which I use a lot.

So what do I do next?

What Does Colemak Look Like?

Here's a diagram of what the Colemak keyboard layout looks like:[7]

In addition to changing the position of the most frequently used character keys, Colemak remaps the Caps Lock key as a second Delete key. This change is one of the biggest innovations in Colemak. No one (aside from Internet trolls) uses the Caps Lock key on a regular basis, but it occupies prime real estate: it's an easy reach for the left-hand pinkie finger, and it's right next door to the A key on the home row.

Changing Caps Lock to Delete allows Colemak typists to correct errors without moving their right hand off the home row to hit the Delete key on the far top right of the keyboard, saving a lot of effort. That single change results in a 15- to 20-percent reduction of finger distance compared with QWERTY. The more mistakes you make that you correct with your left pinkie, the more efficient Colemak becomes.

How Do You Turn On Colemak Mode?

With computers, changing keyboard layouts is easy: it's just a matter of telling the computer to use a different layout file, the same mechanism used to switch to a keyboard in another language. This setting is usually located in the computer's primary "Systems and Preferences" panel. Colemak is included in the Mac OS X operating system as of version 10.5, so there's nothing to install.[8]

In addition, some keyboards, like the TypeMatrix 2030,[9] support Colemak in the hardware itself. Instead of configuring the computer to recognize Colemak, the keyboard translates Colemak keystrokes into QWERTY bits, so the correct characters show up on the screen. As a result, you can type in Colemak without changing anything in the computer at all, provided you're willing to spend around one hundred dollars for a nice ergonomic keyboard.[10]

Changing the settings in the computer is the easy part, but that's not the only barrier. Since most English-language keyboards come with QWERTY by default, switching to Colemak means that the letters printed on the keys won't match the characters that will appear on the screen. If you rely on typing odd strings of characters, like complex passwords, that's a recipe for confusion. How do you find a physical Colemak keyboard?

There are two general approaches: you can buy a blank keyboard, or convert a QWERTY keyboard into Colemak format.

Some keyboards, like the TypeMatrix 2030, are available in Colemak versions, which is an easy solution if you're willing to buy a new keyboard. That didn't help me though: I type on a laptop, so the keyboard is built in.

Modifying My Machine

Fortunately, it's easy to pop the keys off of Apple keyboards and rearrange them without damaging the computer. Since Apple uses flat "Chiclet" style keys that all have the same dimensions, converting the keyboard to Colemak was a five-minute project.[11]

Using a small slotted screwdriver, I gently lifted the top right side of each key, inserted the tip of the screwdriver, then moved it down along the right edge of the key. Once the screwdriver gets to the middle of the key, the key pops off the keyboard's built-in "scissor" mechanism, which makes the key bounce back after it's pressed.

Once you get the hang of it, it's very easy to pop off the keys that need to be changed. I then used a Colemak layout diagram to put the keys back on the keyboard in the correct places. All it took was a gentle press, and the keys clicked permanently into place.

It's a simple procedure, but it's worth noting that this likely voids the warranty on my laptop. For safety's sake, I tested this with a spare Apple wireless keyboard first, then changed the keys on my MacBook Air once I was comfortable with the process.

Now I have a native Colemak keyboard on my laptop. How cool is that?

This is an example of spending a little time changing the environment to support practice. Now that my keyboard is in Colemak, it will be easier to make the switch. If I have trouble remembering which key is which, I can look if necessary.

How Fast Do I Type?

Now that my keyboard is ready, I'm closer to making the big switch. Before I go ahead, however, I want to get an idea of how fast I currently type, which will help me determine my target performance level.

In this case, my target performance level is simple: I want to be able to regain my QWERTY typing speed on Colemak as quickly as possible. I'm not looking to exceed it, since typing speed isn't a limiting factor in my work. I just want to be able to type as well as I'm used to with less effort.

The only piece of information I really need before my switch is my current typing speed, so I searched for a basic online typing speed test.[12]

The test is straightforward: when you push the Start button, the program shows you one hundred random words from an old book.[13] Your job is to type the sample as fast as you can, with as few errors as possible. When you're done, you hit the Stop button, and the program gives you your typing speed and error rate.

My plan is to take the test first using QWERTY, then repeat the test after I switch to Colemak, just to see where I'm starting from. I hit the Start button, and begin typing.

When I was finished, I hit the Stop button and received my results: sixty-one WPM, 100 percent accuracy, zero errors. Not bad: I type right at the threshold David Allen recommends. I'm not a speed demon, but I can type well enough to get the job done.

I have everything I need: I know how fast I type, my keyboard is in Colemak mode, and I know how to enable the layout in the operating system. There's nothing left for me to prepare.

This is it. Am I ready to leave QWERTY behind?

Flipping the Switch

It's now or never. I switch my computer into Colemak mode, then close the settings panel. From now on, I won't be able to type anything in QWERTY until I've completed the experiment.

My web browser still has the typing test loaded. I start the timer with my mouse and begin typing.

Here's my first impression: #%&@.

At the risk of sounding melodramatic, *it feels like part of my brain has been removed.*

I'm used to words flowing effortlessly from my brain into the computer. Now, I don't know where *any* of the keys are. I have to hunt for most of them, even the keys that haven't changed from QWERTY, which doesn't make any sense.

I see something on the screen, and my fingers move unconsciously, so I'm typing gibberish, which I then have to erase. It takes me several seconds to type simple words, and I'm concerned that I'm wearing out the Delete key.

Each word is a new struggle. I look up at the clock, and it's taken me several full minutes to type two sentences. I'm not even halfway done. I seriously consider quitting, but choose to press on. As the minutes pass, I almost quit at least ten times.

In the end, it took me almost twenty minutes to type one hundred words. My new typing speed: five words per minute.

Kill me now.

I write for a living, and I just learned how to program. Now, I can't do either. How will I answer e-mails? How will I work? What have I done?

I Have Seen the Enemy, and It Is Me

This is the primary barrier that prevents most people from learning a new keyboard layout. The technical aspects of switching are trivial compared to the *emotional* aspects.

When you're used to a certain level of speed or ease in completing a task, anything less seems awful. This is particularly true with typing: if you're used to typing being effortless, and it suddenly requires a lot of effort, continuing to press on feels downright painful. What's even worse is the knowledge that if you just went back to the way you used to do things, everything would be better again.

Our minds don't help us here: our brains have a stubborn tendency to assume that what we're experiencing in the moment will continue to be true in the future. Right now, my mind is freaking out. If I'm only able to type five words per minute, I won't ever be able to work again! My career will be over! My family will starve!

That's not true of course, but it *feels* true in that moment. That emotional experience is the largest barrier to learning.

I close the computer and take out a notebook and pen. I need a plan to get up to functional typing speed on Colemak, and I need it *now*.

Remapping My Brain

The first and most pressing order of business is that I don't know where the new keys are located. Sure, I have a printed reference sheet, and the physical keys on the keyboard are in Colemak format, but my brain isn't currently capable of mapping the desire to type a letter to a specific finger movement.

Helping my brain map the new layout into motor skills is my first priority. I need to be functional as quickly as possible.

Fortunately, people have been learning to touch-type for decades now, so there are well-developed commercial tools that can help. Typing tutorials, like Mavis Beacon[14] and Typing Trainer,[15] have been available for decades, and don't cost very much.

Unfortunately, these programs assume that you want to learn how to touch-type in QWERTY, since it's a safe bet most customers want to learn how to touch-type using the standard layout. These programs usually begin with the keys on the home row. QWERTY's home row and the Colemak home row are different, so QWERTY tutorials won't help me.

Dvorak has been around long enough that some programs support it, but Colemak is relatively new. It's probably a good idea to use some sort of typing tutorial, but I'll need to find one that's capable of supporting Colemak.

Fortunately, I have a lead. As I was browsing Hacker News during my programming research, I found a post on Keyzen,[16] an open-source typing trainer created by Rye Terrell. Terrell developed Keyzen to help programmers learn how to type faster. The program runs in a standard web browser, and includes uncommon punctuation marks like parentheses, brackets, and slashes: characters that programmers use quite often, but most typing trainers skip. Terrell posted the full source code for Keyzen on GitHub, and invited other programmers to use or modify it.

The program itself is quite simple: it displays a set of seven characters, beginning with letters on the home row. Your job is to type the characters in that sequence.

As you type, the program plays sound effects. A correct character creates a classic typewriter *clack*, while an incorrect character produces a *thwack!* and turns the character red.

Once you complete a set, the program serves up a new one. If you type a character incorrectly, the program will automatically introduce that character into later sets. If you type all of the characters correctly for three sets in a row, you'll hear a very satisfying *ding!*, which means you've leveled up. Keyzen then introduces a new character, and the training continues.

Modifying Keyzen

Keyzen, like most typing trainers, supports QWERTY by default. Since the program is open source, however, I may be able to modify it to make it suitable for learning Colemak.

My programming practice is about to come in very handy.

I made a copy of the Keyzen source code, then opened the program files on my computer. The program itself is simple, so it was easy to find the section of the program that controlled which characters were displayed, and it was just as easy to rearrange them however I wanted.

The original program introduced characters on QWERTY's home row first, starting with the index fingers, then adding characters until the home row was complete. Next came the top row, progressing from the middle of the keyboard to the periphery, then the bottom row, following the same pattern.

Using Keyzen's training pattern as a model, I edited the progam to use the Colemak character set. The physical key pattern remained the same, but the sequence now taught Colemak instead of QWERTY.

When I closed the program, I had my very own Colemak typing tutorial. Success!

If you're interested, you can try the program yourself: it's at http://first20hours.com/keyzen-colemak.

Fine-Motor Skills

I have my first typing tutorial, and my first goal is simple: learn where each key is located on the keyboard.

I fire up Keyzen and start typing (⎵ represents a space):

```
nn⎵nn⎵n
n⎵nn⎵n⎵
nnn⎵nn⎵
tntt⎵tn
t⎵tntt⎵
tttttnt
```

This type of practice isn't at all glamorous, but it's necessary. By drilling the location of each character in semi-random order, I'm helping my brain translate seeing (or thinking) a character into a fine-motor movement in my fingers.

In addition, Keyzen is helping me learn efficiently in a number of ways. First, Colemak is designed to place the most commonly used letters on the home row, under the strongest fingers. Keyzen introduces these characters first, so I'm mastering ARSTDHNEIO before getting to QWZXYM.

When I make a mistake, Keyzen reintroduces the character into the practice sequence. As a result, I'm spending most of my time practicing the letters I have the most trouble with. This is a form of spaced repetition, which happens to be combined with instant feedback, making the practice extremely efficient.

I set up a practice schedule: at least two sessions of twenty minutes, with a short break in between, at the end of the day, just before bed.

There's a method to my madness: acquiring any type of motor skill requires *physically changing the structure of your brain*, and as it turns out, sleep is instrumental in that process.

Learn While You Sleep!

Over the past four decades, motor skill acquisition has been a very active area of psychological research. If you go to any well-provisioned academic library, you can find shelf after shelf of research on skill acquisition in general, and motor skill acquisition in particular.

I did just that. I wandered the cognitive psychology stacks at Colorado State University, searching for useful information on skill acquisition. I had no trouble at all finding books and studies. Unfortunately, most of this research is very wonkish, full of academic jargon.

Fortunately, it's not all gibberish. Here's an excerpt from a study that caught my eye:

Stages of Motor Skill Learning (2005)[17]

Successful learning of a motor skill requires repetitive training . . . This article covers the growing evidence that motor skill learning advances through stages, in which different storage mechanisms predominate. The acquisition phase is characterized by fast (within session) and slow learning (between sessions). For a short period following the initial training sessions, the skill is liable to interference by other skills and by protein synthesis inhibition, indicating that consolidation processes occur during rest periods between training sessions. During training as well as rest periods, activation in different brain regions changes dynamically.

"Interference" and "consolidation" are the key words here. As you practice a skill, your brain is extremely active, working to find patterns and store them in memory. In the case of motor skills, those patterns involve associating what you see, hear, feel, taste, and think with the firing of neurons that control the muscles in your body. The stronger these neural connections, the better you're able to perform.

During practice, your brain is busy making these connections and associations, but that doesn't mean they're stored instantly in the structure of your neurons. It takes a while for these patterns to take hold, which happens during a process called *consolidation*. Consolidation is happening all the time, but it's particularly effective while you sleep.

Here's the first study I found that draws a direct link between sleep and skill acquisition:

It's Practice, with Sleep, That Makes Perfect: Implications of Sleep-Dependent Learning and Plasticity for Skill Performance (2005)[18]

Practice is often believed to be the only determinate of improvement. Although repeatedly performing a new task often results in learning benefits, leading to the adage "practice makes perfect," a collection of studies over the past decade has begun to change this concept. Instead, these reports suggest that after initial training, the human brain continues to learn in the absence of further practice, and that this delayed improvement develops during sleep.

Here's the conclusion of that study:

Although the functions of the sleeping brain remain uncertain, rapidly increasing literature now supports the role of sleep in modifying and improving memory. These reports provide an abundance of converging evidence indicating that sleep-dependent mechanisms of neural plasticity lead to skill memory consolidation and consequently to delayed performance improvements. Different forms of simple and complex skill memory appear to require subtly different types of sleep for overnight memory enhancement, and several studies indicate that sleep within the first 24 hours following initial practice is essential for consolidation to develop.

Effective skill acquisition, particularly motor skill acquisition, seems to require sleep, which plays a major part in consolidating the skill into long-term memory. Recent research suggests that, for greatest effect, it's best to sleep within four hours of motor skill practice: even a short nap is better than nothing at all. Any longer, and your brain's ability to consolidate the information it gathered during practice is impaired.

That's why I'm practicing typing right before going to bed. If I go to sleep within an hour or so of practice, I can help my brain consolidate the motor movements more effectively.

The weird thing is that I can *see this working*. My first practice session was horrible: I couldn't get anything right, made mistakes constantly, and barely progressed past the characters on the home row. After a full night's sleep, when I sat down in front of the computer, I noticed that I was making fewer mistakes. Sleep had consolidated what I'd learned the night before.

Our brains are seriously cool.

Cognitive Interference

Interference is the opposite of consolidation: it's a disruption of the consolidation process. If you practice or use a second, similar skill shortly after practicing a new skill, that practice can interfere with your brain's ability to consolidate the new information.

The critical period for interference also seems to be roughly four hours. If you wait to practice a conflicting skill after consolidation has taken place, you're less likely to interfere with the improvements you gained in the primary skill.

That's why I'm not practicing QWERTY immediately after practicing Colemak. It would disrupt my brain's ability to consolidate my Colemak practice, slowing down my rate of skill acquisition.

It's also interesting to note that, after seven total hours of Colemak practice, I'm suddenly having a hard time typing in QWERTY, even though I've been touch typing in QWERTY for a very long time. My brain is mapping typing motor movements to Colemak, which seems to be making it more difficult to access QWERTY, at least for the time being.

After my brain adjusts to Colemak, I can go back and reacquire QWERTY if I want to: based on what I've read from other Colemak typists, it's possible to become "keyboard bilingual," and switch back and forth on demand. For now, however, I'm focusing exclusively on Colemak to minimize interference. Reactivating QWERTY can wait.

Breaking the Looking Habit

I now have seven hours of deliberate practice under my belt, averaging forty-five minutes every evening. I'm completing the entire Keyzen sequence without much difficulty. I still make mistakes, but those mistakes are coming less frequently. When I retake the typing speed test, my results are much better: twenty words per minute.

During the day, I'm getting some ambient practice in the form of important e-mails that require an urgent reply. When I sit down to type, it's not as painful. I'm slow, but I can express myself. That's progress!

I'm noticing, though, that I'm looking at the keyboard a lot. Having the correct keys on the keyboard is very handy for typing odd strings of characters, like passwords, but it's also a crutch: whenever I feel uncertain, I look down. If I want to touch-type, I have to break myself of that habit as quickly as possible, but that's difficult, since it takes so little effort to look down.

Das Keyboard

To break myself of the looking habit, I decided to pick up a new learning tool: a completely blank keyboard.

Das Keyboard is the most badass keyboard you'll ever find. The "Ultimate Model S"[19] has no markings on it whatsoever. If you can't touch-type, you can't use Das Keyboard . . . period. It's funny to watch re-actions when people see it: even skilled touch typists are intimidated.

I plugged in Das Keyboard and covered my laptop keyboard with a piece of paper, so I couldn't see any key markings at all. The sensation was similar to when I switched to Colemak for the first time: I was confused and frustrated, but only for a moment. The motor skills I'd picked up in the first seven hours of practice kicked in, and I found that I could type reasonably well. Whenever I forgot a letter, I'd have to hunt for it for a few seconds by trial and error, but I could function.

With nowhere else to look, I focused on the screen. Das Keyboard was serving its purpose. By changing the keyboard, I changed my behavior au-tomatically.

Along with Das Keyboard, I modified my training method. Typing random characters gets old, so I switched to a program called Type Fu.[20] In addition to random characters and words, Type Fu contains a database of proverbs and quotations, which makes practice a bit more entertaining. The program also keeps track of which characters you miss most often, which is handy. I'm finding J, U, V, and B difficult at the moment.

Every night, I practiced for forty-five minutes. After a total of fourteen hours of deliberate practice, I'm now typing at a rate of forty WPM.

At this point, I'm perfectly functional: I can use e-mail and surf the web relatively normally. I was even able to type a five-page proposal with-out too much trouble. It took me longer than usual, but it wasn't the most frustrating thing I've ever done.

Deliberate Practice vs. Ambient Practice

Since I'm able to function, I want to test a hypothesis: How much does de-liberate practice matter?

Currently, I'm practicing in two ways: my Keyzen and Type Fu ses-sions are *deliberate* practice, since I'm focusing on the task and working ac-tively to improve. My typing during the day is *ambient* practice: whenever I write an e-mail or an essay, I'm typing in Colemak, even though I'm fo-cusing more on the content of the message than my technique.

I wonder: What if I drop the deliberate practice for a while and just continue typing e-mails and surfing the web? I'm two-thirds of the way to my target performance level of sixty WPM after only fourteen hours of deliberate practice. Can ambient practice carry me the rest of the way, without additional focused effort?

I decided to do an experiment: I'm going to suspend my deliberate practice for thirty days and see what happens. I'll continue typing normally in Colemak, without switching back to QWERTY. With as much time as I spend on the computer, I should be able to get enough ambient practice to hit sixty WPM, right?

After thirty days, I retook the typing test. Want to guess my typing speed?

Forty WPM. Zero improvement.

Even though I was typing quite a bit, I wasn't actively focused on improving my skills. Ambient practice wasn't enough to improve.

If you want to improve a skill, you need deliberate practice, at least in the early stages of skill acquisition. Lesson learned.

The Final Push

Back to deliberate practice: there's another test I want to try.

Human languages, including English, follow a power law curve called Zipf's law: a very small set of words makes up the vast majority of actual usage. Based on an analysis of *The Brown Corpus* (1964), a 1 million-word collection of 500 modern English documents, only 135 words account for 50 percent of all English usage.[21] The word "the" itself accounts for 7.5 percent, while "of" accounts for 3.5 percent.

You can take this idea even further: within most words, there are common sets of two- and three-character groupings that appear over and over again, like TH, AN, ING, and NCE. These groupings are called *n-grams* (or sometimes *n-graphs*): "n" is a variable that stands for the number of characters you're grouping.

I was able to find a list of the most common n-grams in a book titled *Cryptological Mathematics* by Robert Edward Lewand (2000). N-grams are a major area of study in fields like cryptography. If you're able to identify patterns in an encrypted message, that gives you a clue about the contents. By comparing the n-grams in an encoded message with the most commonly used n-grams in the target language, cryptographers can solve complex ciphers.

Let's put this theory to work. Here's Lewand's list of the most common English 2-grams (*digrams*), in order of frequency of usage:

th, he, in, en, nt, re, er, an, ti, es, on, at, se, nd, or, ar, al, te, co, de, to, ra, et, ed, it, sa, em, ro

And here are the most common 3-grams (*trigrams*), in order of frequency of usage:

the, and, tha, ent, ing, ion, tio, for, nde, has, nce, edt, tis, oft, sth, men

These lists are very useful. The better I'm able to type these sequences of characters, the faster I'll be able to type in general.

Our brains are very good at this type of thing: *procedural memory* is the term cognitive scientists use for motor skills that happen in a certain order. By practicing the most common n-grams, I can train the procedural memory involved in typing directly.

To do this, I downloaded a free program called Amphetype,[22] which is designed for this sort of practice. The program allows you to create custom training sets, as well as set certain thresholds of performance, like words per minute and error rate.

When you begin a session in Amphetype, you can have the program generate the practice set in any number of ways. I set the program to display each n-gram three times, to display three sets of items, and to repeat the sequence three times.

As a result, the first digram practice set looked like this:

th he in th he in th he in en nt re en nt re en nt re er an ti er an ti er an ti

My goal was to type the entire sequence at over sixty WPM with at least 95 percent accuracy. If I fell short of those criteria, I'd have to repeat the entire sequence.

Practicing in this way wasn't entertaining, but it was very, very effective. I drilled each sequence over and over again until I got it, then focused on mastering the next.

Every day, when I sat down to practice, I started from the beginning. The improvement from day to day was noticeable: sequences that took me five tries the day before took one or two tries the next. In no time, I was able to complete the whole set.

Once I mastered digrams, I moved on to trigrams. From there, I found a list of the most common English words, which was compiled by Dr. Peter Norvig.

Norvig is the director of research at Google. A few years ago, he published a set of the most common English words based on Google's "trillion word corpus," which contains every unique word Google's search engine spider has ever indexed.[23]

Norvig's intent in publishing the data was to help programmers build useful utilities like spell-checking tools, but in my case, it was the perfect training set. I pulled the top hundred most commonly used words, added them to Amphetype, and kept drilling.

After eight additional hours of deliberate practice, I took a typing speed test. The result, after several consecutive tests to ensure it wasn't a fluke: sixty WPM, with bursts of seventy to eighty WPM, at 98 percent accuracy. Total time spent in deliberate practice: twenty-two hours.

Mission accomplished!

Impressions from Sixty WPM

I like typing in Colemak a lot. I'm no longer frustrated. Instead, I'm wondering how I coped with QWERTY for so long.

Typing on QWERTY feels like your hands are flying all over the keyboard: lots of movement in every direction. The layout doesn't make any logical sense at all: characters you use all the time are in some of the hardest to reach areas of the keyboard.

Colemak, by contrast, feels like you're twiddling your fingers to make words appear on the screen. Your hands visibly move much less, and you spend a lot less time reaching for characters on the top and bottom rows. It's a nice change from QWERTY, and I can't imagine going back.

Reviewing the Method

Let's review the core of the method I used to relearn how to touch-type:

- I learned how to change my keyboard layout to Colemak.

- I created a fast feedback loop by rearranging the physical keys on the keyboard, so if I forgot where a character was located, I could find it easily.

- I used the Keyzen typing tutorial to learn the placement of characters by touch, learning the most-used characters first. Keyzen reintroduced characters to the training set as I made mistakes, so I spent most of my time practicing difficult characters until my accuracy improved.

- I practiced for forty-five minutes every night, just before going to bed, so my brain could consolidate the motor skills into long-term memory most effectively.

- Once I got to functional speed (twenty WPM), I switched to Type Fu, focusing on typing sentences as fast as possible with over 99 percent accuracy.

- When I reached forty WPM, I used Amphetype to train using the most common English digrams and trigrams, further increasing my speed and accuracy.

- Once I mastered the n-gram sets, I switched to training that used the most common English words in Amphetype until I reached sixty WPM sustained with 98 percent accuracy, which happened at the twenty-two-hour mark.

Where I'm Going from Here

Now that I'm typing a solid sixty WPM on Colemak, I have no pressing need to keep training for raw speed. At this level, I'm able to write as fast as I need to. Since my typing speed is no longer the limiting factor in my output, speed training is no longer my biggest priority.

Speed typing is a skill in itself. Some of the fastest typists in the world can clock in excess of 180 WPM on normal keyboards, but improvements in test speed do not necessarily equate to improvements in speed of writing or coding. These tests always involve typing what you see on the screen, so the primary skill speed typists are practicing involves looking farther ahead in the text and keeping it in short-term memory long enough for the fingers to type it.

While I'd love to be able to write finished prose at over 180 WPM, that's beyond even the fastest typists. Typing is harder and slower when you have to create whatever it is you're putting on the page.

I can, however, benefit from continuing to decrease my error rate. In that spirit, I'm continuing to practice common words, digrams, and trigrams with Amphetype, and practicing using my left pinkie finger for error correction. By decreasing my error rate, my efficiency will increase, and my speed will most likely increase with it.

What surprised me most about learning Colemak was how easy it was to overwrite almost twenty years of previous experience touch typing using QWERTY. I assumed that two decades of muscle memory would take way more than twenty hours to replace. I was wrong.

Our brains are easier to change than we think.

7

Go

Lesson: Explore, Then Decide

Go uses the most elemental materials and concepts: line and circle, wood and stone, black and white, combining them with simple rules to generate subtle strategies and complex tactics that stagger the imagination.
—IWAMOTO KAORU, 9-DAN PROFESSIONAL GO PLAYER

■ ■ ■

For supplementary images, video, and commentary about this chapter, visit http://first20hours.com/go.

I am the sword in the darkness, the watcher on the wall.

The night is cold: snow is falling. Behind me, torches cast flickering light over my compatriots. We stand on the castle's rampart, watching. Waiting.

On the far side of the castle bridge, a host of enemy soldiers is massing just out of range of our catapults, preparing to strike. Warriors, thieves, and rangers are sharpening deadly weapons. Necromancers are summoning armies of disgusting undead creatures. Engineers are preparing mortars and flame rams: powerful weapons designed to breach our gates.

This horde intends to steal my realm's most treasured possession: a glowing orb of great power. They will not take it. Not on my watch.

We are well prepared. To either side of where I'm standing, soldiers are manning ballistas and arrow carts, ready to unleash their deadly payloads on the invading force. Between the defenses elementalists are preparing to rain fire and lightning on the enemy host. Our guardians and mesmers have set runes and reflective shields along the perimeter, granting us protection from arrow and spell, at least for a while.

We wait. The snow falls, and the torchlight dances on my polished steel armor.

We will not fall. We will not break. We will fight, and we will win.

Out of the darkness, an enormous boulder appears, flying high above the enemy forces. The rock crashes into the castle gate and shatters, splintering the reinforced wood.

The enemy roars, then charges across the bridge.

In an instant, my sword and shield are in hand. My battle cry echoes off every stone, carrying might and fury to every defender on the wall.

"FOR GREAT JUSTICE!"

Away Put Your Weapon, I Mean You No Harm

Leading an army in large-scale siege warfare is an enjoyable way to spend a Saturday evening.

I'm not a fan of watching television, movies, or sports. Instead, you're likely to find me playing video games like *World of Warcraft* or *Guild Wars 2* for an hour or two.

I enjoy games: preferably challenges that involve casting spells, battling monsters, and outwitting enemy players. Since a young age, I've loved epic stories about wizards, warriors, and heroic quests, and video games make it possible to become a character in these adventures, at least for a while.[1]

My generation was the first to grow up with immersive video and computer games. Beginning with the early Atari and Nintendo consoles, games have grown in detail and complexity. Now, it's possible to fight Internet dragons and other players in real time with allies from all over the world.

Part of what appeals to me about games like these is the skill that's required to play well. Anyone can create a character, but to wade into battle and emerge victorious, you have to know what you're doing.

We've come a very long way from Mario jumping on enemies and shooting the occasional fireball. Now, it's common for video game characters to have close to one hundred potential abilities. To play well, you have to know what those abilities are, when to use them, and how to customize your character for greatest effect.

There's a lot to learn. Which abilities do the most damage, or protect you from harm? What can enemy monsters do? What's the best strategy when fighting other human players?

The more I play, the better I become. That's why it's fun.

Video games, historically speaking, are brand new. Games of skill and chance, however, have been part of the human experience for thousands of years.

The Oldest Strategic Board Game in the World

A while ago, I stumbled upon an interesting game. Compared to what I'm used to playing, the game is quiet, almost serene. Beneath the surface, however, there's high drama. The board is a map of a great war, and the players are generals, battling against each other to win ultimate supremacy.

Go is the oldest game in the world still played in its original form. Based on historical records, Go originated in ancient China, and has existed under its current rule set for at least three thousand years, with some historians estimating upward of four thousand years. If age is any indication of quality, Go has a lot going for it.

The Chinese name for Go is *weiqi*. *Wei* (圍) means "surrounding" and *qi* (棋) means "board game." Together, these characters become *weiqi* (圍棋, simplified: 围棋), which means "game of surrounding." That's a nice, simple description of the game's victory condition: surrounding the opposing player.

Go was introduced in Europe and the Americas via Japan, so the English Go is a simplification of the Japanese word for the game, *igo* (囲碁). Whether you refer to the game as Go, *weiqi*, *igo*, *baduk*, or some other term, the game is the same.

The Art of War

In the West, chess is the most popular strategic board game, so we can use it as a contrast. On the surface, the games have many similarities.

Each game is played by two players, Black and White. The game takes place on a square board. Black moves first. The players take turns making moves until the game is over. You can think of the game as a military conflict, where the players are opposing generals.

That's where the similarity ends.

Chess is played on a board that's eight squares by eight squares, for a total of sixty-four squares. Each chess piece occupies a single square. The board resembles a battlefield, and the pieces are the soldiers.

Here's what a chessboard looks like at the beginning of a game:

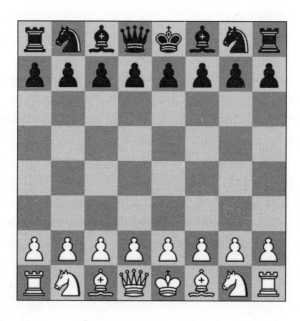

Go, on the other hand, is played on a board made up of nineteen vertical lines that intersect with nineteen horizontal lines. Stones are played on the intersections, not on the squares. As a result, there are 360 intersections available for play on a Go board, 5.625 times as many as on a chessboard.

Here's what a Go board looks like at the beginning of the game:

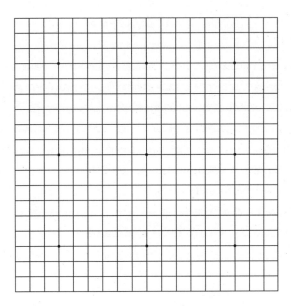

Notice the difference? Not only is the Go board much larger, but the game begins with no stones on the board. In Go, stones are generally *added* during the course of the game. In chess, pieces are *removed* as they're captured.

Notice that the *goban* (board) is square. The little dots on the board (called "star points") are perfectly symmetrical. Those points are important, and we'll come back to them in a bit.

In chess, there are six different types of pieces, and each piece has special rules and abilities. *Pawns* always move straight ahead, except when they move to capture other pieces. *Bishops* can move diagonally, but can't move vertically or horizontally. *Rooks* can move horizontally or vertically, but not diagonally. *Knights* can jump other pieces, but have to move two squares horizontally and one square vertically, or else two squares vertically and one square horizontally. The *queen* can move horizontally, vertically, or diagonally, but can't jump other pieces. The *king* can move in any direction, but can only move one square at a time, unless it jumps a rook using a special move called a "castle." There's a lot to remember.

Every Go move, in contrast, is the same: a stone is placed on an intersection. Unless a stone is "captured" later in the game, a stone laid is a stone played.

Chess pieces are captured by one of the opponent's pieces, like single combat on a battlefield. The rook bashes the bishop over the head with a huge mace, and the bishop exits the game.

Go stones are captured when they are surrounded on all sides by the opponent's stones. When Black's army is surrounded on all sides by White's, Black's stones surrender, and are taken hostage.

Professional chess games usually contain 30 to 40 moves. In a game of Go, the first 30 or so moves are considered opening moves: the endgame begins around move 100. Complete games of Go regularly top 250 moves.

In all ways, the scale of Go is much larger than that of chess. If every game of chess is a battle, the goban is a map of a massive war.

So how do you play Go, exactly? Let's dig in.

The Rules of the Game

Believe it or not, Go has only seven major rules, and we've already covered two of them:

1. Stones are played on the intersections.
2. Black and White take turns placing stones on the goban.

The next five rules define the game's progression and victory conditions:

3. Stones are "captured" when they are surrounded on all sides by the opponent's stones.

4. Playing a stone that's immediately captured ("suicide") is prohibited.

5. Repeating the same sequence of moves over and over again in an infinite loop (a situation called *ko*) is prohibited.

6. The game ends when the players run out of stones, one player concedes the game, or both players pass.

7. The player who surrounds the most territory on the board at the end of the game wins.

In competition play, a few more rules are introduced to remove ambiguities (such as "what constitutes a repeating loop?"), specify the scoring method, and prevent ties. Otherwise, those are the rules.

Pretty simple, right?

Learning the rules of Go is easy: it only takes a few minutes. The rules themselves aren't complicated.

There's a very old Go proverb, however: "a few moments to learn, a lifetime to master." Combine these simple rules with a simple board and simple stones, and you get mind-blowing complexity.

The Size of the Universe

While the baroque rules of Chess could only have been created by humans, the rules of Go are so elegant, organic, and rigorously logical that if intelligent life forms exist elsewhere in the universe, they almost certainly play Go.

—EDWARD LASKER, CHESS GRANDMASTER AND AUTHOR OF *GO AND GO MOKU*

Let's say we want to create a computer program that plays Go intelligently, similar to Deep Blue, the famous artificial intelligence program that defeated Garry Kasparov, the reigning world-champion grandmaster, in 1996.

Typically, computers outwit human players through sheer computational power: they calculate all of the possible legal moves on the board, then choose the move that has the highest mathematical probability of success, based on a vast library of past game data.

On a chessboard, this type of computation isn't easy, but it's possible. There are sixty-four squares, and each piece's movement is constrained by specific rules. Since each piece can only move in certain ways, the program only needs to consider a small range of options.

In a game of Go, the active player can place a stone on *any* open intersection on the board. The game begins with 360 possible choices, so from the beginning, our fledgling AI program has a lot more analysis to do.

Let's do some quick math. How many possible sequences of five moves can be played on a Go board, assuming it's the beginning of the game and neither player captures the opponent's stones?

Here's the calculation:

$$360 * 359 * 358 * 357 * 356 = 5,880,282,488,640$$

That's over 5.8 *trillion* possible sequences, and that's only the first five moves.

The math gets crazy very, very quickly. Remember when I mentioned that it's common for Go games to last 250 moves? Depending on your assumptions, there are approximately 2.08 times 10^{170} sequences of legal moves on a nineteen-by-nineteen-size Go board.

If that math is correct, there are more possible legal games of Go than there are *subatomic particles in the known universe.*

It's a mathematical certainty that every Go game that has ever been played has never been played before in the history of the universe, even if you're willing to throw in the possibility that there are billions of advanced alien civilizations somewhere out there that also happen to play Go.[2]

Given current technology, it would take even the most sophisticated computers running the best brute-force algorithms about four hundred years to calculate a single optimal move, assuming the program completed a calculation every few milliseconds.

Mind = blown. This game is *huge.*

So How Do Players (and Computers) Play Go?

If human players relied on brute-force analysis to play Go, they'd go insane. They obviously don't: skilled human players can identify the best moves on the board in a few seconds. How do they do it?

Go players rely on pattern recognition to identify high-value moves. Players use a lot of words that invoke intuition, like "shape" and *sente* (initiative). The best Go players seem to rely as much on geometry, aesthetic beauty, and emotion as they do on rigorous logic and analysis.

That makes sense: the human brain isn't very well equipped for brute-force number crunching, but it's awesome at pattern recognition. By noticing patterns in the stones on the board, as well as patterns in how the stones are being played, skilled Go players are capable of reading the current situation, then finding the best move: all in less than four hundred years.

Even more impressive: the very best players are able to anticipate how stones will be played in the future, often thirty to forty moves ahead. If you find yourself playing with a professional, it will probably feel like they're reading your mind.

An Actual Game

The difference between a stone played on one intersection rather than on an adjacent neighbor is insignificant to the uninitiated. The master of Go, though, sees it as all the difference between a flower and a cinder block.

—DAVE LOWRY, AUTHOR OF *THE CHALLENGE OF GO:*
ESOTERIC GRANDDADDY OF BOARD GAMES

Here's what a game of Go looks like in progress:

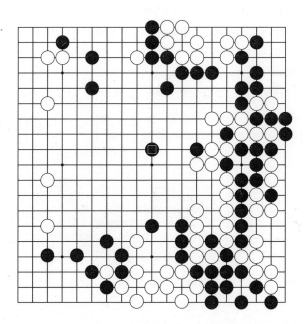

This is a diagram of a real game: one of the most famous games in the history of Go.[3]

In 1846, Shusaku of House Honinbo, a seventeen-year-old 4-dan, was invited to play Gennan Inseki, an 8-dan. Inseki was the head of

House Inoue, one of the four major professional Go schools in mid-nineteenth century Japan.

Shusaku accepted the honor, and the match attracted an audience. No one expected Shusaku to win, but he was strong enough to put up a fight.

After playing a short game in which Inseki granted Shusaku a two-stone handicap, it was clear Shusaku didn't need it. Inseki conceded to start a second game with no handicap stones: even odds.

Shusaku, as the challenger, took Black. The early game was flawless, except for a minor mistake by Shusaku in an exchange on the lower right side of the board. One hundred and twenty-six turns into the game, Inseki held the lead, as expected. After all, who could best the master?

Shusaku's next play changed the game. You can see the stone yourself: it's the Black one just above the center of the board that's marked with a square.

After Shusaku's move, a spectator noticed something odd: Inseki's ears were red. The master was angry.

Shusaku's move at 127 was good: very, *very* good. The single central stone simultaneously lent support to Shusaku's stones at the top, right, and bottom of the board while establishing new influence to the left. The move was the perfect balance of offense and defense.

Inseki was in trouble, and he knew it. With a single stone, Shusaku was able to influence the entire board. The game continued, with Inseki suddenly fighting for control.

Here's what the game looked like at move 325:

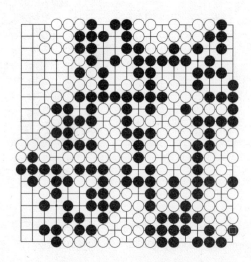

Take a moment to study the board. Which areas are surrounded by Black, and which are surrounded by White? Who has surrounded more territory on the goban?

Inseki admitted defeat, and Shusaku won by two points. The game would go down in history as the Ear Reddening Game, and move 127 the Ear Reddening Move.

"Invincible Shusaku" went on to become one of the most celebrated Go players in history, renowned for his nineteen consecutive castle game victories, which were hosted annually by the Shogun. He died on September 7, 1862, at age thirty-three, after tending to victims of a cholera outbreak.

Pattern Recognition

There's something we can learn from these diagrams. Here's the Ear Reddening Move again:

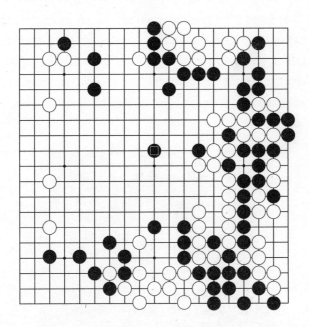

Go games are usually presented from Black's perspective. We're seeing the board the way Shusaku saw it during the game.

Here's how Inseki (White) viewed the board, a rotation of 180 degrees:

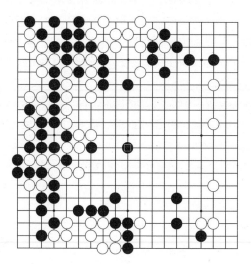

In chess, there are only two primary perspectives: Black sits across from White, and both players begin the game with all of their pieces on their respective sides of the board. Chess is never played with White's and Black's pieces arranged on the left and right sides of the board. In addition, chess moves have a general pattern: *away* from the player, *toward* the opponent's side of the board.

As a result, chess players can learn to recognize specific patterns of moves on the board. Here's a famous pattern, called the King's Gambit:

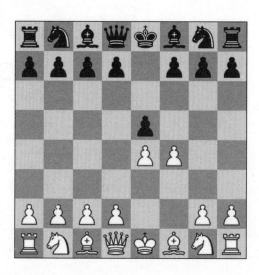

A large portion of training to become a chess grandmaster involves memorizing common patterns that appear in games. The best chess players can see a pattern developing on the board in an instant, since the patterns always look the same. If you try to play a King's Gambit, a grandmaster will notice immediately, and will know exactly how to respond.

While pattern recognition in chess isn't easy, it helps that players never have to look at the board rotated ninety degrees to the left or right, which makes the patterns much easier to learn.

In contrast, since a goban is perfectly symmetrical, no side of the board has any special meaning. As a result, you can view the goban from any of the four sides of the board.

At the beginning of a Go game, any handicap stones are placed by Black on the star points, those little black dots, in a symmetrical pattern. Otherwise, the board is empty.

Go stones can be placed on any empty intersection at any time. A player can play on the top of the board one turn, and the bottom of the board the next. They can play on the left side, then play on the right. There's no universal, predictable direction of play like there is in chess.

Let's go back to the Ear Reddening Move. Here's Shusaku's perspective:

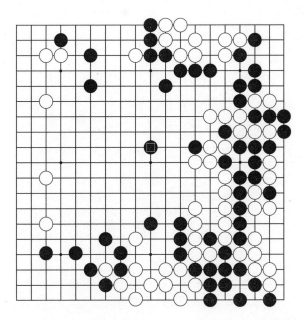

Again, here's Inseki's perspective:

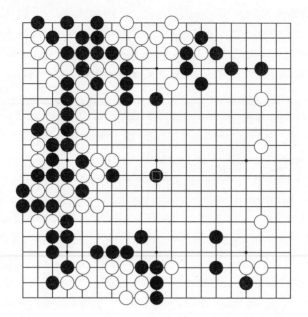

Now, here's the perspective from Shusaku's right, or Inseki's left:

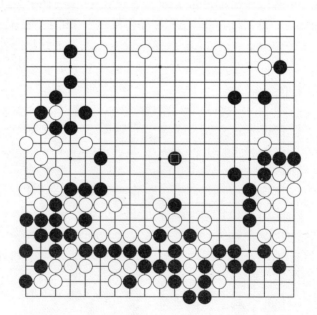

And Shusaku's left, or Inseki's right:

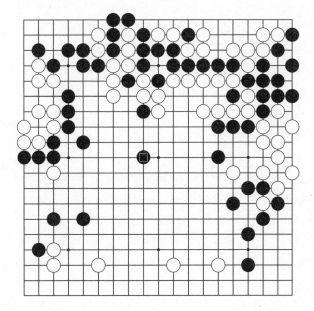

The symmetrical nature of the goban makes pattern recognition even more difficult than it normally is. These four diagrams of the Ear Reddening Move are *exactly the same* from a strategic standpoint, even though they *look* completely different to the untrained eye. If you wanted to, you could rotate a Go board ninety degrees after every move without dramatically affecting the game.

Go players can't rely on the more straightforward techniques of game memorization that chess players count on to identify developing patterns during a game. Every pattern Go players learn needs to be mastered from *four* perspectives, not just one.

That's why Go players rely on intuition so much. The game is much too large to memorize or calculate, so skilled players train themselves to see developing patterns at a much higher level: general shapes, directions of movement, and impressions of strength and weakness.

Use Your Feelings . . .

[Go requires] the tactic of the soldier, the exactness of the mathematician, the imagination of the artist, the inspiration of the poet, the calm of the philosopher, and the greatest intelligence.

—ZHANG YUNQI, IN AN INTERNAL DOCUMENT OF THE CHINESE WEIQI INSTITUTE, 1991

One of the early articles I read about Go made an interesting argument: mastering the game isn't really about competing with or dominating the opponent. It's about mastering *yourself.*

Games of chance have been around since the dawn of human civilization. When you're rolling dice, Lady Luck (or rather, Mama Physics) decides who wins. Skill isn't a factor.

Games of skill, by contrast, usually focus on outwitting or outperforming other players. Who exhibits the most aptitude and control? Who can find the biggest opportunities first? Who is better at exploiting the weaknesses of their opponent? Chess falls into this category: becoming great involves mastering tactics and reading your opponent.

Go is a unique game in this respect: the introduction of handicap stones is a built-in way of intentionally making strong players weaker. If your opponent begins the game with a few stones on the board in key strategic positions, that dramatically influences how you play. Here's where the handicap stones are placed:

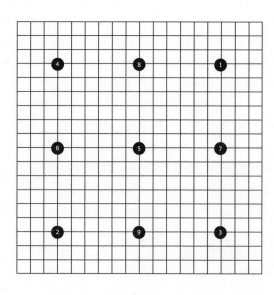

In a properly handicapped game of Go between two players of roughly equal skill, each player should win about half the time. If one player dominates the other, in the next game, the losing player begins with one or two additional stones on the board.

Because of this handicapping feature, you can think of Go as a game you play against yourself. Sure, you're making decisions based on the actions of your opponent, but winning the game is not the only goal.

As your skills increase, the number of handicap stones you need goes down. When you play strong opponents, you'll be able to do battle on even terms. Eventually, you'll be giving stones to weaker opponents.

Go history takes the self-mastery aspect of the game to an extreme: learning to play well requires mastering your thoughts and emotions. Advanced players can learn to see signs in the stones that reveal their opponent's mental and emotional state.

According to the stories, ancient masters could read a game transcript and identify when each player was feeling anger, confusion, envy, or greed, as well as pinpoint the precise moment "when the maid entered to serve tea."

Stone Ninja

Throughout the centuries, Go's handicapping system evolved into a ranking system: the difference in rank determines how many stones the lower ranked player can place at the beginning of the game.

Believe it or not, the "belt" system of ranking in the martial arts is derived from Go rankings. As players increase in skill, he or she moves up in ranking.

Beginners start at a rank of 35 kyu (similar to a white belt). As the player gets stronger, his or her rank decreases until it reaches 1 kyu.

The next rank up from 1 kyu is 1 dan, the game's equivalent of a black belt. From there, the ranks increase until the player reaches 9 dan, the highest official rank; 10 dan is an honorary title reserved for winners of the top world tournaments.

Determining a player's rank can be done in several ways. The first is competition: if a player can win most of the time on even terms against 12 kyu players, but loses most of the time against 8 kyu players, his or her strength is probably in the 10 kyu range. The more games a player completes in ranked competition, the more accurate his or her rank becomes.

The other way of estimating rank is by completing Go problems: structured puzzles that present a situation, then ask the player to determine the best move that achieves a specific result, like "capture Black's group" or "White to save." As the player moves up in rank, his or her ability to solve problems correctly increases as well.

Since Go has been around for such a long time, a huge library of Go problems is available for study. These problems are ranked by difficulty: a 20 kyu player will struggle with 10 kyu problems, while a 1 dan player will think the 10 kyu problems are easy and obvious. Kiseido, a specialty publisher of Go books, publishes a very handy series of ranked problems, titled *Graded Go Problems for Beginners*, that's very useful for this purpose.

The existence of ranked problems makes Go a game you can study as much as you play. Completing the problems in these books is a good way of practicing Go skills on your own, as well as estimating your relative strength.

I'm ready to get started. What do I need to practice?

Gearing Up

It's difficult to play a game of Go without a board and stones, so I picked up a nice set from Yellow Mountain Imports,[4] a company that distributes Go products from all over the world in the United States.

Go boards and stones vary widely in price and quality. Inexpensive boards and simple glass stones can be acquired for a few dollars, so a basic game set is easy to obtain.

On the other end of the spectrum, superior quality boards made of fine *kaya* wood, the traditional material used in Japan, sell for tens of thousands of dollars. Likewise, you can purchase stones made of genuine slate and shell, but they'll cost you dearly.

After doing some research, I settled on a nice *shin-kaya* (imitation *kaya*, typically white spruce) floor board and a set of Yunzi stones, which are made by a company of the same name in China. The company considers the composition of their stones a trade secret: the stones feel nice and solid, create a very satisfying sound when you place them on the board, and are reasonably priced. The stones come with traditional wooden bowls, which are placed beside the goban during play.

In addition to purchasing the goban and the stones, I also picked up several Go books for beginners, including:

- *Go: A Complete Introduction to the Game* by Cho Chikun (2010)
- *The Second Book of Go: What You Need to Know After You've Learned the Rules* by Richard Bozulich (1998)
- *How Not to Play Go* by Yuan Zhou (2009)
- *Lessons in the Fundamentals of Go* by Toshiro Kageyama (1996)
- *Opening Theory Made Easy* by Otake Hideo (1992)

I found these books via a very useful website called Sensei's Library,[5] which has hundreds of pages of information and commentary about Go history and technique. One page is a huge list of opinions about the best Go books available, compiled by advanced players, which is solid gold at this stage of the learning process. I read the entire page, which lists close to one hundred books.

Here's how I chose which books to read first: *Go: A Complete Introduction to the Game* was easily the top recommendation for beginners, so that was a no-brainer. Likewise, *The Second Book of Go* was highly recommended as a beginning text on strategy. The book assumes you already know the basic rules, so it spends more time on fundamental techniques.

How Not to Play Go is an example of an inversion, which I was happy to see: you can learn a lot about how to do something well by studying common mistakes. For most skills, you have to research the inversion yourself, but in this case, there's a whole book put together by an expert. That's great!

Lessons in the Fundamentals of Go, often called "The Yellow Book," is the book that most advanced players cite as the single text that helped them improve their game most dramatically. It looks a bit too advanced as a starter text, so I'll read it after I've learned the basics.

Finally, I chose *Opening Theory Made Easy* because it's clear, even from my basic analysis, that the opening of the game is extremely important. Since the goban is empty at the beginning of the game aside from any handicap stones, the first thirty to forty stones that are played create a structure that profoundly influences the rest of the game. If you don't know how to play the opening correctly, and your opponent does, you'll probably lose, making openings a subject well worth studying from the beginning.

Follow the White Rabbit

In addition, modern technology has made practicing Go a bit easier. SmartGo, a program available for iPhones and iPads, includes a very good built-in AI program, a database of ranked Go problems, and annotated historical games to study.

SmartGo is designed to take advantage of the device's touchscreen, so you can place stones on the "board" by touching the appropriate intersection. This makes completing Go problems much easier. Instead of imagining the solution, then looking up the solution by hand in the back of a printed text, the program gives you instant feedback. This fast feedback loop makes it much, much easier to practice problems, particularly problems that require more than one move to solve.

I'm all set. I have everything I need to learn how to play. There's only one more thing I have to do . . . ensure that I spend my time playing Go instead of playing something else.

Eliminating Distractions

Go isn't as viscerally compelling as an action-packed video game. Learning Go will require time and concentration. I'm already playing other games, but I have a very limited amount of leisure time. If I want to progress in Go as quickly as I'm able, I'll need to focus.

That means I need to eliminate potential distractions. The biggest immediate threat is other games: time spent whomping digital monsters is time *not* spent learning Go. If I keep playing video games, I won't have any time to learn.

Remember, time is never found: it's *made*.

Accordingly, I'm choosing to not play other games until I've invested at least twenty hours in Go. I can't afford the distraction if I want to learn quickly.

Here's a useful tactic in these sorts of situations: the best way to change your behavior is to change the structure of your immediate environment. If you don't want to do something you're currently doing, make it impossible to do. If you can't make the behavior impossible, make it as difficult, expensive, or prohibitive as you possibly can. The more effort required, the less likely you are to go back to your previous behavior.

Farewell, *World of Warcraft* . . . it's been nice knowing you.

Before embarking on my Go adventure, I canceled my *World of Warcraft* account and deleted the game from my computer. If the game's not installed, I can't play it even if I want to. I won't play video games under any circumstances until my Go experiment is officially complete.

The Rules of the Game, Reexamined

The best place to begin is by reexamining the rules. I've already read them, but I need to see what they look like on a goban.

There's a nice Go feature that makes it easier to learn: you can change the board size. Since the goban is symmetrical, you can make the board larger or smaller, as long as you choose an odd number of lines. The same rules and tactics still apply.

Competition boards are nineteen by nineteen, but for learning purposes, it's best to start with a seven-by-seven board. That's big enough to have space to learn the key ideas, but small enough that the board isn't overwhelming.

Let's see what the rules look like on an actual board.

Give Me Liberty, or Give Me Death

Let's begin with the third rule of Go: Stones are "captured" when they are surrounded on all sides by the opponent's stones.

When you play a stone on an intersection, the intersections adjacent to that stone are called *liberties*. Imagine soldiers on a battlefield: if there's a safe place to retreat close by, the soldiers can't be captured.

The maximum number of liberties a stone can have is four:

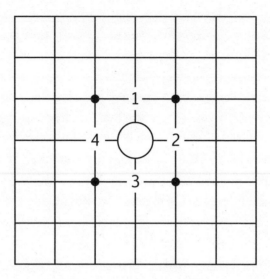

Liberties are reduced when the opponent attacks by placing a stone immediately adjacent to yours. This attack reduces White's stone to three liberties:

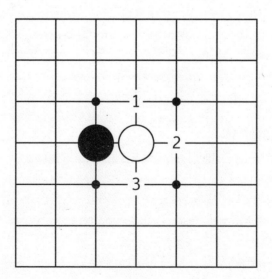

Another attack reduces White's stone to two liberties:

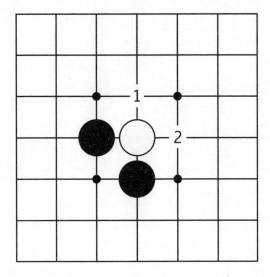

Look out, White! Only one liberty left:

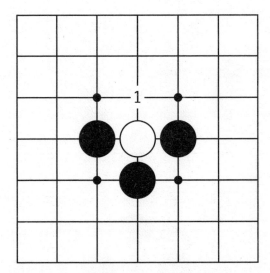

This situation is called *atari*.[6] If Black eliminates White's last remaining liberty, White's stone is taken prisoner, and is removed from the board:

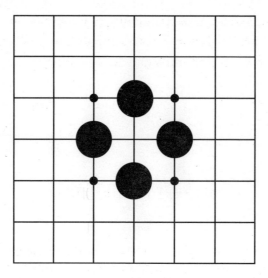

Pretty simple so far. If you don't want your stones to be captured, you need to make sure they have as many liberties as possible. If you want to capture your opponent's stones, remove their liberties.

No Suicide, Please

This is a good opportunity to look at the fourth rule: Playing a stone that's immediately captured ("suicide") is prohibited.

Let's look at that last situation again:

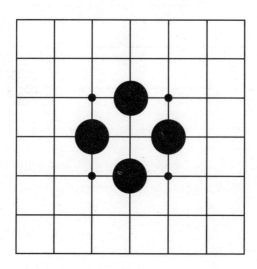

This shape is called a *ponnuki*, and it's very common in Go. The space in the middle of the Black stones has no liberties, so if White plays a stone there, it would be captured immediately. The fourth rule prohibits "suicide" moves like this.

This rule becomes very important when we start looking at larger groups of stones, so we'll come back to it in a bit.

Backing into a Corner

In the middle of the goban, stones typically have many liberties until they're attacked. On the corners and the sides of the board, there are fewer liberties, since there aren't as many intersections in the vicinity.

Here, Black has only one liberty remaining: the intersection labeled "a":

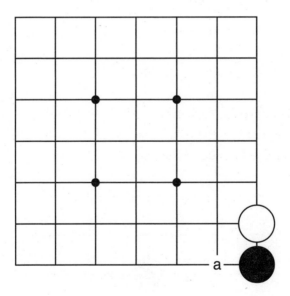

Black is in *atari*. If White plays at "a," Black is taken prisoner:

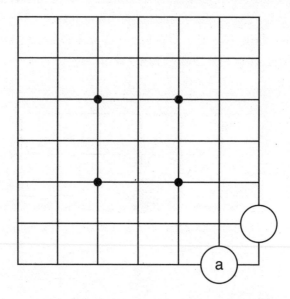

This example illustrates the difference between the corners and the middle of the board. In the corner, it only takes two stones to capture. In the middle, it takes at least four. On the sides, it takes three stones to capture.

As a result, it's usually easiest to establish and defend territory along the corners of the board. Sides are a bit harder, and the middle is hardest of all, since it takes so many stones to trap the opponent.

That's why, if you look at the beginning of Go games, skilled players follow a general pattern. First, they'll establish positions in the corner of the board. Once that early territory is secure, they'll branch out to the sides. The middle of the board is the last priority, and is reserved for late in the game. That's why Shusaku waited until move 127 to play the Ear Reddening Move.

To Infinity, but Not Beyond

Now that we've learned the rules of capture, let's examine the fifth rule: Repeating the same sequence of moves over and over again in an infinite loop is prohibited.

This is a situation called *ko*, which is the Japanese word for "infinity." Infinite loops are possible in Go, and if they were allowed, they'd ruin most games.

Here's what ko looks like. Black can capture White's stone, which is marked with a triangle, if they play at point "a":

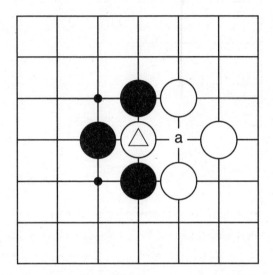

Notice what happened? We have the same pattern, only in reverse. Now, if White plays at "a," they can take back the stone:

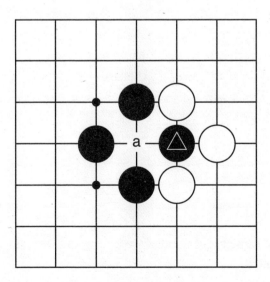

Without a rule against ko, White and Black could battle over this stone until the end of time. That's why the rule exists: in a ko fight, the player that loses their stone first can't retake the ko until at least one turn has passed, preventing the infinite loop.

In tournaments, there's usually an additional rule called "super ko." Imagine there are two or more ko fights on the board. Players could just cycle through ko fights in a larger infinite loop. Once a pattern is established, super ko kicks in, and players have to do something else, or the game ends.

Victory Conditions

Now, let's look at how the game ends. Here's rule six: The game ends when the players run out of stones, one player concedes the game, or both players pass.

Simple enough. How do we determine who wins?

That's rule seven: The player who surrounds the most territory on the board at the end of the game wins.

Let's look at an example. On a seven-by-seven board, there are forty-nine intersections. Let's assume the board is divided like this:

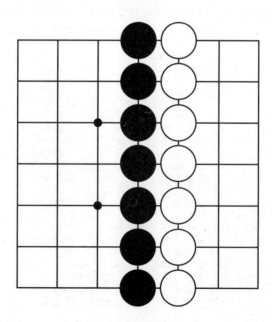

Black controls the left side of the board, which accounts for twenty-eight spaces of territory. White controls the right side, which equals twenty-one spaces. Black wins.

Here's a variation: Black has managed to invade just a bit into White's territory. Black now has twenty-nine spaces, and White has twenty:

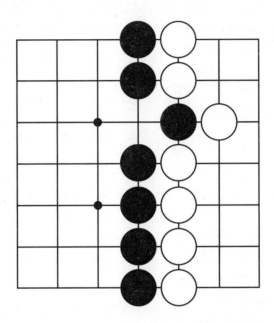

The counting gets trickier when the board is larger, and groups are scattered all over the place, like the end of the Ear Reddening Game:

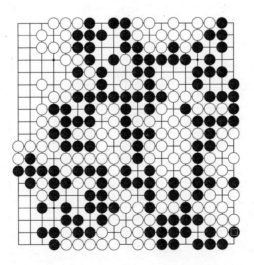

The general principle of counting territory is this: if territory is contested, neither side gets points for it. Sometimes advanced players will concede territory to the opponent without playing the full resolution, so that territory counts as captured. If there's a dispute about who controls what territory at the end of the game, play resumes until the dispute is resolved.

Estimating territory is a skill, and it requires practice.

En Garde!

That covers the basic rules. Now, what about common tactics?

The first thing to know is what an attack looks like. Direct attacks remove a liberty from one of your opponent's stones. Here, Black is attacking the White stone marked with a triangle:

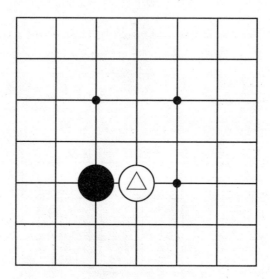

You can also attack indirectly, by placing a stone close to your opponent. Indirect attacks are a way to strengthen your position in an area before your direct assault begins. Here, Black is threatening the White stone marked with a triangle:

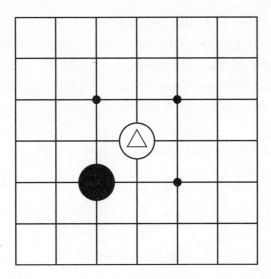

Charge of the Knights

Attacks are the basic elements of offense. The basic elements of defense are called *connections* and *joints*. Moves that balance offense and defense are called *approaches*.

One common approach is called the "knight move," which gets its name from the movement of the knight in chess:

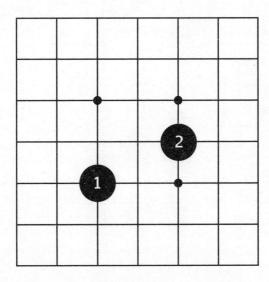

The knight move is evenly balanced between offense and defense: it's close to other stones, so it's easy to connect if necessary, but it extends your influence more than a one-step move.

There's also a large knight move that's even more aggressive:

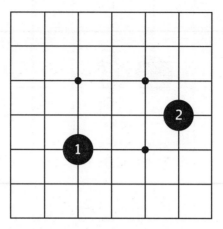

This move trades defense for influence: it extends the player's range, but the stone will be harder to defend if it's attacked.

Bamboo Is Stronger Than Steel

On the defense side of strategy, there's a shape called a bamboo joint that's very solid. Here's what it looks like:

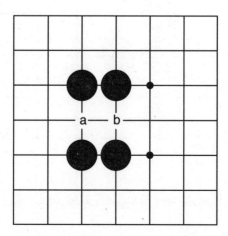

Bamboo joints are very strong because, no matter how your opponent tries to attack it, it's easy to connect your stones into a strong shape.

In this case, if White attacks at "a," Black can connect at "b":

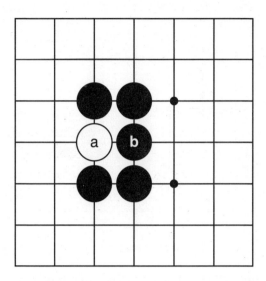

Likewise, if White attacks at "b," Black can connect at "a":

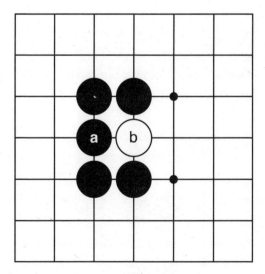

Once Black connects the bamboo joint, it would take White nine additional stones to capture the group. That level of protection is hard to beat.

Easy enough: attacking, defending, and capturing seem relatively straightforward, and knight moves and bamboo joints are easy tactics to remember and understand.

Tempered by a Hundred Battles?

Now that I know the rules, as well as the rudiments of strategy, I have a choice to make. Should I try to improve my game by facing off against human opponents, or is the most straightforward path to skill studying the game by reading books and solving ranked problems?

Expert players on Sensei's Library have mixed opinions. Several skilled players invoke Sun Tzu, author of *The Art of War*, opining that it's best to be "tempered by a hundred battles." Others believe studying Go problems and reading books on strategy and tactics is the best way to improve at first.

I'm not sure what to think. There's a local Go club that meets every Wednesday, but they meet in the early evening, which conflicts with family time. I'd love to play, but that doesn't work for me at the moment.

There's another option: playing on Internet Go servers. Players from all over the world congregate online to play, and servers are up 24–7. Even better, these games are ranked, so you can estimate your relative strength if you play enough games. It's not a tournament ranking, but it's something.

I decided to check out the two most popular online Go destinations: IGS (Internet Go Server) and KGS (Kseido Go Server). Playing is simple: you create an account with your e-mail address, download a Go program, and log in. From there, you can ask other players for a game, or watch other players battle in real time.

I created accounts on both systems, then looked for my first real opponent. I didn't have a ranking, since I'd just created an account, so I invited another unranked player. He accepted, and the game started.

Since we were both unranked, there were no handicap stones. I played

Black, and thought my early game was solid. We took turns establishing territory in the corners first, then on the sides. Thirty or so moves into the game, I was feeling pretty good.

Then, White attacked. I wasn't worried: my territory looked strong, so I connected my stones to strengthen my position.

My study up to this point didn't prepare me for what was about to happen. Turn by turn, White *destroyed* me.

Territory I thought was secure was brutally invaded. Stones I thought were safe were taken hostage.

I tried to counterattack, and my advances were blocked. I tried to defend, and my protections failed.

I kept trying to gain ground, but an hour into the game, it was clear my cause was hopeless. I conceded.

After the game was over, I asked my opponent how long he'd been playing.

"Years," he said. "I just created an account on this server, so I don't have a ranking yet."

No wonder he destroyed me! I told him I was a brand new player, and asked for advice on how to improve.

"Watch 10 to 20 kyu games. You'll learn a lot."

I thanked my opponent for the game, then logged off.

What went wrong?

Looking back on the game, I thought I was building defensible groups of stones, but I obviously wasn't. Understanding why my groups were captured requires looking at how large groups can be attacked.

One Eye Bad!

Remember the rule against suicide moves? There's an important wrinkle in that rule: if a move that would otherwise be suicide captures one or more of the opponent's stones in a way that creates new liberties, it's allowed.

Here's an example. The intersection at "a" has zero liberties for White, since it's surrounded by Black:

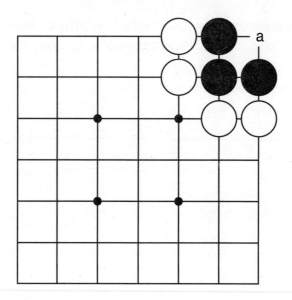

Normally, White wouldn't be allowed to play at "a" under the suicide rule, but in this case, White has Black surrounded. Black's last remaining liberty just so happens to be "a." When White plays at "a," Black's group is captured:

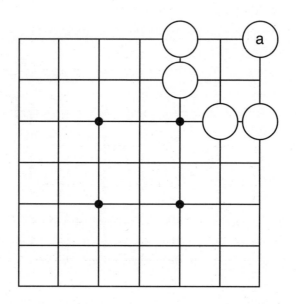

In Go, these types of spaces are called *eyes*. Depending on the situation, they can be sources of either strength or weakness. If a group has only one eye, it's weak.

Here, Black is in trouble:

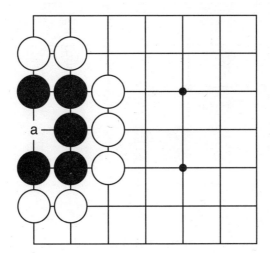

White captures at "a":

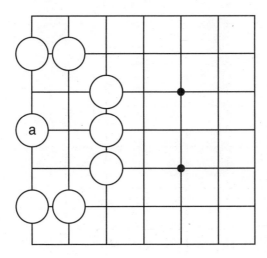

White's in trouble now:

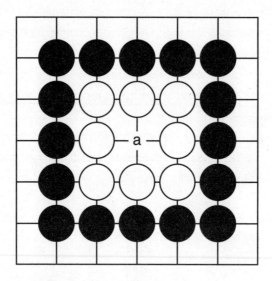

Black captures at "a":

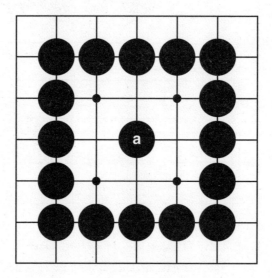

This takes a bit of getting used to. Groups with only one eye are easy to capture, so they're fundamentally insecure.

Two Eyes Good!

That doesn't mean eyes are bad: they're necessary. That seems weird until we examine the suicide rule again.

The exception to the rule against suicide only works if the stone results in the capture of the opponent's group. If it doesn't, the move isn't allowed under the suicide rule.

That means that groups with two eyes are invincible. It's like building a fortress in the middle of enemy territory: no matter how many stones the opponent attacks with, they won't be able to capture the group.

Here, Black's group has two eyes:

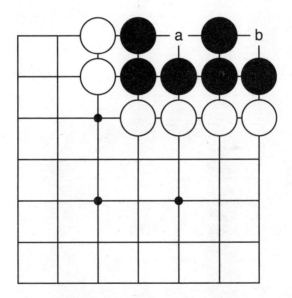

If White plays at "a," it's suicide. If White plays at "b," it's suicide. White can't play at "a" and "b" at the same time, so Black is safe, even though the group is surrounded on all sides.

Here, a group of White's stones has two eyes on a side:

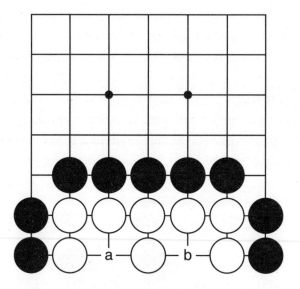

Here, a group of White's stones has two eyes in the middle:

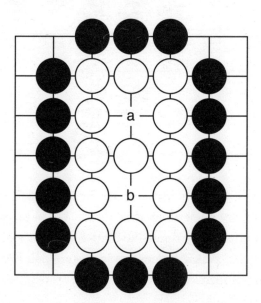

Notice how it took six stones to form two eyes in the corner, eight stones to form two eyes on the side, and thirteen stones to form two eyes in the middle? That difference in efficiency is why corners are easiest to defend, and the middle is always difficult to secure.

The False Eye (of Sauron?)

If having two or more eyes in a group makes it invincible, forming eyes as quickly as possible becomes a huge priority. Unfortunately, it's not always easy to figure out whether or not a shape that *looks* like an eye actually *is* an eye.

Often, groups will form eyes that look solid, but are vulnerable to attack. These shapes are called *false eyes*, and they're deadly.

Here's an example. Black's group looks like it has two eyes, but the stones at the top marked with triangles are vulnerable:

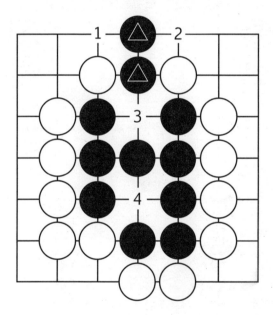

Let's say it's White's turn. White can attack at 1 or 2, removing a liberty. Black may try to escape along the top side, but in the very next move, White will cut off the escape route. No matter how Black responds, White will then capture the marked stones by playing at 3. That leaves the rest of the Black group vulnerable, and the entire group will be captured when White plays at 4. Ouch!

A major part of Go strategy involves creating groups with two eyes, avoiding false eyes, preventing your opponent from building true eyes, and destroying your opponent when they build false eyes. It takes a lot of experience and skill to create true eyes, and to notice when eyes are false.

The "Dismantle"

That leads us closer to understanding the cause of my first major loss. I thought I was creating secure territory, but in reality, I was vulnerable to attack, and I didn't realize it in time.

Here's a simplified example: look at all of the eyes Black has created. With four eyes, that group has to be invincible, right?

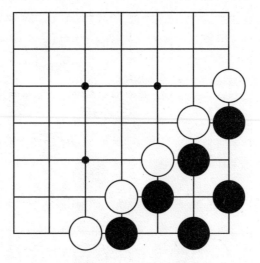

Unfortunately for Black, that's not the case. If White plays at 1 or 2, "a" or "b" will be captured:

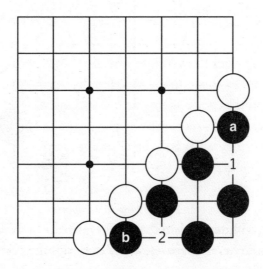

Then, if White plays at 3, "c" and "d" will be captured:

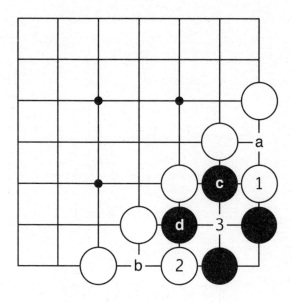

Finally, if White plays at 4, "e" and "f" will be captured:

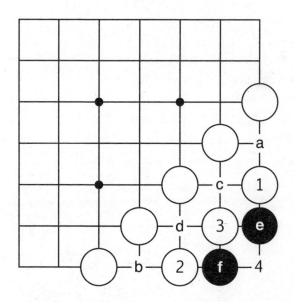

As a result, White is able to completely dismantle Black's "invincible" group. They were never true eyes, and Black pays the price:

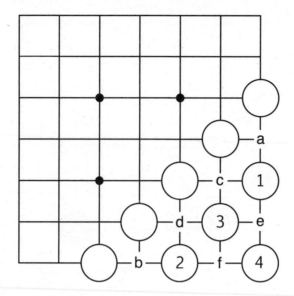

That's the essence of what happened to me. I thought I was building secure territory in the corners and on the sides, but I wasn't building two real eyes. As a result, my opponent was able to dismantle everything I built. Lesson learned.

Chutes and Ladders

There are a few other important strategic concepts I didn't fully appreciate until I saw them in action.

The first is called a *ladder*. Whenever an attack occurs, the other side has a choice: they can counterattack, or they can run. Often, trying to escape is the better option. If the opponent chases, a capturing race begins.

Let's look at an example. Here, White's stone (marked with a triangle) is about to be attacked:

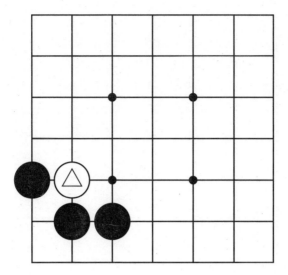

Black attacks at 1, and White escapes at 2. Black attacks at 3, and White escapes at 4. Black attacks at 5, White escapes at 6, and so on. Eventually, we find ourselves here:

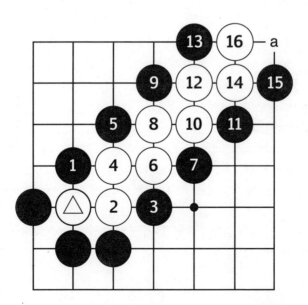

It's Black's turn, and White has no place to run. When Black plays at "a," all of White's stones are captured, and Black controls the entire board. Game over!

There's an old Go proverb: "If you don't know what a ladder is, don't play." This situation is a good illustration of why that's a valid position.

Now, let's reexamine the same situation with a slight twist: White has a stone (marked with a circle) on the far right side of the board. What happens?

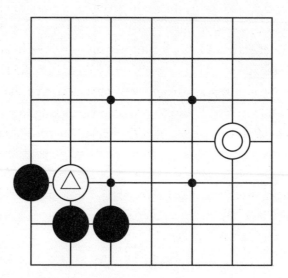

The first part is the same: Black attacks at 1, and White escapes at 2. Black attacks at 3, and White escapes at 4. The pattern progresses until White escapes at 10. At that point, we see this:

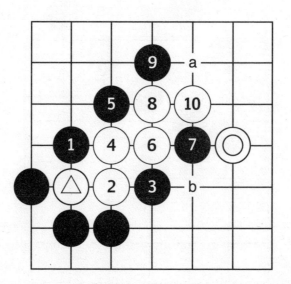

If Black attacks at "a," continuing the pattern, White will capture Black at 7 by playing at "b." If Black tries to defend at "b," White escapes Black's wrath by playing at "a."

A single stone on the opposite side of the board saved White from total annihilation. That's what makes Go so interesting: a stone that looks disconnected and remote from the main action is capable of changing the course of the game.

Reading ladders is a skill. On a nineteen-by-nineteen board, there are many ways to start a capturing race, or find yourself on the receiving end of an attack you want to escape from, creating a ladder. In these instances, you need to be able to read ahead to predict who's going to win the race.

If you don't think you can win, it's better to sacrifice a stone or two than lose an entire group. If you predict victory, it's in your interest to provoke your opponent into playing a game they can't win, ultimately giving you a huge advantage.

Throwing Nets

Throwing a stone in the path of a potential ladder can be a very good play. Likewise, trapping your opponent by placing a stone in a surrounding position can be a good strategy.

Here, White wants to capture the Black stone (marked with a triangle). Instead of attacking directly, White casts a *net* that encircles Black indirectly:

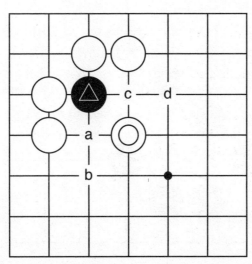

If Black tries to escape at "a," White blocks at "b." If Black tries to escape at "c," White blocks at "d." No matter how much Black struggles, he can't escape White's net.

Aside from the eye issue, my opponent was much better at provoking me to overextend. I found myself in ladders I couldn't win, or trapped in nets I didn't notice until it was too late.

All of these things are what make skilled practitioners good at the game. If you don't know basic shapes like eyes, ladders, and nets, you're going to lose to players who know how to create and take advantage of them.

Maximizing Practice Time

After my loss, I took my opponent's advice to heart, and tried to look for games with players ranked between 10 and 20 kyu. Unfortunately, there weren't many to watch.

Internet Go servers aren't the most beginner-friendly places on the net. The major servers and programs have been around for a long time, so the interfaces are straight out of the 1990s, and it takes a while to figure out how to use them.

There also don't seem to be many low-ranked players around. And if you don't know how to play the game very well, getting stomped over and over again isn't the most enjoyable experience. Most of the active matches I found were between players 8 kyu and above.

I tried watching a few games, but my rate of learning was very slow. I was able to follow the moves just fine, but not the reasons why the players were making them. Sometimes sequences of moves happened too fast, and I wasn't able to keep up with the analysis. I was sure there was a motive behind each stone, but I was too inexperienced to figure out what it was.

Full games of Go can take over an hour to complete, which was another barrier. Several times, I began watching a game, only to have to step away to wrangle Lela or help Kelsey with a chore. Since the games were happening in real time, that meant I couldn't follow the game to resolution.

I tried the "hundred battles" approach, and based on my early experiment, it wasn't the most efficient way to improve as a beginner. I decided to change my strategy, substituting unenlightened floundering with structured study.

Man Against Machine

Every evening, I spent forty-five minutes studying Go problems, first using the SmartGo program on my iPad, and later by working through Kiseido's *Graded Go Problems* series of books.

After studying problems, I then played a game against SmartGo's built-in AI program on a small nine-by-nine board. At first, SmartGo stomped me, even with an eight-stone handicap. Embarrassing!

As I studied, however, my games began improving quickly. I learned to take advantage of my handicap stones by going on the offense, attacking White quickly and forming strong connections whenever possible.

It didn't take long to reduce my handicap stones to six, then five, as I won games against the AI. After thirty games, I'm around the four-stone handicap mark.

Estimating the score is challenging: sometimes I think I'll be doing well, but when I peek at the score, I'm behind by a significant margin. Since winning the game requires making profitable moves that increase the amount of territory you control, that's a problem. Often, a move I think increases my territory doesn't, wasting a move and creating an opening for the opponent.

Failure Modes

In conjunction with studying Go problems, I read the books I picked up from the Sensei's Library reading list. What I learned helped me considerably.

Studying *How Not to Play Go* was an extremely good use of time. According to Yuan Zhou, the author, beginners make several common mistakes that cost them dearly:

- **Inexperienced players follow their opponent blindly.** For example, when attacked, poor players will automatically respond by defending, escaping, or counterattacking in the same local area, instead of considering all available options.

- **Inexperienced players don't pay attention to the entire board.** Sometimes, the best move isn't where the action is taking place; it's on the other side of the board, far away from everything. Battle is exciting, and poor players can be blind to the opportunities present in quieter areas of the goban.

- **Inexperienced players don't make the most profitable move.** Go requires thinking in terms of profit and cost: every move costs a stone, and you always want to get the best bang for your buck. Often, this involves sacrificing a stone or two, provided you'll reap larger benefits elsewhere.

- **Inexperienced players don't value *sente*.** In Go, "initiative" is a big deal: you want to dictate your opponent's responses as much as possible. Instead of focusing on their agenda, you want your opponent to be so worried about preventing potential losses that they ignore securing gains. Whoever establishes and keeps *sente* almost always wins.

- **Inexperienced players aren't good at estimating territory.** As a result, they'll spend a lot of time fighting a local battle or securing a small corner of the board while their opponent takes over a huge amount of territory uncontested.

- **Inexperienced players get jealous of the opponent's position.** Zhou calls this the "red eye problem," and it usually results in a player making a wildly unprofitable move just because they feel their opponent's territory is getting too big.

- **Inexperienced players succumb to wishful thinking.** It's very easy to be enticed by a group of stones that you could capture with only two stones, and fail to take into account that you can't take two moves in a row: your opponent gets to respond to what you do. As a result, you waste precious stones, all in the vain hope that your opponent is too dumb to notice what you're doing.

These qualities hit home for me, particularly the wishful thinking bit. How many times have I attacked a group, hoping the opponent overlooked my plan? How many times have I been drawn into a local battle, ignoring the bigger picture?

After reading *How Not to Play Go*, my game improved immensely. One of the biggest things I had to correct was the visceral feeling that capturing the opponent's stones was the shortest path to victory. In chess and checkers, that's true: in Go, it's not.

Capturing stones is helpful, but it's not the victory condition. Securing *territory* is the goal of Go, and very often, you can do that without capturing the opponent's stones at all. That lesson took a while to sink in: capturing stones feels good, even if it's actually counterproductive.

Proverbial Wisdom

Aphorisms are very common teaching tools in Go. Since the game is so complex, rules of thumb help players remember how to play in common situations.

One of the earliest examples of this teaching approach is "The Ten Golden Rules of Go," which are attributed to Wang Jixin, who played sometime during the Tang dynasty, which ruled in China from roughly 600 to 900 CE:[7]

1. "The greedy do not get success."
2. "Be unhurried to enter the opponent's territory."
3. "Take care of oneself when attacking the other."
4. "Discard a stone to gain *sente*."
5. "Abandon small to save big."
6. "When in danger, sacrifice."
7. "Make thick shape, avoid hasty moves."
8. "A move must respond to the opponent."
9. "Against strong positions, play safely."
10. "Look for peace, avoid fighting in an isolated or weak situation."

A lot of Go wisdom is like that. There are countless Go proverbs:

- The enemy's key point is your key point.
- When in doubt, *tenuki* (play somewhere else).
- There is death in *hane* (a stone that reaches around to attack).
- Beginners play *atari*.
- A *ponnuki* is worth thirty points.
- Nets are better than ladders.
- Make a fist before striking.
- Sacrifice plums for peaches.
- A rich man should not pick quarrels.
- If you ride a tiger, it's difficult to get off. (Don't start what you're not willing to finish.)

There's a lot to learn: not only is it wise to learn the proverbs and why they exist, you need to understand when to ignore them. After all, one of the proverbs is "Don't follow proverbs blindly."

There are also proverbs that apply to beginners. My favorite is "Only after the tenth punch will you see the fist," which is usually followed by "Only after the twentieth punch will you be able to block it." In my experience so far, that's very true: skilled players can attack me in ways I can't even *recognize*.

I have a lot to learn.

"Five Stone" Questions

Almost a month into learning Go, I found an essay by Sam Bleckley that described his experiences learning the game.[8] In the essay, Sam relayed the advice of a friend, who suggested that he ask himself four specific questions about the situation on the board before placing a stone:

1. Can I ensure one of my groups *lives*? (By forming two eyes, connecting, etc.)
2. Can I *kill* one of my opponent's groups?

3. Can I *secure* my territory?

4. Can I *invade* my opponent's territory?

Those four questions capture the essence of the four major priorities in Go: live, kill, secure, invade. By working through the questions in that order before you make a move, you'll immediately gain "five stones" in strength by making better decisions and avoiding poor tradeoffs.

This is a very effective technique. It's easy to memorize and recall a list of four priorities. By asking yourself a few simple questions before you play a stone, and by considering the highest-value moves before lower-value moves, you ensure that your decisions in the moment correspond to your true priorities.

Go requires making decisions with incomplete information in a changing environment, so techniques like this are very useful. Questions like these provide structure and logic in uncertain circumstances. Even better, it's possible to indentify and use "five stone" questions in other areas of your life. Whenever you find yourself in a situation that requires making decisions with incomplete information, assigning priorities, and accepting tradeoffs, it's very likely there's a simple, obvious set of "five stone" questions that can help you make better decisions.

Reaching the Twenty-Hour Mark

Based on my notes, after about a month of study, I've reached the twenty-hour mark. Where am I, and what have I accomplished?

According to the database in SmartGo, I've solved around 150 ranked problems, and I've progressed to the 18 kyu set. I've played thirty-three games, and I currently have a four-stone handicap against the AI.

I've also completed the first volume in the Kseido *Graded Go Problems* series, which are rated 30 to 25 kyu. I'm in the middle of the second book, which is rated 25 to 15 kyu, so it's safe to estimate I'm somewhere in the 18 to 20 kyu range. Not bad.

Reviewing the Method

Let's review the core of the method I used to learn how to play Go:

- I learned the basic rules of the game.

- I purchased a goban, stones, and several books on Go strategy aimed at beginners.

- I found several ways of studying the most important strategic principles by working on ranked Go problems, both in a computer program and in books.

- I focused my initial practice on solving ranked problems, repeating the exercises I couldn't answer or explain on the first try.

- I practiced problems and played games until I hit twenty hours. At that point, I was comfortably solving 20 kyu problems, an improvement of fifteen ranks from the beginner rank of 35 kyu.

Where I'm Going from Here

I have mixed feelings about Go. I've learned enough about the game to appreciate just how deep it is and how far I am from mastering it. I've progressed considerably since I started, but to be truly good at the game, I have a *very* long way to go.

On the other hand, my leisure time is limited, and Go seems to require the same sort of intense, focused concentration that writing and programming demand. While Go can be fun, at the end of a long day, Go feels a bit too much like *work*.

In addition, full nineteen-by-nineteen games can take over an hour to complete, and it's not very polite to human players to have to quit the game if family duties call. So far, most of my games have been played against the computer, since it's always available and doesn't care if I have to go do something else for a while.

I've grown to appreciate the brain-teaser qualities of Go problems, so I'll likely keep doing them when I feel like solving puzzles. I enjoy Go exercises far more than crossword puzzles, sudoku, and other similar sorts of games, so my Go programs will stay on my phone, ready for use when I have a few spare moments.

I'm planning to teach Lela how to play when she's a little older. The rules are simple enough for a four-year-old to understand, and I have fond memories of playing chess with my dad when I was young. Go is a good way to teach important skills like analysis, strategy, and tradeoffs, and I think we'll have a lot of fun playing in the years to come.

Other than that, I don't have a burning desire to spend more time mastering Go. I've learned enough about the game to satisfy my curiosity, and continuing to progress to mastery isn't a major priority.

That's perfectly okay. There's no universal law that says you have to master everything you ever learn. Life requires tradeoffs, and there's nothing wrong with exploring something new, learning a lot, and then deciding to explore something else.

You don't have to be a black belt in everything to live a satisfying life.

8

Ukulele

Lesson: Isolate, Practice, Repeat

Today, like every other day, we wake up empty and frightened.
Don't open the door to the study and begin reading. Take down a musical
instrument. Let the beauty we love be what we do. There are hundreds of
ways to kneel and kiss the ground.

—RUMI, THIRTEENTH-CENTURY PERSIAN POET

■   ■   ■

For supplementary images, video, and commentary about this
chapter, visit http://first20hours.com/ukulele.

A few years ago, I read a thought-provoking set of books by Tom Hodgkinson titled *How to Be Idle* (2005) and *The Freedom Manifesto* (2007). Hodgkinson's thesis, in a nutshell, is that we work too much, and all stand to benefit by slacking off. Instead of pushing ourselves to the limit, we should instead learn to relax, kick back, and not take everything so seriously.

The books are primarily a call to ignore consumer culture and careerism. Instead of pursuing material overabundance, Hodgkinson recommends being content with modest means and returning to the pursuits of simpler times: gardening, cooking, and playing music.

In *The Freedom Manifesto*, Hodgkinson recommends learning to play the ukulele:

This four-stringed marvel is very cheap, very portable, and very easy to play. It is therefore even more punk than the guitar. Here are the three chords you need to play most songs: C F G

Get an ukelele, and you will never be bored again.

Hodgkinson's advice resonated with me. At the time, Kelsey and I were living in a 340-square-foot studio apartment on New York City's Upper East Side, and we were both working a lot, hustling to progress in our careers and pay the insane Manhattan rent. A diversion would be welcome, and learning to play the ukulele sounded like great fun.

In high school, I was involved in every music group my school offered. I already mentioned that I learned to play the trumpet, but I also sang in the choir, and really enjoyed it. Once I left for college, however, I stopped doing anything musical, and Hodgkinson's book reminded me of how much I missed it.

Part of the problem is that trumpets are *loud*, and not very fun to play by yourself. I was busy enough with other things and wasn't interested in searching for a band to join. In addition, you can't sing and play the trumpet at the same time, as you can with a guitar, piano, or ukulele.

After a little research, I ended up purchasing a Washburn Oscar Schmidt OU5 Concert Ukulele. It's made of Hawaiian Koa wood, sounds nice, and was reasonably priced: between the ukulele and the case, I spent about $175.

When the ukulele arrived, I plucked the strings for a bit, but I'd never played a stringed instrument before, aside from a very brief experiment with a cheap guitar in college. Without a good idea of how to get started, other matters took priority, and the ukulele sat in the closet beside the guitar, collecting dust.

Ukulele Hero

My interest in playing the ukulele was rekindled when Kelsey and I welcomed Lela into the world. It's amazing how having children shifts your priorities overnight. All of a sudden, I was working less in favor of spending time at home, and I started thinking about music again.

One of my best friends, Nate Siebert, plays his guitar for his sons,

Jackson and Finley, every night before they go to bed. They love it, and over the years it's evolved into a consistent, calming ritual.

As an added benefit, the music is quite likely to be good for them: early exposure to music has been linked over the years to a wide range of measures associated with cognitive development. It's not clear precisely *how* music helps little brains develop, but it does.[1]

I'd love Lela to grow up in a home where playing music is a common event, and I'm all for doing what I can to help her develop into an intelligent, happy little girl. Learning to play the ukulele suddenly seems like a *very* good use of time.

Meet My New Axe

I already had an ukulele, but another instrument has caught my eye. Kelsey's cousin, Erik Smith, happens to be a self-taught master woodworker who makes fine instruments. Erik's company, Crow Hill Guitars,[2] specializes in creating handcrafted custom acoustic and electric guitars, and Erik exhibits them at music festivals all over the United States.

Erik decided to try his hand at making his first tenor ukulele. Meet the Grizzly:

This ukulele is one of a kind: the body is crafted from African mahogany and wenge, with inlays of Spanish cedar, Indian rosewood, curly redwood, and curly maple. A white mother-of-pearl bear claw is embedded in the fretboard, and abalone bear claws adorn the sound hole on the face. I wanted the Grizzly as soon as I saw it.

There was a catch, though: Erik's instruments cost thousands of dollars. They're worth every penny in terms of quality, but was I serious enough about learning to play to justify the expense?

I decided to purchase the Grizzly for two reasons. First, playing on a high-quality instrument, even as a beginner, gives you an important psychological boost: you sound better right away. Compared to the Grizzly, my old Oscar Schmidt sounds downright dull. As a result, playing on the Grizzly is way more fun.

Second, it would be a complete embarrassment to have an instrument this nice in my house and not be able to play it. In addition, if I don't learn to play, I'll have wasted a good chunk of money. I'm now invested substantially in the outcome, so it's more likely I'll make time to practice, making this purchase a great example of using a *precommitment* to change behavior.

Supporting Gear

Along with the Grizzly, I picked up two other important pieces of equipment:

- Snark SN-6 Ukulele Tuner—this inexpensive electronic tuner clips onto the head of the ukulele, making it easy to keep each string tuned to the proper pitch.
- D'Addario J71 Pro-Arte Ukulele Strings, Tenor—extra hard tension nylon classical guitar strings that give the ukulele a fuller sound and make it easier to strum fast.[3] If a string breaks, you have to replace it before you continue, so it's good to have a few extra sets on hand, just in case.

Along with the equipment, I purchased three ukulele books:

- *Absolute Beginners Ukulele, Omnibus Edition* by Steven Sproat (2010), a beginner tutorial
- *Fretboard Roadmaps—Ukulele* by Jim Beloff and Fred Sokolow (2006), which covers advanced techniques
- *The Daily Ukulele* by Jim Beloff and Liz Beloff (2012), a reference book that contains a wide variety of songs ranging from folk to classic rock

An Intriguing Challenge

Shortly after I purchased the Grizzly, I got an e-mail from my friend Chris Guillebeau, author of *The $100 Startup* and *The Art of Non-Conformity*. Each year, Chris hosts a very fun conference called World Domination Summit. Imagine bringing together over a thousand people who are each doing crazy/odd/interesting things in the same general area: that's WDS.

Chris had originally invited me to speak about *The Personal MBA*, but ten days before the event, another speaker canceled their session at the last minute. Chris knew I was working on this book, so he sent me a note: was I willing to lead a second session about rapid skill acquisition?

Sure . . . why not?

World Domination Summit was about to become the first time I presented these ideas in public.

I was drafting the new presentation, which focused on the ideas we discussed in chapters 1–3, when I received another e-mail from Chris, which he sent to every speaker before the event. Among other things, Chris's note contained this advice: "If you can do something special, do it. . . . Anything you can do to surprise [the participants] will stand out and go far."

That got me thinking . . . playing the ukulele would be a great way to demonstrate how these ideas work. Could I learn how to play in ten days?

It will be a stretch, but I think I can do it. I replied to Chris and accepted the invitation.

I now officially have ten days to learn how to play the ukulele.

Crazy for You

With only ten days before my first public performance, I have to make a plan, and fast. This isn't a commitment I can easily back out of, and it will be the first time in twelve years I've done anything musical in public.

After I commit, the part of my brain that wants me to look good in front of other people naturally kicks in. What am I thinking? Am I nuts?

What makes this crazy idea even more nerve-racking is that I'll be by myself: just me and the Grizzly. I won't have a band to back me up, and if I make a mistake, everyone will know. If I'm horrible, everyone will see and hear just how bad I am.

Just thinking about that possibility makes me nervous. I'm considering speaking, playing an instrument I've never played before, and possibly singing in front of people I don't know. Yikes!

All the more reason to know what I'm doing before I take the stage. I have a lot of work to do, and the clock is ticking.

Defining Success

The first part of my target performance level is set: I'm going to play the ukulele in public in ten days. That's a good start, but how can I make that more specific?

I took out a notebook and sketched what I wanted the session to look like. I have an hour to talk. If I explain the main ideas in thirty minutes or so, that leaves twenty minutes for playing and ten minutes for questions.

I'm going to plan on playing for roughly twenty minutes. What do I want to focus on?

The talk isn't a concert. It's primarily a teaching session, so I want to focus on using whatever I play to illustrate a few interesting and important ideas about rapid skill acquisition. It'd also be nice to highlight some interesting things about music.

As I sketch, I start to get ideas . . . this is going to be *fun*.

The "Four Chord Song"

As I was thinking about what I might want to play, I remembered a funny video of a band I saw several months prior.

Axis of Awesome[4] is a comedy rock band based in Sydney, Australia. The group is most widely known for the "Four Chord Song," a medley of past and present pop hits, which has been viewed over 24 million times on You-Tube.

Here's the gag: as the band demonstrates, pretty much every popular song of the past several decades is made up of the same four chords. Play the chords over and over again, overlay some random lyrics, and you have yourself a surefire pop hit.

No artist is immune: Elton John, The Beatles, John Denver, U2, The Red Hot Chili Peppers, Bob Marley, Beyonce, Lady Gaga. Even the venerable Australian folk song "Waltzing Matilda" makes an appearance. The song goes on for five minutes, introducing a new hit every five to ten seconds, accompanied by gales of laughter and applause from the audience.

The "Four Chord Song" is simultaneously hysterical and mind-blowing. By showing the underlying structure of well-known songs, it illustrates that popular music does indeed have a formula. There are many possible variations on the theme, but the human mind seems to gravitate to that particular method of constructing a catchy tune.

Here are the four chords in the "Four Chord Song":

G / D / Em / C

I'm going to learn how to play the "Four Chord Song." If the gag is true, I'll also be simultaneously learning how to play every pop song ever written. Sounds like an efficient place to start!

As it turns out, these four chords are very easy to play once you know how the instrument works. Let's examine the ukulele to see what we're dealing with.

Anatomy of an Ukulele

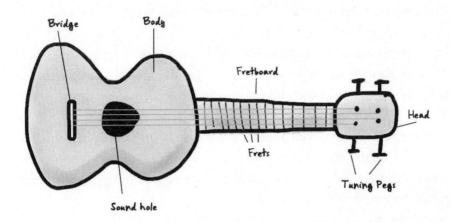

Ukuleles have four strings, which extend along the length of the instrument's body. The long piece that sticks out from the body of the instrument is called the *fretboard*.

Just above the fretboard is a piece of wood called the *head* or *headstock*. Embedded in the head are *tuning pegs*, which securely hold the top end of the instrument's four strings. These strings extend from the head, over the fretboard, past the open *sound hole*, to the *bridge*, which is near the bottom of the ukulele's body. The bridge keeps the strings in place, strung tightly over the sound hole and fretboard.

The ukulele is traditionally played by wrapping the left hand around the fretboard, and using the right arm to hug the instrument close to the chest. The player strums the strings with the fingers of their right hand (usually the right index finger or thumb), while the fingers of their left hand press down on the fretboard to change the pitch of the strings.

Tuning

Each string has a *tuning*: a pitch that's made if you pluck the string without pressing down anywhere on the fretboard. The pitch of each string is adjusted by turning the tuning pegs. If a tuning peg is turned to add tension to the string, the pitch moves higher. If the tuning peg is turned to reduce the string's tension, the pitch moves lower.

Here's the most popular default tenor ukulele tuning:[5]

- 4th string (bottom) = **G** (196 Hz)
- 3rd string = **C** (261.6 Hz)
- 2nd string = **E** (329.6 Hz)
- 1st string (top) = **A** (440 Hz)

Tuning the ukulele is very easy if you have a good tuning device. That's where the Snark SN–9 comes in. When you clip it to the headstock, turn it on, and pluck a string, the tuner measures the string's pitch, translates the frequency into a note, and shows you if the pitch is *flat* (slightly below) or *sharp* (slightly above) the proper frequency. When you have the correct pitch, a signal light appears, and you move on to the next string. When all four strings are in tune, you're ready to play.

Proper tuning is very important: if the strings aren't tuned correctly, the ukulele sounds off in a way that even people who claim to be tone-deaf can notice. The more accurate the tuning, the better the instrument sounds.

Notes and Chords

If you want to play a single note on the ukulele, all you need to do is pluck a string, which causes it to vibrate over the sound hole in the body, creating sound. If you press down on the fretboard as you pluck a string, the string becomes temporarily shorter, and as a result, vibrates faster when you pluck it. The higher the frequency of vibration, the higher the pitch of the sound.

What makes ukuleles, and other stringed instruments, like guitars and pianos, interesting is that they're capable of playing several notes at the same time. If an ukulele player strums every string with their right hand, they can play four notes simultaneously. A skilled player can press the strings on the fretboard in ways that make the pitches each string generates complement one another, creating a *chord*.

Chords are what make stringed instruments sound so rich and vibrant. By playing combinations of notes instead of single notes, the player can create both melody and harmony at the same time. In a sense, chords allow the player to become their own accompanist.

Even better, unlike the trumpet, clarinet, flute, or saxophone, stringed instruments only require the player to use their hands. With enough practice, it's possible to play complex chords and sing at the same time, which is why instruments like the guitar and piano are so popular with vocalists.

Playing Chords

Since I'm starting from scratch, I have a choice to make: I can focus on learning how to play individual notes by reading sheet music, or practice playing chords. Since chords are new to me, and I'd like to be able to sing and play at the same time, I'm leaning in that direction.

Chord diagrams are visual representations of which strings to press on the fretboard with the fingers of your left hand. If you press the strings in the combination shown in the diagram, you'll play the chord.

Here are the four chords in the "Four Chord Song":

G / D / Em / C

Here's what these chords look like on the ukulele:

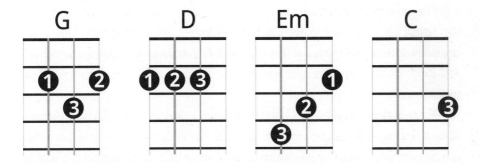

If you hold the ukulele upright, it looks just like the diagrams. The thick bar at the top of the diagram represents the top of the ukulele's fretboard, which is called the *nut*. Each line below that is a fret, which corresponds to the raised metal pieces sticking out of the fretboard.

Frets make it much easier to produce clean-sounding notes when you press down on the fretboard. When you play, you don't press down on the frets themselves: you press down on the spaces between them. As you press down, the fret below your finger also presses on the string, shortening it to a precise length, and altering the pitch accordingly.

Chord diagrams indicate which strings you need to press down on, and where you need to press, in order to play certain chords. The strings are represented by the four vertical lines: the string on the left is the 4th string, which is the string on the top if you're holding the ukulele in playing position. The string on the right is the 1st string, which will be on the bottom.

The black circles show where to press, and the numbers stand for which finger you should use:

1 = index finger

2 = middle finger

3 = ring finger

4 = little ("pinkie") finger

According to the diagram, to play a G chord, I'll need to press down on the bottom three strings with my index, middle, and ring fingers. My index finger should push on the third string above the second fret; my middle finger should be in the same position on the first string, and my ring finger should press on the second string above the third fret.

That's a lot to say, but in practice, it's easy to do. Once you figure out which finger goes where, playing chords becomes a standard motor skill: learning what shape your fingers need to take, and where you need to push, to create a given chord.

To practice chords, it's useful to have a set of reference diagrams that show how to play common chords. A brief Internet search led me to the "Kiwi Ukulele Indispensable Chord Chart,"[6] a downloadable guide to playing chords on the ukulele. The guide was created by Mike Dickison, author of *Kiwi Ukulele: The New Zealand Ukulele Companion* (2008).

There are many places to find chord charts: pretty much every ukulele book contains a set of chord diagrams. What makes Mike's chart unique is that it's organized by frequency of use. Common chords, like the chords featured in the "Four Chord Song," are listed first. Rare chords, like G#ᴋᴍᴋ4, are listed at the bottom, since you'll rarely see them used.

This type of frequency analysis is very, very useful: the power law applies to music as well. To be able to play songs, you don't need to know hundreds of chords. Ten to twelve chords cover most songs.

Chord Practice

I pick out the diagrams of the chords in the "Four Chord Song," and spend some time learning which fingers go where. When I make the appropriate shape with my fingers on the fretboard, I strum all four strings. It works: I'm able to produce chords that sound nice!

The biggest challenge early on is pressing each string down in a way that ensures the fret does its job. If you don't press down hard enough, the string won't produce a clear tone. Instead, you'll get a very unattractive "buzzing" sound along with the pitch you want, which is distracting.

Once I learn the four chords, I spend an hour practicing playing each one, repeating the sequence over and over again:

G...D...Em...C...
G...D...Em...C...
G...D...Em...C...

This is the first stage of motor skill acquisition: helping my brain associate certain thoughts, like the name of a chord, with a pattern of muscle movements in my left hand. Later, I'll be able to play an **Em** chord whenever I want to, but to get there, I need to practice making the right shapes with my fingers, pressing down hard enough on the fretboard, and switching between the chords in a sequence.

I'm also practicing before bed, using the same strategy I used to relearn to touch-type. By practicing before I sleep, I can ensure that my brain is able to consolidate these movements as efficiently as possible.

Strumming Patterns

The next day, I'm able to play all four chords well, and switch between them at will. Not bad for an hour of practice. Now that I have some idea of what my left hand is doing, I need to focus on my right.

While the left hand is busy playing chords, the right hand is responsible for strumming the strings to produce sound. Up to this point, I've been strumming using a very basic pattern: counting to four and strumming with each number:

1 2 3 4

1 2 3 4

1 2 3 4

Most songs, when they're put in musical notation on paper, are written in what's called 4/4 time. Without going too far into the details, the songs in 4/4 time are organized around four strong beats.

The next time you hear a song, try counting from one to four in your head in time with the beat. More often than not, you'll notice the pattern fits.

Of course, if every song consisted of playing notes or chords in a simple, predictable pattern over and over again, music would get boring very quickly. To add interest and variation to music, musicians intentionally break this simple pattern of counting by using a technique called *syncopation*.

Syncopation means playing in a way that strays from the regular progression of beats. Here's what it sounds like: with one of your hands, tap a simple beat on a flat surface in front of you—a table, desk, or counter is perfect. Keep the beats strong and regular. As you tap, count from one to four over and over:

1 2 3 4

1 2 3 4

1 2 3 4

Pretty simple, right?

Now, as you tap the beat, add a twist. Use your other hand to tap *between* the beats, like this:

1 and 2 and 3 and 4 and
1 and 2 and 3 and 4 and
1 and 2 and 3 and 4 and

That's very basic syncopation. The taps on "and" are off the standard beat, which adds a bit of variation that makes the rhythm more interesting.

Skilled musicians spend a lot of time experimenting with syncopation. Each beat can split into many parts. It's very common for beats to be split into four sections, which are counted like this:

1e&a 2e&a 3e&a 4e&a

That's "one-e-and-a, two-e-and-a, three-e-and-a, four-e-and-a." The "e" is long, like in "eagle," and the "a" is short, as in "ah."

By emphasizing or accenting certain beats, and by leaving some beats out entirely, the musician can create all sorts of interesting rhythms that fit into the song.

This is important to know because the right hand on the ukulele keeps the rhythm. If I want to be able to do anything aside from strum on the beat, which is boring, I need to spend some time figuring out an interesting strumming pattern.

After some experimentation, I settle on a pattern:

1 &a e&a 3 &a e&a

It takes me a while to train my right hand to strum the rhythm, but I pick it up eventually. First, I play a simple C chord while I strum. Once I'm comfortable, I start moving through the four-chord sequence, changing chords on the 1 and 3 beats:

G   D
1 &a e&a 3 &a e&a
Em   C
1 &a e&a 3 &a e&a

At this point, I'm playing the actual song: I'm hitting the chords in the correct order with my left hand, and keeping up the strumming pattern with my right.

For the first time, I'm playing a song on the ukulele. It's simple, but it works!

I keep repeating the sequence over and over again. Once I'm comfortable, I close my eyes, and try to play without looking at the fretboard or strings. I make more mistakes, but I'm able to keep the song moving, and get back on track when I make an error.

Not bad after only two hours of practice.

Playing and Singing at the Same Time

Now that I'm able to play the chords and keep up the strumming pattern, I have one more layer to add. Can I figure out how to sing and play at the same time?

The "Four Chord Song" is funny because it's easy to recognize the songs. Without the lyrics, it just sounds like I'm playing the same thing over and over again. That's the point, of course, but without the words, the song doesn't make sense.

Over the years, I've met many very cool people through my business. Among the coolest is Derek Sivers, the founder of CDbaby.com. Derek is an accomplished singer and guitarist, so I asked him for advice on how to proceed. Here's what he recommended:

> Memorize the song by just singing first! It's important to separate instrument-knowledge from song-knowledge. You need to be able to just sing the whole thing, no instrument in hand. (Voice quality doesn't matter: sing, hum, whistle, anything.)
>
> Once you have the song memorized, sing the note-names instead of the lyrics. Memorize the song like this, eyes closed.
>
> Finally, add the instrument, singing the note-names as you play them on the strings.

This is a brilliant example of deconstruction: breaking a complex process into simpler parts. To sing and play at the same time, you have to know the song's words and melody well enough to remember them as you play the chords and keep the strumming pattern going. By separating the song learning from the instrument at first, you ensure you know the song well enough to not have to think about it too much when you add the instrument.

Once you have the words down, switching the lyrics to the chord names helps you get a feel for when to change chords as you play. Since the lyrics have a rhythm of their own, you can use them to remember when to switch: one less thing to keep track of!

Finally, by singing the chord names in rhythm with the chord changes and strumming pattern, you're helping your brain put the pieces together. If you can keep everything together, switching from the chord names to lyrics is simple, since you already have them memorized.

I took Derek's advice to heart, and begin memorizing the words to the "Four Chord Song" by listening to it over and over again to pick up the tune. I then practiced the words by writing them down in a notebook, then repeating them over and over from memory.

Then, I played the song on the ukulele while whistling the tune, keeping the names of the chords in my head. It was easy to notice when to change chords, and suddenly, I began playing and whistling at the same time.

Adding the lyrics came easier than I expected. Every once in a while, I forgot the words or messed up a chord, so I stopped, went back, and tried again.

After five hours of practice, I'm able to play and sing my first full song. It's rough in spots, but all of the pieces are there.

Five days until showtime. I'm able to perform well enough by myself, but how will I hold up when people are watching me?

Making It Automatic

In order to make sure I'm able to play when it counts, the remainder of my practice on the song is pure repetition, always right before bed. The goal is simple: I want to make changing chords, maintaining the strumming pattern, and singing the words take as little mental effort and attention as possible.

This part of practice isn't glamorous, but it's important. Everything up to this point has been part of the cognitive phase of motor skill acquisition: analyzing, deconstructing, and experimenting. Now, I need to push into the associative phase, and begin to allow my muscles to take over without conscious thought.

Every day, I play and sing the song over and over again: I've lost count of how many times. My chord transitions are becoming smoother, the strumming pattern is getting more consistent, and I'm remembering most of the words. A few of the transitions between songs are tricky, so I spend extra time practicing them.

Before I know it, it's time to travel to Portland. I won't be traveling alone: this time, the Grizzly is coming with me.

Showtime

My performance is on the last day of the conference. The good news is that the schedule gives me at least two more hours to practice. The bad news is that it gives me two days to feel anxious about how it will go.

The day of the talk, I tune the Grizzly and practice one last time an hour before my session. Then, ukulele in hand, I walk to the venue.

I wasn't sure how many people to expect, so I'm relieved that it's a relatively small room. I'm not sure how I'd handle an auditorium right now.

The place fills up, and attendance is great. The room seats forty, but more people come, so a few folks are standing on the sides. The energy in the room is high.

After explaining my research and the method, I pull out the ukulele, and everyone is visibly excited. I'm trying my best not to be visibly terrified.

Here goes nothing. I start to play, then sing.

It went really well: way better than I expected. It wasn't a Carnegie Hall–worthy performance, to be sure, but I played the entire song without screwing up the chords, missing a beat, or forgetting the words. The audience smiled, tapped their feet, laughed at the lyrics, and applauded at the end.

My training paid off: instead of looking at the fretboard or the strings the entire time, I was able to look out into the crowd and enjoy the moment.

Finger Picking

After the song was over, I showed the audience another trick I figured out while I was practicing: you can play songs that sound complicated if you pluck individual strings in a sequence instead of strumming them all at the same time. The chords are exactly the same.

This technique is called *finger picking*, and there are many ways you can do it. The pattern I demonstrated is very simple: plucking the 1st string, 4th string, 2nd string, and 3rd string on the beat, in that order. By repeating this pattern while the left hand plays chords, each note naturally complements the next. The result sounds nice and complex, even though it's not really any more complicated than strumming.

The talk was a success, and fun besides. I'm glad I took a risk, pushed myself, and practiced well. Going from zero to first public performance with ten total hours of practice isn't bad at all.

One-Four-Five

By chance, I happened to run into a fellow WDS participant, Melissa Dinwiddle, outside the main auditorium. Melissa's an artist, and she just so happened to bring her ukulele with her, so we broke out the instruments and jammed for a while.

One of the things Melissa taught me that day was a song structure called the "12 bar blues," which is based on a chord progression referred to as one-four-five.

Without getting into too much music theory, every note has an associated chord, as well as a "family" of chords that complement the root. If you can play the root chord, as well as the chords in the associated family, you can suddenly play thousands of common songs.

Take, for instance, "Twinkle, Twinkle, Little Star." The entire song can be played using three chords, which follow this progression:

C / F / G

Here are the chord diagrams:

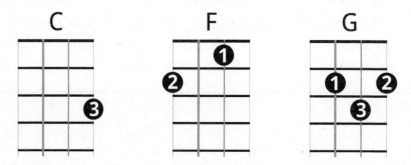

In this case, C is the root, or **I** chord. F and G are the other two chords in this family. F is the **IV** chord, and G is the **V** chord.

Using only these three chords, you can play all sorts of fun songs, like:

- "The ABC Song"
- "Frosty the Snowman"
- "Elmo's Song"

That means I can figure out how to play children's songs for Lela when I get home, as well as some fun blues songs.

My next ten hours of practice are devoted to exploring all of the new songs I can play. Between working through *The Daily Ukulele* (Beloff, 2010), picking up new strumming patterns from the *Absolute Beginners Ukulele* (2009), and learning more basic music theory from *Fretboard Roadmaps—Ukulele* (2006), the hours fly.

Tom Hodgkinson was right: if you pick up an ukulele, you'll never be bored again.

Reviewing the Method

Let's review the core of the method I used to learn how to play the ukulele:

- I obtained an ukulele, strings, a tuner, and other necessary equipment.
- I decided to begin by focusing on learning the most common

chord progressions and strumming patterns, which allowed me to play thousands of popular songs.

- Once I was able to play chords and strum without looking at the fretboard or strings, I practiced until I could maintain the pattern and change chords without thinking about it.

- When I was comfortable with basic chords and strumming patterns, I began learning songs by humming along as I played, learning where the words and chord changes overlapped, then adding lyrics until I could sing and play at the same time.

- I experimented with finger picking the same chord progression instead of strumming, which allowed me to play more complex songs.

- I learned the I, IV, V chord progression, which helped me figure out how to play even more songs.

Where I'm Going from Here

I love playing the ukulele. Between *The Daily Ukulele Songbook* and looking up songs online, I can figure out how to play pretty much any song I want. Some chords are harder than others, and there are thousands of strumming and finger-picking patterns to learn, which will keep me busy for a long time.

One of the best parts about playing the ukulele is that it's low pressure. Aside from my initial experiment, I'm not playing to prepare for a performance, or because I expect to be a professional musician in the future. When I pick up the ukulele, I can just relax and fiddle around for a while, learning a new song, finger-picking technique, or strumming pattern.

Lela's getting old enough to remember songs now, and my old dusty Oscar Schmidt is coming in handy: it's now Lela's ukulele, and it serves as a decoy while I practice, or as our primary instrument when she wants to sit in my lap and strum the strings as I change chords. Now that I can play songs she recognizes, she asks to play the "ukuyaya" before we go to bed.

It's nice to have music in our life.

9

Windsurfing

Lesson: Environment Matters

We wrestle not with flesh and blood, but with epoxy, carbon fiber, monofilm,
and our own egos, dreams, and indomitable wills.

—CHRIS ZEITVOGEL, WINDSURFER

■   ■   ■

For supplementary images, video, and commentary about this
chapter, visit http://first20hours.com/windsurfing.

I'm in the middle of the lake, trying desperately to raise my sail. It's difficult: the muscles in my arms, legs, and back are screaming.

A strong northwest wind is kicking up small crested waves, bouncing
my sailboard back and forth beneath me. I let the sail drop back down into
the water and pause, taking a moment to rest and adjust to the rocking of
the board beneath my feet.

I look to the west: a storm is blowing up, pushing dark clouds over the
mountains. It's time to head back in.

I reach down, retrieve the uphaul line, then pull, hoisting my sail out
of the water for at least the thirtieth time in the past thirty minutes. I hope
I'm able to return to land before the storm hits.

It will be close . . . I'm not very good at steering this odd contraption, but I have to learn. Paddling back to shore gets old fast.

Life on the Water

I have very fond memories of summers spent on the water. Growing up, I was very involved with the Boy Scouts of America, and spent several summers serving as a staff member at two camps in Northern Ohio: Camp Firelands and Camp Avery Hand.

During my last summer at camp, I had the honor of serving as assistant director of aquatics under the legendary "Aqua" Bob Sliney. Bob traditionally leads the pool program: swimming, lifesaving, and mile swim. I was responsible for watercraft activities of all kinds: canoeing, rowing, sailing, and motorboating.

I loved every minute of camp. Each day, I got to spend most of my time on the water, teaching younger Scouts how to enjoy using watercraft safely. It was a challenging and exhausting job in all of the best ways.

When I went off to college, I left the water behind. My first corporate job in Cincinnati was time-consuming, and the Ohio River, the closest large body of water, isn't ideal for recreational boating. Later, when Kelsey and I moved to the middle of New York City, the closest we came to boating was a ride in the gondola in Central Park. When we settled in Colorado, I felt sure my boating days were done: after all, this part of the world isn't exactly known for its wealth of water.

Recently, however, I was able to arrange access to a small private lake just north of town, a few miles from home. I'm giddy: it's the first time in *years* I'll be able to spend time on the water.

What should I do first?

Catching the Windsurfing Bug

My first idea was to take up rowing: the lake is big enough for rowing sculls. Unfortunately, standard rowboats are large and bulky, and even the smallest sculls are very long and relatively fragile, which is a pain, since I don't have the ability to safely store large or long craft at the lake.

The same problems apply for sailboats, with the added downside of expense: even basic equipment can cost a pretty penny. Aside from the mooring complications, I'd rather not drop ten grand on gear.

Canoeing is easier and less expensive, but it's not very fun to do by yourself: the length of most canoes makes them better for two-person paddling. Motorboats and Jet Skis are out of the question, since the lake's owners restrict motors to 9 horsepower or less, and I prefer human-powered craft in general.

As I researched my options, I chanced upon a video shot by James Douglass, a marine biology professor at Florida Gulf Coast University. In addition to his biology expertise, Jim is an accomplished windsurfer who publishes excellent information about the sport on his personal blog.[1]

In the video, Jim rigs up a Formula-class sailboard with a waterproof HD video camera, which is attached to the end of the sail's boom, capturing all of the action at once.[2] He then *flies* over the water, jumping small waves and executing fast, impressive turns.

I was hooked, and I watched that video several times in a row. I've never been on a sailboard before, but suddenly I wanted to try.

Windsurfing meets all of my criteria: I can do it by myself, and the necessary gear isn't huge or unwieldy. It's also, based on my cursory research, not exorbitantly expensive: I'll need to buy gear, but a basic setup won't break the bank.

Windsurfing looks fun, but before I jump in, I want to be sure it's safe. I'm not by nature an adrenaline junkie or thrill seeker. If windsurfing turns out to be dangerous, I'd be just as happy doing something else.

If I'm going to sailboard, I want to know the risks *before* I commit. What can go wrong?

Is Windsurfing Dangerous?

Windsurfing is often labeled an "extreme" sport, but the degree of extremity depends on what type of sailboarding you want to do. On flat, enclosed, small lakes of the type I'll be learning on, it's more intense than piloting a small sailboat, but it's not crazy.

Windsurfing in the ocean, on the other hand, carries much more significant risks. Waves crashing into the shore make launching more difficult, and losing your rig far from shore is a very big deal. The ocean adds elements of fun, like jumping waves, but it also adds risks. Compared to ocean sailboarding, windsurfing on an inland lake is very safe.

No matter what kind of sailboarding you do, however, there are significant risks, most notably, drowning and hypothermia. There's no getting around it: when you're standing exposed on a floating piece of Styrofoam in the middle of a large body of water, holding a large sail upright by hand on a windy day, bad things can happen if you're not prepared.

The risk of drowning has two primary factors: injury and exhaustion. If you fall in a way that results in a major limb injury or concussion, you risk losing consciousness in the water. If you get so tired you can't get back on the board or make it back to shore, drowning is possible.

The best way to prevent drowning is to (1) wear a personal flotation device (often called a PFD or life jacket); and (2) always go out with someone close by, either on the water or on shore. If you get into trouble, you want someone nearby who can help.[3]

Hypothermia can be just as deadly. In cold, wet, and windy conditions, your body loses heat very quickly. Once your core body temperature drops below ninety-five degrees Fahrenheit (thirty-five degrees Celsius), your heart, lungs, and nervous system begin to shut down, leading to death unless core body temperature is restored to normal operating levels, which are between ninety-eight and one hundred degrees Fahrenheit.

What makes hypothermia particularly dangerous is that it occurs gradually. As core body temperature drops, symptoms like shivering, confusion, loss of coordination, and fatigue set in, impairing physical dexterity and judgment. If you're relying on good judgment and physical skill to get you home, the onset of hypothermia is a major threat that's all too easy to overlook.

At water temperatures above sixty-five degrees Fahrenheit, hypothermia isn't a huge risk factor. Below that threshold, it pays to ensure you have insulation before you risk entering the water. That's where wet suits come in.

Wet suits are made of thin and flexible materials that insulate in water, like neoprene. Modern wet suits are rated in terms of millimeters of thickness, and are usually designed to be thicker in the torso than the limbs. This design serves two purposes: more insulation around the torso preserves body heat more effectively, while less material around the limbs preserves range and ease of motion. For windsurfing in cold conditions, you need both insulation and flexibility.

A combination of two wet suits provides the widest range of protection in common weather conditions. A short-sleeve "shorty" wet suit, which keeps the arms and legs exposed, is best for warmer temperatures: 3 millimeters in the torso and 2 millimeters in the limbs (3/2) is sufficient. In water temperatures below sixty-five degrees, a full-body 5/4 wet suit with boots, gloves, and a neoprene hood or hat is best.[4]

California's coastal areas are popular windsurfing destinations, so the state's department of boating and waterways put together a handy list of safety tips:[5]

1. Consider local weather and tidal forecasts.

2. Always advise someone of where you plan to sail and when you expect to return.

3. Wear clothing that suits the conditions.

4. Wear a U.S. Coast Guard-approved life jacket with a whistle attached.

5. In hot, sunny, humid conditions, drink plenty of water.

6. Check your equipment for signs of damage or fatigue.

7. Sail with a buddy.

8. When the winds are offshore, sail no more.

9. Cold can kill. The first time you shiver, return to shore and warm up.

10. Always stay with your board—never try to swim ashore.

The state also provides a simple prelaunch checklist:

Before Launching . . .

1. Double-check your safety leash.

2. Be wary of dark clouds on the horizon—storms strike fast.

3. If in doubt, don't go out.

4. A smart sailor will always try to take the safest course of action before rescue is the only way out.

That's common sense, but it's important. Windsurfing is fun. Dying is not. With a bit of preparation and planning, however, windsurfing's major risks can be minimized.

Where Do I Start?

As you might expect, northern Colorado is not a major windsurfing hot spot. There's enough wind to make it worthwhile if you have a place to practice, but in contrast to major destinations like Washington's Columbia River Gorge, local winds are variable and unpredictable, not strong and sustained.

In addition, large bodies of accessible water aren't very common in northern Colorado. Since much of the Front Range is high-altitude, semi-arid steppe, large bodies of water like lakes don't form naturally. Most of the "lakes" in the area are artificial reservoirs designed to hold water for local farmers, fed by rivers like the wild and scenic Cache La Poudre, which carries snow runoff down from the mountains to the plains below.

As a result, the local geography supports a very developed white-water kayaking scene, but not much windsurfing. I don't happen to know anyone who windsurfs on a regular basis, and it doesn't look like there are any local retailers that sell boards or equipment. Likewise, after searching for instructors in the area, it looks like I'm on my own. The closest place I can find that gives lessons is in Denver, an hour's drive. That makes scheduling tricky: some days it's windy, and some days it's not, so scheduling a lesson would carry a significant risk of cancellation.

While it would be ideal to start with some personal instruction, work and family responsibilities are keeping me close to home for now. I'm confident that if I can get the right equipment, I can pick up the technique once I'm on the water.

That's a big if: how do I buy gear if there are no stores close by? From what I understand, windsurfing boards and sails are bigger than the packages companies like FedEx and UPS usually ship.

If I can't get the appropriate equipment, this project will be over before it begins.

Gearing Up

My first source of information is Jim's website, which has a ton of how-to posts for beginners. One of the first essays I read was a post titled "Top 18 Windsurfing Questions Answered,"[6] which includes a tutorial on necessary equipment.

From the Q&A, it looks like I'll need, at minimum, a board, a sail, a PFD, and a wet suit. I read every windsurfing post on Jim's site, made a list of various pieces of gear that looked useful, tried to edit them down to what I believed were the two best options, then wrote Jim an e-mail to say thanks, as well as ask for his advice.

Of primary importance was the type of board and sail I should get. Jim's video of flying around on a Formula-class board was impressive, and I'd love to get to that point, but I'm not sure if starting with a Formula board is a good idea. The other option, from my research, is a well-rounded board called the Rio, which is manufactured by a company called Starboard. The Rio's developed a reputation of being very beginner-friendly, as well as a good general-purpose board for most conditions: it won't fly as fast as a Formula, but it will perform in a wider range of conditions.

I didn't know what to do, so I asked Jim for his advice:

I'm completely new to windsurfing—haven't stepped on a board yet. I was hoping you could give me some advice on getting started.

I'm looking to pick up a full set of gear, and I'm trying to decide between the Starboard Rio Medium and the Starboard Formula 167.

The Rio sounds like a good beginner board, but I'd like to learn to [hydroplane] as quickly as possible. I'll only be windsurfing on flat water, and I'd like to be able to sail in less wind (4–5 knots).

Formula boards, from what I've read so far, [hydroplane] more quickly and work better in less wind.

Here's my question: is it insane to learn on a Formula board? I have a very high tolerance for early frustration, and I'd rather buy a single board vs. multiple boards. If I learn on a Formula, do I run a significant risk of breaking the equipment or getting injured?

Thanks for any advice you can pass along—I appreciate your help!

An hour or so later, Jim replies:

1. The thing about formula boards being better in light winds is misleading. They do have the potential to plane in lighter winds than any other board (7–8 knots), but you have to be a very good sailor flapping a huge 11–12 square meter sail to tap into that potential. And a formula board when it is NOT planing is a dog because it's so short and wide and has no daggerboard. For non-planing conditions (realistically, anything under 10 knots) a longer narrower board with a daggerboard (Like the Rio M) is a lot faster and easier to navigate than a formula board.

2. You are unlikely to injure yourself trying to learn on a formula board, unless it's hurting your back trying to uphaul too big a sail. The reason you are unlikely to injure yourself is that you probably won't be able to make the board go at all! You could very well injure the board however, because formula boards have a thin skin that will ding easily when you drop the rig during a fall.

3. The Rio M is probably the best board ever for fast learning and getting comfortable planing and using the foot straps, although the GO 171 would also be good.

4. My strategy would be to have a few different sized sails so you can be pushing the limits of how much power you can handle regardless of the wind strength. For the first steps and for high winds later on, you're going to want a sail smaller than 6 square meters . . . I have a windsurfing calculator that will give you an idea of about what size sail you'll need to have a chance of planing in a given wind strength.[7]

5. Your best chance of planing is going to be with smaller sails

when the wind is strong, because it requires less technique to plane with a small sail in strong wind than with a big sail in light wind.

This type of information is absolute gold. Jim cleared up several misconceptions I had about the type of board I need to start on, as well as the type of sails I should start with. Jim's kindness in sharing his advice saved me several thousand dollars and a lot of frustration.

Jim also introduced me to Isthmus Sailboards,[8] a shop in Madison, Wisconsin, that sells windsurfing gear online. I called Isthmus, and Gary Stone, one of the owners, helped me put together a list of the gear I'd need to get started.

Here's what I ended up ordering:

- Starboard Rio M board
- Chinook Powerglide 4.7 square meter sail
- Chinook Sport AL boom
- Chinook 400cm mast
- Chinook US mast extension
- Chinook US 1-bolt mast base
- Chinook bungee uphaul
- Mystic Crossfire 5/4 full wet suit + neoprene boots, gloves, and hat
- Mystic Crossfire 3/2 shorty wet suit + neoprene Vibram Five Fingers
- Dakine Surface personal flotation device

Total investment: about three thousand dollars, including delivery. Windsurfing isn't cheap, but if I take good care of the gear, it should last a long time.

At first, I was leaning toward purchasing a larger sail, but Gary's been teaching people how to windsurf for over two decades, and quickly talked me out of it. Large sails, he said, can be great for lower wind conditions, but only if you know how to use them.

The downside of large sails is that they're heavier and more difficult to lift out of the water. If I start with a large sail while I'm still getting the hang of balancing and turning, I'll, in Gary's words, "hate my life."

I'd rather not hate my life, so I took Gary's advice and opted for the smaller sail. Once again, it pays to take the advice of more experienced mentors before making decisions. After half an hour on the phone with Gary, I placed my order with Isthmus.

As it turns out, commercial freight shipping companies are able and willing to deliver surfboard-sized objects wherever you like, so getting the equipment was easier than I expected. Gary estimated that it would take about a week to receive the gear, so in the meantime, I started educating myself about how to use it.

Avast, Ye Lubbers!

A bit of time browsing the Internet led me to a few introductory windsurfing resources:

- *A Beginner's Guide to Zen and the Art of Windsurfing* by Frank Fox (1988)
- *Windsurfing* by Peter Hart (2005)
- *Learn Windsurfing in a Weekend* by Phil Jones (1992)
- *Beginner to Winner* (DVD) by Jem Hall (2006)

These resources all do a good job of explaining windsurfing terms, theory, and basic technique. Jem Hall's instructional DVD is particularly good at explaining how to handle the board in the water: it's easier to explain complex movements by demonstrating them. Books are at a disadvantage there, since even the best illustrations can be confusing to parse compared to a detailed how-to video.

One thing that struck me immediately was how much traditional sailing terminology is used in windsurfing. It makes sense, since a sailboard is basically a sailboat that uses a surfboard instead of a hull, but it still surprised me. Windsurfers are referred to as "sailors," and the terms used in instruction come directly from sailing.

It's been several years since I've sailed, so I need to review. If you don't know the terms, reading instructional books can be frustrating, so it's important to know the key ideas. Here are a few:

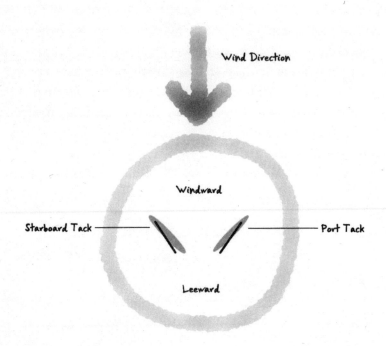

- **Wind direction**—directions like north, south, east, and west aren't very useful in sailing, since the wind changes. Directions are given relative to the wind direction: *windward* means traveling into the prevailing wind, and *leeward* means traveling with the wind.

- **Craft direction**—likewise, "left" and "right" are relative to the current orientation of the craft. *Port* means the left side of the craft, while *starboard* means the right.

- **Front and back**—the front of the craft is called the *bow*, and the back is called the *stern*. Toward the bow is called *fore*, and toward the stern is called *aft*.

- **Turning**—the terms for turning the board are *tacking* and *jibbing*. The difference between them is which end of the board happens to be passing through the wind during the turn. If you're moving into the wind (to windward) and you turn, you're tacking. If you're moving away from the wind (to leeward) and you turn, you're jibbing.

Combining these terms is where it starts to get tricky. If you're headed toward the wind and you turn the bow of the craft to the right (to starboard), you're on a "port tack," since the wind is coming over the left (port) side of the craft.

It's confusing, so it takes me a few hours to decode the instructions in the book and imagine them on the water. This mental simulation process will be helpful when I'm on the water: by imagining the concepts applied to a real craft, I'm making it easier to recall them when it counts.

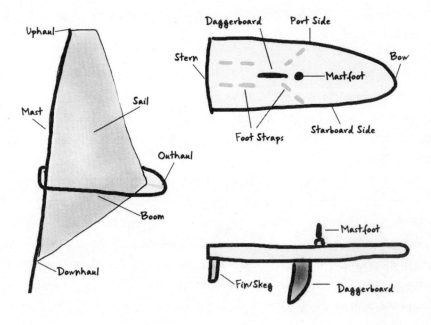

The parts of a sailboard also have distinctive names:

- **The board**—we've already covered bow, stern, port, and starboard, but that's not all we need to remember. Windsurfing boards typically have additional pieces, like a large fin in the center (*daggerboard*) and a smaller fin at the stern (*fin* or *skeg*), both of which extend down into the water. On the top of the board, there's a place to attach the sail (*mastfoot*), which is secured by a mechanical base (*mast base*). There are also typically foot straps on the top of the board, which help the sailor stay balanced and in the correct position when the board really gets moving.

■ **The sail**—windsurfing sails are roughly triangular, and are attached to the board via a large vertical pole called a *mast*. The mast is inserted into a pocket in the sail (*mast sleeve*) that extends from the mastfoot to the top (*head*). Once the mast is in place, a horizontal handhold (*boom*) is placed roughly perpendicular to the mast and is secured to the mast with a clamp. The three sides of the sail are tied to mast and boom with nylon rope (*line*), which is tightened by wrapping it around the end of the boom, then threading it through a special rope-holding device called a *clew*. Once the sail is fully rigged, the mast is attached to the mastfoot, making the board ready to sail.

Properly rigging the board requires judgment and experience. There are several ways to attach the mast base to the board, and each variation changes the board's center of gravity. Depending on the board, there may also be different ways to set up the stern fin and foot straps, all of which affect the board's performance on the water.

Likewise, the way you rig the sail has a huge impact on how the board handles. The two biggest variables are the *downhaul* and *outhaul*, which refer to how tight you make the ropes that secure the sail to the bottom of the mast and the far side of the boom. Less downhaul and outhaul creates a larger "pocket" in the sail, which means the sail is able to catch more wind, producing more power. Adding more downhaul and outhaul reduces the size of the pocket, reducing the potential power, which makes the sail more manageable in very windy conditions.

Stand Back, I'm About to Do Physics!

Sails are fascinating devices. Contrary to popular belief, sailboards (and sailboats in general) don't move because the wind pushes on the sail. The full story is a bit more complicated than that.

Sails work by creating differences in air pressure on the front and back of the sail. In most conditions, as air flows around the sail, the flow creates an area of low pressure in the front (toward the bow), and an area of high pressure in the back (toward the stern). The combined effect of these two different pressure zones creates a force that moves the craft in the direction of the low-pressure area.

As a result, the wind *pulls* the sail as much as it pushes it. Airplane wings work much the same way.

That's important to know when you're on the water, trying to move. If your mental model of how sails work is "maximize the amount of sail the wind can blow on," you'll have a hard time adding power, as well as sailing in any direction other than where the wind happens to be blowing.

All of this information is tough to keep track of, but I'm glad I have a bit of time to learn the basic theory before I try my hand at sailing. Windsurfing is primarily a motor skill, but if I don't understand how the craft works, I risk spending a lot of time practicing the wrong moves.

Watching the Wind

In addition to reading books, I also began paying much closer attention to the weather. Before becoming interested in windsurfing, I never noticed the wind unless it was blowing abnormally hard. Now, I'm finding myself watching it constantly, scrutinizing the tops of trees to estimate wind speed.

Technology helps here: websites like Weather Underground,[9] Windfinder,[10] and iWindsurf[11] collect wind information from locations all over the world, making it much easier to check wind speed in various locales.

Of course, the only wind that really matters is the wind that's over the water where you intend to windsurf. To check wind speed and direction at the lake, I picked up a Kestral 3000 Pocket Wind Meter.[12] This handy little device lets me check the current wind speed at the lake, so it's more accurate than the information online. The unit is also capable of measuring both air and water temperature, so I can make sure I'm not going out if the hypothermia risk is high.

As I watch the wind over the course of a few days, I begin to notice patterns. At the lake, light winds tend to come from the east in the morning, then pick up and shift to blow from the north-northwest in the afternoon, usually around four p.m. Since I'll be launching from the east side of the lake, it will be best to go out in the afternoon. Four is also a good time for my schedule in general: if I plan my workday well, I can go out for an hour or so without major distractions.

You Can't Windsurf Without Wind

I also notice that the winds aren't very predictable here: There's a lot of variability. Some days it's windy, and some days it's not. Based on what I've read, if the wind is less than five to six miles an hour, it isn't worth rigging up.

That means I'll need a backup plan. Fortunately, I have an idea: I've seen people out on the lake on stand-up paddleboards, which also looks like a fun activity that also meets my boating criteria. If I'm generating my own power with the paddle, I don't need the wind, so paddleboarding will be a good alternative on days when I can't windsurf.

I already have a PFD and two wet suits, so all I need is a decent stand-up paddleboard and a long paddle. After a bit of research, I settle on the following equipment:

- Ocean Kayak Nalu 11' paddleboard
- Quick Blade Kahana Elite 80" paddle

The paddleboard comes delivered on the same freight truck as my sailboard. Between my sailboard and paddleboard, I can spend time on the water regardless of the wind conditions.

Putting Together the Pieces

Now that I have all of my gear, I need to figure out how to put the board and sail together, a process called *rigging*.

Fortunately, Isthmus has me covered. Rigging is a common trouble area for new sailboard owners, since it's a complicated process that involves several different parts. When you're trying to figure out which rope goes where, it's easy to get confused.

Isthmus solved this problem by providing detailed rigging videos,[13] so you can watch as a pro rigs a board in real time. Instructional video is ideal for this type of learning: I watched the instructions several times and made notes before trying it with my own gear.

Armed with my notes, I was able to rig my board in about thirty minutes: not bad for my first attempt. I'm in my wet suit, my board is ready, and the wind is blowing. Time to launch.

The Maiden Voyage

I carry my board and sail down to the edge of the water, attach the mast to the base, then float the rig out into the lake until the water is waist high: deep enough to lower the daggerboard. The wind is coming from the northwest at about twelve miles an hour, creating a good bit of chop on the lake's surface. No matter: I've got this.

I push myself up onto the board, stand up, then lean over to grab the uphaul, a braided bungee cord attached to the mast. By yanking on the uphaul, I can pull the sail out of the water until it's straight, roughly perpendicular to the board.

As the sail leaves the water, the outhaul naturally moves to leeward, away from the wind. That allows me to raise the sail without adding power, so I stay roughly where I am, holding onto the mast with both hands. This "neutral" position is the starting point of windsurfing, so I'm feeling pretty good about myself. So far, I'm doing great.

My next order of business is to *sheet in* the sail: move one of my hands off the mast, grab the boom, and pull. By doing this, I'll add power, and start moving.

Here goes nothing . . .

At the Mercy of Mother Nature

I was not prepared for what happened next.

As I pulled the boom toward me, several things happened at once. The board started moving faster than I expected, and combined with the rocking of the board under my feet, I panicked and lost my balance. My center of gravity shifted backward, and before I could process what was going on, I was in the water.

My hands were still holding the boom, so the last thing I saw before submerging was the mast moving very quickly in the direction of my head.

Did I mention I wasn't wearing a helmet?

I'm not sure what I expected falling off of a sailboard to feel like, but it certainly wasn't this *violent*. Fortunately, the mast missed my head by a foot, but the fall knocked the wind out of me, and I swallowed a few mouthfuls of nasty lake water. Below the surface, I couldn't tell which way was up.

Fortunately, I wasn't under water long: my PFD brought me to the surface, coughing and sputtering. That's when I noticed my next problem: I couldn't see anything.

I rely on glasses to correct my vision. Contact lenses don't work well for me, so I gave up on them years ago. Before going out on the water, I didn't think about my prescription sunglasses, and of course, I wasn't wearing any sort of strap to keep them attached to my head. As a result, my first fall tore my glasses from my face. They're currently adorning the lake bed, never to be seen again.

I'm five minutes into my first windsurfing excursion, and I'm already soaked, blind, and shaken after narrowly avoiding a concussion.

This is not going well.

I grit my teeth and swim toward the board. By the time I'm able to reorient myself, the wind has blown it ten to fifteen feet away from me. I grab the board, hoist myself up, and uphaul once more.

Self-Rescue

In the forty minutes I was on the water that day, I fell in every possible fashion: backward, forward, sideways. I swallowed enough water to cause nausea, and my legs, arms, and back were aching from uphauling the sail over and over and over again.

Eventually, I decided enough was enough. I was cold, sick, and exhausted. Time to go home.

Unfortunately, I don't know how to steer this damn board, and every time I try to raise the sail, I end up inhaling more water. The wind is blowing me south, away from my launching spot. I couldn't maneuver back there if my life depended on it.

At that point, I decided it was time to practice a self-rescue technique I learned from one of the books I'd picked up. I laid down on the board and arranged the sail so that it was laying flat on top of me, with the top of the sail pointing back toward the stern. Then, I started paddling with my arms, slowly pulling myself toward the shore.

It was slow going. I wasn't very far out, but it took me ten minutes of hard paddling to get back. Arms aren't very efficient paddles in even the best of circumstances, and these were *not* the best of circumstances.

When I finally landed, my trials weren't over. Since I was quite a ways from my launching position, that meant my first outing ended with a proper "walk of shame." I forced my exhausted body to carry my gear back to the car, drove home, and collapsed.

Not an auspicious beginning.

Post-Traumatic Event Analysis

After resting, I reviewed the outing. What happened out there? What went wrong?

First, the wind conditions were too strong for an absolute beginner. For someone with any experience, they were probably fine, but for my first time on a board, it was too much, too fast. Lesson learned.

Second, I have no experience balancing on any sort of board. I've never surfed, never skateboarded, or done anything else that required balancing on a moving surface. The waves created by the wind were rocking the board, and that freaked me out.

Third, adding power to the sail shifts the center of gravity on the board. If I don't shift my body in the right way to compensate, I'm likely to fall. If I don't let go of the sail quickly enough if I sense I'm out of control, I'll probably take a dive. I need to get comfortable shifting just enough in any direction to stay on the board, particularly during wind gusts.

Fourth, I didn't have all of the proper safety gear. I clearly need a helmet to protect my head from the mast in case I fall. I had a close call once, and I got lucky. I won't make the same mistake again: I'm ordering a helmet immediately.

Learning from the Past

There are a few things I can do to help prevent my next practice session from resembling my first.

First, I can ensure my next session takes place on a day with less wind. It may not be as exciting, but it will let me practice without being overwhelmed.

Second, I can get a feel for balancing on the board by taking it out without the sail attached, using my eighty-inch paddle to maneuver. By removing the variable of the sail, I can get a feel for what it's like to balance on the board, and learn how far I can lean in any direction without capsizing. It won't be a perfect test, since the sail will change the board's center of gravity once it's attached, but it's better than constantly falling.

Third, I can focus my next practice with the sail on learning to sense the sail's balance. If I pay attention, I'll be able to feel which direction the sail is moving, and how that affects the board. I can learn when to shift my weight back to counterbalance the force of the sail, when to let up to avoid falling backward, and when to let go if a wind gust suddenly makes the sail too much to handle.

The next few days are calm, which gives me a chance to isolate balancing on the board. That test is a success: by the end of my practice session, I'm no longer freaking out as much, and later, a high-wind day gives me the opportunity to practice balancing on the board when the water is choppy. I still have to get over the oddness of looking down and seeing the water moving beneath my feet, but just experiencing the sensation for a while goes a long way in calming my nerves.

A few days later, it's sunny and warm, with a brisk but not-too-crazy breeze. I rig up, launch, and uphaul into neutral. Am I about to have a repeat of day one?

Not at all: I only fell twice that day. Isolating balancing on the board helped a lot, and I was able to avoid falling when I sensed the board getting out of control. I uphauled a lot that day, but that's okay: it's better than drinking lake water. I practiced adding power to the sail, and suddenly I was moving.

How Do You Turn This Thing?

Getting the board to move without falling is a victory, but it introduces a new pressing problem: How do you turn?

I experimented with things I learned from the books and DVD: spinning the board under my feet while I held the sail in neutral position helped a lot. It also helped to remember that sailboards (and sailboats in general) can't move directly into the wind.

There's a "dead" or "no-go" zone that extends forty-five degrees to either side of windward: try to sail anywhere inside that zone, and you'll find yourself "in irons," and you'll stop, or start moving backward. To move into the wind, you have to point the board at least forty-five degrees to either side of windward, sheet in the sail, then tack to move in the other direction after you move for a while. By tacking back and forth, you can zigzag your way to your destination, even if it's upwind.

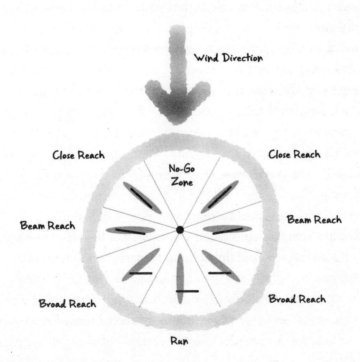

It's also important to be able to turn the board under power. When you're moving, shifting the sail to the left or right changes the *center of effort*, the focal point of all of the force the wind is generating on the sail, relative to the board's *center of lateral resistance*, the focal point of the resistance between the board and the water. By shifting the sail to fore, aft, port, or starboard, the relationship between these focal points changes, and the board turns to compensate.

When you're getting back on the board after falling, it's common to find yourself in an odd position. Ideally, you want the board to be perpendicular to the wind, with the sail pointing downwind. In this position, you can uphaul the sail without too much difficulty.

If the sail is pointing upwind, however, you're in danger of the boom smacking you in the face as you uphaul when it catches the wind. Likewise, you can find your board pointed into the wind, straight into the dead zone.

To compensate, it's best to use your feet to rotate the sail so it's perpendicular to the board, regardless of the wind's direction. Once the sail and board are perpendicular to each other, you can uphaul slowly, allowing the wind to rotate the board into the correct position. Once the sail is on the downwind side, you can uphaul completely, then tack in whichever way you want to go.[14]

After a few hours of practice, I'm getting the hang of it. I'm not very agile or fast, and my turns aren't pretty, but I can launch the board, sail out to the middle of the lake, and get back to roughly where I started. Compared to my first windsurfing experience, it's a huge improvement.

For Everything, There Is a Season

Autumn hits fast and hard on the Front Range of Colorado, typically at the end of September. One day it's seventy-five degrees and sunny, the next, it's thirty degrees and threatening to snow.

I've been out on the water as much as possible each afternoon, trying to maximize my practice time before the weather changes. The water temperature is stable at sixty-eight degrees: a bit chilly, but not in the hypothermia danger zone. With a wet suit, the initial shock of entering the water is the worst part: after that, falling in is no big deal.

On days when the wind is over six miles per hour, I rig up the sailboard. On days when the winds are calm, I paddleboard instead.

I've been doing more paddleboarding than windsurfing: it's difficult to sailboard when there's no wind. It's frustrating, since I want to get as much windsurfing practice as I can, but I can't negotiate with Mother Nature. The wind is either blowing strong enough when I'm able to get out on the water, or it's not.

One morning, the temperature plummets to forty degrees. Over a period of three days, the lake's water temperature drops to a frigid fifty degrees. With my 5/4 wet suit, I could survive for a while, but risking hypothermia or drowning isn't high on my list of priorities. For me, windsurfing season is over.

I tally up my total practice hours, and come up short of my goal: nine hours of practice in total, far less than the twenty I wanted to spend by this point. I spent more time than that on the water paddleboarding.

There's an important lesson here: environment matters. It's easy to be disappointed that I didn't hit my practice target, but my desire to learn can't make the wind blow. Even then, it wasn't wise to spend too much time on the water, since exhaustion is a major risk factor. As a result, each day I was able to practice at all clocked in at a total of thirty to forty minutes on the water.

Even though I fell short of twenty hours, I learned a ton. I have a solid rig, learned how to assemble it properly, figured out how to launch in various wind conditions, and practiced getting back on the board from the water more times than I can count. I can raise the sail, point myself in the right general direction, and control the board under power without capsizing. I can turn the board when I need to, and get back to shore safely, in roughly the same area of the beach I launched from. That's a lot of progress in a short period of time.

As a bonus, I picked up a mini-skill: paddleboarding. The setup and technique is nowhere near as complex or demanding as windsurfing, but it's a lot of fun. Even when the wind isn't blowing, I really enjoy gliding on top of the water, chasing ducks from one end of the lake to the other. It's nice to paddle as the sun goes down, and between the exercise and the scenery, it's a great way to unwind.

Reviewing the Method

Let's review the core of the method I used to learn how to windsurf:

- I acquired the necessary equipment: a board, sail, wet suit, personal flotation device, helmet, and other important safety gear.
- I learned how to rig the board and sail, as well as disassemble, maintain, transport, and store the rig safely.
- I learned how to protect myself from major risks, including drowning, concussion, and hypothermia.
- I learned how to launch the board from shore, raise the sail into neutral position, and add power to the sail to start moving.
- I learned how to turn the board (tack/jibe), and how to position the sail to move in various wind conditions.
- I learned how to avoid falling off the board, and how to get back on the board and uphaul the sail if I fall.

Where I'm Going from Here

By the time you read this, it will once again be windsurfing season. I'll be out as soon as the weather and water conditions are out of the hypothermia danger zone, reacquiring the basics of rigging, balance, and turning.

I'll reacquire this basic level of skill quickly, so I'm preparing for the next challenge: getting the board to *hydroplane*, which increases speed dramatically. "Planing" is only possible in high-wind conditions, and the increased speed increases the risk of crashing and injury, so I need to be completely comfortable with the basics before attempting it.

I'll also be sporting a bigger sail. The generally low (and variable) wind conditions on the lake make using a larger sail a good idea, so once I'm comfortable using the 4.7-square-meter sail, I'm going to start practicing with a 7.5. Between the two sails, I should be covered: I'll use the large sail for lower-wind days, and the smaller sail for high-wind days.

All in all, windsurfing is great fun. I enjoy my time on the water, particularly now that I'm not falling so much. I'm looking forward to the next season, and to taking advantage of the windy days whenever they appear.

I can't control Mother Nature, but I can control how I practice when the conditions are favorable. That's enough.

Afterword

■ ■ ■

In less than a year, I learned six complex skills.

I'm not a genius or a freak of nature. I'm not naturally talented. I didn't quit my day job. I didn't drop everything and move to the other side of the world. I didn't ignore my family.

I just set aside an hour or so every day to practice, and I practiced in an intelligent way. Skills that began as a complete mystery became comprehensible in a matter of days, often hours. All it took was a bit of research and around twenty hours of consistent, focused, deliberate practice.

Even better, my practice became routine: these skills are now a part of my daily life. Learning the most important subskills first makes it very easy to keep progressing. By the time you read this, I'll be even better in each of these areas. How *much* better will depend on how much I practice.

If you want to acquire a new skill, you have to practice. There is no other way.

You can prepare. You can research. You can eliminate distractions and alter your environment to make it easier to practice. You can find intelligent ways to make your practice more effective or efficient. But, in the end, you must practice.

What feels like the long way is the shortest way. Zero-practice shortcuts don't exist. No practice, no skill acquisition. It's as simple as that.

Why don't we practice? Simple: we're busy and we're scared. Shakespeare said it well a long time ago, in a play titled *Measure for Measure*: "Our doubts are traitors, and make us lose the good we oft might win, by fearing to attempt."

The major barrier to rapid skill acquisition is not physical or intellectual: it's *emotional*. Doing something new is always uncomfortable at first, and it's easy to waste a ton of time and energy thinking about practicing instead of practicing.

Fortunately, the frustration barrier is deceptively easy to break through: skill acquisition always *feels* bigger than it actually is. By creating time for practice, doing a bit of early research, and leaning into the initial discomfort, you will always see major progress in the first ten to twenty hours of practice. All it takes to reap the rewards is a small burst of effort, persistence, and a bit of grit.

You don't need to pick many skills to acquire: just choose one. Take a skill on your "want to do" list and commit to trying it. Learn that language, play that instrument, explore that game, work on that project, cook that dish, create that art. It's easier than it feels.

Precommit to practicing that skill for an hour or so a day for the next month. Once you actually start practicing, you'll always pick it up more quickly than you expect. Break it down, make the time, try new things, and your brain will begin picking up the technique automatically: that's what brains do. When you get stuck or confused, test a new approach.

Remember: once you start, you can't stop until you reach your target performance level or the twenty-hour mark. Struggle if you must, but don't stop. Show your grit, and keep pushing forward. You'll get there: all it takes is practice.

One final thought: the only time you can choose to practice is *today*.

Not tomorrow. Not next week. Not next month or next year. Today.

When you wake up in the morning, you have a choice. You can choose to invest your time acquiring skills that will make your life more successful, enjoyable, and rewarding . . . or you can squander your time doing something else.

What will you do today?

Acknowledgments

■ ■ ■

To Kelsey and Lela: I love you. Thanks for everything.

To Dave, Sheri, and Zulema: thank you for the Lela-wrangling that made this book possible.

To Leslie Kaminoff, Derek Sivers, Jim Douglass, and Gary Stone: thanks for your generosity and help. I've learned so much from you.

To Lauren Baker: thanks for making the illustrations in this book print worthy.

To Lisa DiMona: I am fortunate beyond measure to have your help and support.

To Adrian Zackheim and Joel Rickett: viva Portfolio!

To Emily Angell: you wield the red pen with finesse. Thanks for your insight and diligence.

To Will Weisser, Margot Stamas, Richard Lennon, and Allison McLean: books without readers aren't very fun. Thanks for everything you do to spread the word.

To Joe Perez and Dan Donohue: when people judge books by their covers, you always make your authors look great. I appreciate your hard work bringing this idea to life.

To Bria Sandford, Samantha LaBue, Sarah Katie Coe, Thomas Dussel, and the entire production and distribution team at Penguin: thank you for everything you've done, and continue to do, to bring this book to readers worldwide.

To You, Dear Reader: you're the reason I do what I do. I hope you enjoyed this book, and find the information useful in the years to come. Good luck!

Notes

■ ■ ■

CHAPTER 1

1.   Ericsson, K. Anders, Neil Charness, Paul J. Feltovich, and Robert R. Hoffman, eds. *The Cambridge Handbook of Expertise and Expert Performance* (Cambridge: Cambridge University Press, 2006).

2.   http://www.chirunning.com/.

3.   Undergraduate college programs usually take four years due to convention and self-interest: colleges bring in more revenue for every year the student is enrolled. That's not to say it's not possible to complete even the most demanding programs in less time: Scott H. Young completed MIT's undergraduate computer science curriculum in less than one year. See http://www.scotthyoung.com/blog/mit-challenge/.

4.   VanLehn, Kurt. "Cognitive Skill Acquisition." *Annual Review of Psychology* 47, no. 1 (1996): 513–539.

CHAPTER 2

1.   If you can relate to my frustration, I recommend reading *The Renaissance Soul: Life Design for People with Too Many Passions to Pick Just One* by Margaret Lobenstine (New York: Harmony, 2006). Reading this book helped me realize that my diversity of interests is a strength, and that it's possible to structure my efforts to take advantage of my natural inclination to learn many things at once.

2.   http://www.newyorker.com/reporting/2011/10/03/111003fa_fact_gawande.

3.   I use an Enso Pearl programmable interval timer: http://www.salubrion.com/products/ensopearl/. You can use any sort of timer you like, including basic kitchen timers, but the Enso has built-in intervals and a very nice-sounding chime, which is more important than it seems. When you're practicing a lot, strident electronic beeps get old fast.

4.   Snoddy, George S. "Learning and Stability: A Psychophysiological Analysis of a Case of Motor Learning with Clinical Applications." *Journal of Applied Psychology* 10, no. 1 (1926): 1.

5.   Newell, Allen, and Paul S. Rosenbloom. "Mechanisms of Skill Acquisition and the Law of Practice." *Cognitive Skills and Their Acquisition* (1981): 1–55.

6.   Logan, Gordon D. "Toward an Instance Theory of Automatization." *Psychological Review* 95, no. 4 (1988): 492.

CHAPTER 3

1.   http://ankisrs.net/.

2.   http://www.supermemo.com/.

3.   http://smartr.be/.

4.   This isn't a book about academic study techniques, but since you're diligently reading the endnotes, here's a deceptively simple study method that works wonders: pick an idea, take out a blank sheet of paper, then try to explain that idea completely using very simple language, as if you're teaching a beginner. The gaps in your knowledge will become clear very quickly, which makes it easy to go back to the source material to learn what's missing. Scott H. Young, a study skills researcher, calls this the "Feynman Technique" (in honor of the renowned physicist Richard Feynman), and it's quite effective. For more details, see http://www.scotthyoung.com/learnonsteroids/grab/TranscriptFeynman.pdf.

CHAPTER 4

1.   There's something really, really fun about sprinting as fast as you can toward a waist-high barrier and leaping over it without breaking stride. The closest I've ever come to feeling like Superman was the time my foot connected squarely with the center of a hurdle during a race. The wooden bar of the hurdle shattered, and I sailed through without losing speed. It was awesome.

2.   http://www.youtube.com/watch?v=IMC1_RH_b3k.

3.   http://www.nytimes.com/2009/07/26/magazine/26FOB-consumed-t.html.

4.   http://www.gilhedley.com/.

5.   You can watch Gil's famous "fuzz speech" here: http://www.youtube.com/watch?v=FtSP-tkSug. Be advised that the video contains footage of a dead human body, so you may want to skip it if you're squeamish.

6.   Sarno, John E. *Healing Back Pain: The Mind-Body Connection* (New York: Grand Central Life & Style, 2010).

7.   I'm about to attempt to explain thousands of years of very complex history in a few

paragraphs. Books about these topics can fill entire libraries, so please excuse my brevity. If you're interested in a more detailed overview, I recommend reading *The Great Transformation: The Beginning of Our Religious Traditions* by Karen Armstrong (New York: Anchor, 2007).

8.   Armstrong, Karen. *The Great Transformation: The Beginning of Our Religious Traditions* (New York: Anchor, 2007).

9.   Desikachar, T. V. K., and R. H. Cravens. *Heath, Healing, and Beyond: Yoga and the Living Tradition of Krishnamacharya* (New York: North Point Press, 1998). A short biography is also available at http://www.yogajournal.com/wisdom/465.

10.   How *much* Krishnamacharya consciously adopted from non-hatha sources like British gymnastics is a matter of debate. At a minimum, many of the poses and movements Krishnamacharya included in his sequences bear a very strong resemblance to gymnastics and military training exercises of the time.

11.   http://www.nytimes.com/2012/01/08/magazine/how-yoga-can-wreck-your -body.html?_r=3&pagewanted=all.

12.   http://www.manduka.com/us/shop/categories/products/gear/manduka-pro -black-sage/.

13.   http://orthoinfo.aaos.org/topic.cfm?topic=A00063.

CHAPTER 5

1.   http://personalmba.com/best-business-books/.

2.   http://wordpress.org.

3.   For the curious: my standard WordPress stack consisted of PHP5 with PHP-FastCGI, NGINX, APC, MSMTP, and WP-Supercache on a Slicehost.com VPS running Ubuntu 8.04 LTS, all with custom configuration files.

4.   http://jekyllrb.com.

5.   http://github.com.

6.   For some reason, almost every programming tutorial begins with showing you how to display or print "Hello, World!"

7.   http://stackoverflow.com.

8.   http://news.ycombinator.com.

9.   http://rubyonrails.org/.

10.   http://www.sinatrarb.com.

11.   http://37signals.com/.

12.   http://rubysource.com/rails-or-sinatra-the-best-of-both-worlds/.

13.   http://paulstamatiou.com/how-to-wordpress-to-jekyll.

14.   https://github.com/sstephenson/rbenv.

15.   In practice, "hacking" is nothing like how it's portrayed in movies, which I find highly disappointing.

16.   https://toolbelt.heroku.com.

17.   http://www.heroku.com/.

18.   http://git-scm.com/.

19.   Versions of Ruby before 1.9.3-p125 required a program called GCC to complete the installation. GCC is available at https://github.com/kennethreitz/osx-gcc -installer.

20.   Programmers coined the acronym "RTFM," which stands for "read the (freaking) manual," as a standard response to questions about issues covered in a program's official documentation.

21.   http://www.ruby-lang.org/en/documentation/.

22.   http://0xfe.muthanna.com/rubyrefresher/.

23.   https://code.google.com/p/ruby-security/wiki/Guide.

24.   The term for advanced modification of Ruby's core objects, classes, and methods is called *metaprogramming*. I picked up a book called *Metaprogramming Ruby: Program Like the Ruby Pros* by Paolo Perrotta (Raleigh, NC: Pragmatic Bookshelf, 2010), and it's way over my head at the moment. First things first.

25.   http://www.ruby-doc.org/core–1.9.3/index.html.

26.   http://ruby.learncodethehardway.org/.

27.   https://devcenter.heroku.com/articles/keys.

28.   https://devcenter.heroku.com/articles/ruby.

29.   https://devcenter.heroku.com/articles/rack.

30.   http://macromates.com/.

31.   https://devcenter.heroku.com/articles/bundler.

32.   http://www.sinatrarb.com/intro.

33.   http://backpackit.com.

34.   http://tom.preston-werner.com/2010/08/23/readme-driven-development.html.

35.   http://www.postgresql.org/.

36.   http://datamapper.org/.

37.   http://stackoverflow.com/questions/1152299/what-is-an-object-relational
-mapping-framework.

38.   http://en.wikipedia.org/wiki/SQL.

39.   http://www.sqlite.org/.

40.   http://pow.cx/.

41.   https://github.com/rodreegez/powder.

42.   http://twitter.github.com/bootstrap/.

43.   I have no idea why it's called a slug, and I agree it's weird.

44.   See http://www.regular-expressions.info/ for examples of common regular expressions.

45.   http://daringfireball.net/projects/markdown/.

46.   http://www.httpwatch.com/httpgallery/authentication/.

47.   Using SSL on a custom domain is more complicated: you have to go through a
long process to verify your identity and obtain a "certificate" that secures each user's
session.

48.   https://github.com/SFEley/sinatra-flash.

CHAPTER 6

1.   Here's a fun fact: Tiger Woods is the only professional golfer in history to win the
U.S. Masters with three different golf swings. Tiger retrained with Butch Harmon after
his Masters win in 1997, won again in 2001 and 2002, retrained again in 2002 with Hank
Haney, then won in 2005. Most recently, Tiger began his third swing retraining with
Sean Foley in 2011, making this Tiger's fourth swing since becoming a professional golfer.

2.   Vector keyboard image via http://wowvectors.com/object/mac-keyboard-vector/.
Distributed under the Creative Commons Attribution 3.0 Unported license.

3.   For a very interesting history of the development of the QWERTY typewriter,
see "The Fable of the Keys" by S. J. Liebowitz and Stephen E. Margolis, available at
http://www.utdallas.edu/~liebowit/keys1.html.

4.   http://www.google.com/patents?id=qSVdAAAAEBAJ.

5.   http://mkweb.bcgsc.ca/carpalx/.

6.   http://mkweb.bcgsc.ca/carpalx/?colemak.

7.   http://colemak.com.

8.   Other operating systems may need to install a small software package that enables the layout. Packages for most popular systems are available at http://colemak.com.

9.   http://www.typematrix.com/2030/features.php.

10.   On TypeMatrix keyboards, you can activate Colemak hardware mode by pressing Fn+F5.

11.   This won't work on all keyboards: many models have different-sized keys on the top, middle, and bottom rows. If that's the case, it's probably easier to either get another keyboard or order stickers that can be affixed over each key.

12.   http://www.typeonline.co.uk/typingspeed.php.

13.   Test corpus material comes from books are in the public domain, which are freely distributed online via Project Gutenberg. See http://www.gutenberg.org/.

14.   http://www.mavisbeacon.com/.

15.   http://typingtrainer.sourceforge.net/.

16.   http://github.com/wwwtyro/keyzen.

17.   Luft, Andreas R., and Manuel M. Buitrago. "Stages of Motor Skill Learning." *Molecular Neurobiology* 32, no. 3 (2005): 205–216.

18.   Walker, Matthew P., and Robert Stickgold. "It's Practice, with Sleep, That Makes Perfect: Implications of Sleep-Dependent Learning and Plasticity for Skill Performance." *Clinics in Sports Medicine* 24, no. 2 (2005): 301–317.

19.   http://www.daskeyboard.com/model-s-ultimate-silent/.

20.   http://type-fu.com.

21.   Milton, James. *Measuring Second Language Vocabulary Acquisition* (Bristol, UK: Multiligual Matters, 2009).

22.   http://code.google.com/p/amphetype/.

23.   http://norvig.com/ngrams/.

CHAPTER 7

1.   In my opinion, the most disappointing aspect of reality is the lack of magic: given how much I read, I'd be at *least* a level 80 wizard by now. Alas, using my mind to manipulate the fabric of the universe is still beyond my capabilities.

2.   Here's another fun fact: if you shuffle a deck of cards thoroughly, the resulting sequence of cards has never been seen before in the history of the universe. "52 factorial" is a very large number: 8.065 times 10^{67}, or over 80 *unvigintillion*, possible combinations.

3.   Other famous games include the Blood Vomiting Game, in which one of the master players died after the match, and the Atomic Bomb game, in which the match was interrupted by the explosion of the atomic bomb over Hiroshima. After the bomb went off,

the players took a break for lunch, replaced the stones on the board, and resumed the game. See http://senseis.xmp.net/?FamousGoGames for more famous games.

4. http://www.ymimports.com.

5. http://senseis.xmp.net/.

6. Yes, that's where the name of the Atari video game console comes from.

7. http://senseis.xmp.net/?TheTenGoldenRulesList.

8. http://diiq.org/five_stone_questions.html.

CHAPTER 8

1. http://cdp.sagepub.com/content/14/6/317.short.

2. http://www.crowhillguitars.com.

3. http://www.daddario.com/DADProductDetail.Page?ActiveID=3769&productid=264.

4. http://www.axisofawesome.net.

5. http://www.ukuleles.com/Technology/strings.html.

6. http://www.kiwiukulele.co.uz/Kiwi-Ukulele-Chord-Chart.pdf.

CHAPTER 9

1. http://jimbodouglass.blogspot.com/.

2. If you want to see what it looks like to go really fast on a Formula board, check out Jim's boom-cam video: http://jimbodouglass.blogspot.com/2010/01/formula-windsurfing-boom-mount-video.html.

3. The Boy Scouts call this the *buddy system*, and it's the cardinal rule of water safety.

4. Wet suits trap a layer of water close to the body, which is then warmed by body heat, acting as an insulating layer. Below water temperatures of fifty degrees, it's best to use a dry suit, which prevents water from touching skin.

5. http://www.dbw.ca.gov/Pubs/Windsurf/index.htm.

6. http://jimbodouglass.blogspot.com/2008/02/top–16-windsurfing-questions-answered.html.

7. http://jimbodouglass.blogspot.com/2010/11/updated-windsurf-calculator-online.html.

8. http://www.isthmussailboards.com/.

9. http://www.wunderground.com/.

10. http://www.windfinder.com/.

11. http://www.iwindsurf.com/.

12. http://www.kestrelmeters.com/products/kestrel-3000-wind-meter.

13. http://www.isthmussailboards.com/info_technical_help.asp.

14. For a detailed guide on how to do this, complete with diagrams, see http://jimbodouglass.blogspot.com/2012/10/beginner-windsurfing-how-to-reorient.html.